## Get the eBook FREE!

(PDF, ePub, Kindle, and liveBook all included)

We believe that once you buy a book from us, you should be able to read it in any format we have available. To get electronic versions of this book at no additional cost to you, purchase and then register this book at the Manning website.

Go to https://www.manning.com/freebook and follow the instructions to complete your pBook registration.

## That's it!
## Thanks from Manning!

# *React Hooks*
# *in Action*

## WITH SUSPENSE AND CONCURRENT MODE

JOHN LARSEN

MANNING

SHELTER ISLAND

For online information and ordering of this and other Manning books, please visit
www.manning.com. The publisher offers discounts on this book when ordered in quantity.
For more information, please contact

Special Sales Department
Manning Publications Co.
20 Baldwin Road
PO Box 761
Shelter Island, NY 11964
Email: orders@manning.com

Manning Publications Co.
20 Baldwin Road
PO Box 761
Shelter Island, NY 11964

| | |
|---|---|
| Development editor: | Helen Stergius |
| Technical development editor: | John Guthrie |
| Review editor: | Aleksandar Dragosavljević |
| Production editor: | Deirdre S. Hiam |
| Copy editor: | Sharon Wilkey |
| Proofreader: | Keri Hales |
| Technical proofreader: | Clive Harber |
| Typesetter: | Dennis Dalinnik |
| Cover designer: | Marija Tudor |

ISBN: 9781617297632
Printed in the United States of America

*To Mum, for all the books. And to Dad, for all the gadgets.*

# contents

v

## 7 *Managing performance with useMemo*   164

## 8 *Managing state with the Context API*   194

## 9 *Creating your own hooks*   218

# *preface*

As a high school teacher and a programmer, I was in a great position to develop applications to support teaching, learning, and organization within schools. I could see firsthand and day-to-day the requirements of students, teachers, and support staff and work with them to build intuitive apps and tools that made it easier to plan, communicate, understand, and play. I started with quiz apps and matching games written in JavaScript, and then created lesson-planning and resource-booking apps that made use of jQuery and templating. Then the science department wanted a way to order equipment for lessons, the leadership team wanted a way for staff to pass on announcements, and the ICT technicians wanted a way for staff to report and manage problems with software and hardware. How about a seating plans app, a content management system for news stories on the website, a bespoke calendar, an interactive duty roster, or a sports match diary, all with a consistent look and feel?

While each project had its own requirements, there was a lot of overlap, and similar methods could be used across apps. To speed things along, I switched to JavaScript end-to-end with Node.js, Express, Handlebars, Backbone, and Marionette. For the most part, it all worked well, although making updates as requirements changed was sometimes fiddly. In particular, the flow of data between the models, views, and controllers wasn't always smooth. The users were happy, but I could see the underlying problems in the code and knew I'd have to get back to it and straighten out the twists and turns at some point.

Then I came across React, and all my problems were solved! Okay, not quite. But React's model of components, props, state, and automatic re-rendering clicked with me in a way no other framework had before. One by one, I converted the existing apps to React. Every time, they became simpler, easier to understand, and easier to maintain. Common components could be reused, and I could make changes and add new features quickly and with confidence. While not quite a React zealot (I'm a fan of framework diversity), I was definitely a convert and enjoyed the developer experience and the user response.

Now with React Hooks, my code has taken another positive step along the simplicity scale. Code that was split across class component life-cycle methods can be collocated, either within function components or in external custom hooks. It's easy to isolate, maintain, and share code for particular functionality, whether it's for setting a document title, accessing local storage, managing context values, measuring onscreen elements, subscribing to a service, or fetching data. And hooking into the functionality of existing libraries like React Router, Redux, React Query, and React Spring has become easier, too. Using React Hooks offers a new way of thinking about React components, and although it has some initial gotchas to look out for, it's a definite change for the better in my view.

The switch to hooks is part of an underlying change in the way React will work going forward. Concurrent Mode will become the new normal, enabling time-slicing wizardry where rendering doesn't block the main thread and high-priority updates like user input can be rendered straightaway, even while the UI for other components is being built. Selective hydration will allow React to load component code just in time for user interactions, and the Suspense API will let developers more carefully specify loading states while code and resources load.

The React team is focused on building a great developer experience so that developers can build great user experiences. Further changes are still to come, and best practices will continue to emerge, but I hope *React Hooks in Action with Suspense and Concurrent Mode* gives you a solid grasp of the existing changes and prepares you for the exciting developments on the horizon.

# *acknowledgments*

This is where I'd normally thank friends and family for their patience as I've been locked away in a bunker, furiously clacking those typewriter keys, creating my masterpiece, as everyone else gets on with life as normal. But, what with one thing and another in 2020, it's been far from life as normal. So, I'd like to thank anyone and everyone who's made things better in any way, large or small, for those around them, in difficult times.

Thank you to Helen Stergius, my editor at Manning, for her patience and encouragement; writing a book is a long process but is made much easier with the support and advice of a great editor like Helen. Thanks also to John Guthrie and Clive Harber for their attention to detail and honest, constructive feedback; they really helped to make the code and explanations clearer and more consistent. I would also like to thank Deirdre Hiam, my production editor; Sharon Wilkey, my copyeditor; Keri Hales, my proofreader, and Aleksandar Dragosavljević, my reviewing editor.

To all the reviewers: Annie Taylor Chen, Arnaud Castelltort, Bruno Sonnino, Chunxu Tang, Clive Harber, Daniel Couper, Edin Kapic, Gustavo Filipe Ramos Gomes, Isaac Wong, James Liu, Joe Justesen, Konstantinos Leimonis, Krzysztof Kamyczek, Rob Lacey, Rohit Sharma, Ronald Borman, Ryan Burrows, Ryan Huber, and Sairam Sai, your suggestions helped make this a better book.

# about this book

*React Hooks in Action with Suspense and Concurrent Mode* is a book for experienced React developers. It introduces the hooks now built into React and shows how to use them when developing apps with React function components, managing state in and across components, and synchronizing component state via external APIs. It demonstrates how the hooks approach is great for encapsulation and reuse, for simplifying component code, and for preparing for changes to come. It also explores some of the more experimental Suspense and Concurrent Mode APIs that the React team is still working on.

## Who should read this book

If you've used React before and want to see how hooks can help improve your code, shifting your components from class-based to function-based and integrating with Suspense and Concurrent Mode to improve the developer and user experiences, then this book will show you the way. You should already be able to create a new app with `create-react-app` and install packages with npm (or Yarn). The code examples use modern JavaScript syntax and patterns like destructuring, default parameters, the spread operator, and the optional chaining operator, so, while there are brief explanations when they're first used, the more comfortable you are with their use, the better.

## *How this book is organized: A roadmap*

*React Hooks in Action* has 13 chapters across two parts. The book's page at Manning's website also includes articles that offer extra examples and explanations that didn't fit within the main flow of the book.

Part 1 introduces the syntax and use of the new, stable, non-experimental, built-in React Hooks. It also shows how to roll your own custom hooks and make the most of third-party hooks made available by existing React libraries:

- We start in chapter 1 with an overview of recent and upcoming changes in React, with a particular focus on how React Hooks help you organize, maintain, and share your component code.
- Chapter 2 introduces our first hook, useState. Components can use it to manage state values and to trigger re-rendering when the values change.
- Sometimes multiple state values are linked together, with a change in one causing changes in others. The useReducer hook, covered in chapter 3, provides a way to manage multiple state changes in one place.
- React aims to keep the UI in sync with your app's state. Sometimes your app needs to retrieve state from somewhere else or display it outside the document, maybe in the browser title, for example. When your app performs side effects by reaching outside its components, you should wrap the code by using the useEffect hook, discussed in chapter 4, to keep all the pieces synchronized.
- Chapter 5 uses the useRef hook to update state without causing a re-render (when working with a timer ID, for example) and to maintain references to elements on the page, like text boxes on forms.
- Our apps use multiple components, and chapter 6 investigates strategies for sharing state, passing it down via props. The chapter shows how to share the updater and dispatch functions from useState and useReducer and how to create an unchanging reference to a function with the useCallback hook.
- Components sometimes rely on functions to generate or transform data in some way. If those functions take a relatively long time to do their thing, you want to call them only when absolutely necessary. Chapter 7 shows how to enlist the help of the useMemo hook to limit when expensive functions run.
- Sometimes the same state values are used widely by many components across an app. Chapter 8 explains how to use React's Context API and useContext hook to share state without passing props down through multiple levels of components.
- React Hooks are just functions. You can move code that calls hooks into functions outside your components. Such functions, or *custom hooks*, can then be shared among components and across projects. Chapter 9 explains why and how you'd create custom hooks, with plenty of examples, and highlights the Rules of Hooks.

- Popular React libraries have been updated to work with hooks. Chapter 10 makes use of third-party hooks from React Router, for managing state in the URL, and React Query for painlessly syncing your UI with state stored on a server.

Part 2 explains how to more effectively load component code for larger apps and use `Suspense` components and error boundaries to organize fallback UI as resources are loading. It then dives into experimental APIs for integrating data loading with Suspense and working in Concurrent Mode:

- Chapter 11 discusses code splitting, combining `React.lazy` for lazy-loading components, `Suspense` components for showing fallback UI as your components lazily load, and error boundaries for showing fallback UI if something goes wrong.
- In chapter 12, we head into more experimental territory, looking at how libraries might integrate data fetching and image loading with Suspense.
- Finally, in chapter 13, we explore some volatile APIs that work only in Concurrent Mode. The `useTransition` and `useDeferredValue` hooks and the `SuspenseList` component are all designed to improve the user experience during state changes in your apps. Exactly how they work is still changing, but the chapter gives you a heads-up about the problems they're trying to solve.

While the book's main example app is built up over the course of the book, you should have no problems if you want to head straight for a certain chapter or hook. If you want to run individual code examples, you can check out the corresponding repo branch and go from there.

The chapters also include exercises to practice the ideas just presented. They mostly ask you to replicate the approach from one page of the example app on another page. For example, the book may show you how to update the Bookables page and then ask you to do the same for the Users page. Getting your hands dirty with the code is an effective learning strategy for many, but you can always check out the solution code from the repo if necessary.

## About the code

The book includes an ongoing example, a bookings app, that we build up from chapter to chapter. The example provides a great context for discussing React Hooks and seeing them in action. But the focus of the book is on the hooks, not the bookings app, so, while most of the app's code is in the book, some updated listings are available in the example app's GitHub repo but are not shown in the book. The repo is at https://github.com/jrlarsen/react-hooks-in-action. I'll point out when you need to go to the repo for the latest changes. Waypoints in the development of the example app are on separate branches in the repo.

Some short examples also are not part of the main bookings app. Their code is either on CodeSandbox for React-based examples, or on JS Bin for vanilla JavaScript examples. The code listings in the book include links to GitHub, CodeSandbox, or JS Bin as appropriate.

The examples were all thoroughly tested using React 17.0.1. Chapter 13 is an exception; it uses the experimental release of React, so its examples are not guaranteed to work with any version other than the one used on its branches in the repo.

This book contains many examples of source code both in numbered listings and in line with normal text. In both cases, source code is formatted in a `fixed-width font like this` to separate it from ordinary text. Sometimes code is also **in bold** to highlight code that has changed from previous steps in the chapter, or because it is the focus of the surrounding discussion.

In some cases, the original source code has been reformatted; we've added line breaks and reworked indentation to accommodate the available page space in the book. In rare cases, even this was not enough, and listings include line-continuation markers (➥). Additionally, comments in the source code have often been removed from the listings when the code is described in the text. Code annotations accompany many of the listings, highlighting important concepts.

## liveBook discussion forum

Purchase of *React Hooks in Action* includes free access to a private web forum run by Manning Publications, where you can make comments about the book, ask technical questions, and receive help from the author and from other users. To access the forum, go to https://livebook.manning.com/book/react-hooks-in-action/discussion. You can also learn more about Manning's forums and the rules of conduct at https://livebook.manning.com/#!/discussion.

Manning's commitment to our readers is to provide a venue where a meaningful dialogue between individual readers and between readers and the author can take place. It is not a commitment to any specific amount of participation on the part of the author, whose contribution to the forum remains voluntary (and unpaid). We suggest you try asking the author some challenging questions lest his interest stray! The forum and the archives of previous discussions will be accessible from the publisher's website as long as the book is in print.

## Other online resources

The official React documentation at https://reactjs.org is a thorough, well-written resource and is in the process of being rewritten. Definitely check it out. This book's page at www.manning.com/books/react-hooks-in-action also has a few articles that expand on certain sections and ideas.

# *about the author*

**JOHN LARSEN** has been programming since the 1980s, starting with BASIC on a Commodore VIC-20 and moving on to Java, PHP, C#, and JavaScript. He's the author of *Get Programming with JavaScript*, also from Manning. A mathematics teacher in the UK for 25 years, he taught computing to high-schoolers and developed web-based programs to support teaching, learning, and communication in schools. More recently, John has taught English in Japan and is working hard to improve his Japanese language skills.

# *about the cover illustration*

The figure on the cover of *React Hooks in Action* is captioned "Femme de la Carie," or Woman from Caria. The illustration is taken from a collection of dress costumes from various countries by Jacques Grasset de Saint-Sauveur (1757–1810), titled *Costumes de Différents Pays*, published in France in 1797. Each illustration is finely drawn and colored by hand. The rich variety of Grasset de Saint-Sauveur's collection reminds us vividly of how culturally apart the world's towns and regions were just 200 years ago. Isolated from each other, people spoke different dialects and languages. In the streets or in the countryside, it was easy to identify where they lived and what their trade or station in life was just by their dress.

The way we dress has changed since then and the diversity by region, so rich at the time, has faded away. It is now hard to tell apart the inhabitants of different continents, let alone different towns, regions, or countries. Perhaps we have traded cultural diversity for a more varied personal life—certainly for a more varied and fast-paced technological life.

At a time when it is hard to tell one computer book from another, Manning celebrates the inventiveness and initiative of the computer business with book covers based on the rich diversity of regional life of two centuries ago, brought back to life by Grasset de Saint-Sauveur's pictures.

# Part 1

Part 1 of *React Hooks in Action with Suspense and Concurrent Mode* introduces React Hooks and covers the key hooks in the first stable release of React 17. You'll see how to manage state within function components, share state with children and deeper descendants, and synchronize state with outside services, servers, and APIs. You'll also learn how to create your own hooks (while following the rules) and make the most of third-party hooks from established libraries like React Router, React Query, and React Spring.

A booking app acts as a consistent context for the examples presented, and you'll see how to load and manage data and orchestrate the interactions between components and react to the actions of users. But first, what are hooks, and why are they a step in the right direction?

# *React is evolving*

*React* is a JavaScript library for building beautiful user interfaces. The React team wants the developer experience to be as great as possible so that developers are inspired and enabled to create delightful, productive user experiences. *React Hooks in Action with Suspense and Concurrent Mode* is your guide to some of the latest additions to the library, additions that can simplify your code, improve code reuse, and help make your applications slicker and more responsive, leading to happier developers and happier users.

This chapter gives a brief overview of React and its new features to whet your appetite for the details that follow later in the book.

## 1.1 What is React?

Say you are creating a user interface (UI) for the web, the desktop, for a smartphone, or even for a virtual reality (VR) experience. You want your page or app to display a variety of data that changes over time, like authenticated user info, filterable product lists, data visualization, or customer details. You expect the user to interact with the app, choosing filters and data sets and customers to view, filling in form fields, or even exploring a VR space! Or maybe your app will consume data from a network or from the internet, like social media updates, stock tickers, or product availability. React is here to help.

React makes it easy to build user interface *components* that are composable and reusable and that react to changes in data and to user interactions. A page from a social media site includes buttons, posts, comments, images, and video, among many other interface components. React helps update the interface as the user scrolls down the page, opens up posts, adds comments, or transitions to other views. Some components on the page might have repeated *subcomponents*, page elements with the same structure but different content. And those subcomponents could be made up of components too! There are image thumbnails, repeated buttons, clickable text, and icons aplenty. Taken as a whole, the page has hundreds of such elements. But by breaking such rich interfaces into reusable components, development teams can more easily focus on specific areas of functionality and put the components to use on multiple pages.

Making it easy to define and reuse components, and compose them into complex but understandable and usable interfaces is one of React's core purposes. Other frontend libraries are out there (like AngularJS, Vue.js, and Ember.js), but this is a React book, so we concentrate on how React approaches components, data flow, and code reuse.

Over the next few sections, we take a high-level look at how React helps developers build such apps, highlighting five of its key features:

- Building UI from reusable, composable components
- Describing UI by using JSX—a blend of HTML-style templating and JavaScript
- Making the most of JavaScript without introducing too many idiomatic constraints
- Intelligently synchronizing state and UI
- Helping manage the fetching of code, assets, and data

### 1.1.1   *Building a UI from components*

Social media sites show rich, hierarchical, multilayered user interfaces that React can help you design and code. But for now, let's start with something a bit simpler to get a feel for the features of React.

Say you want to build a quiz app to help learners test themselves on facts they've been studying. Your component should be able to show and hide questions, and show and hide answers. One question-and-answer pair might look something like figure 1.1.

You could create a component for the question section and a component for the answer section. But the structure of the two components is the same: each has a title, some text to show and hide, and a button to do the showing and hiding. React makes it easy to define a single component, say a `TextToggle` component, that you can use for both the question and the answer. You pass the title and text and whether the text

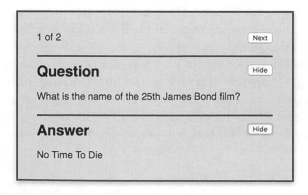

**Figure 1.1   Part of a quiz app showing a question and an answer**

should be shown to each of your `TextToggle` components. You pass the values as properties (or *props*), something like this:

```
<TextToggle title="Question" text="Who created JavaScript?" show={true} />

<TextToggle title="Answer" text="Brendan Eich" show={false} />
```

Wait! What now? Is that HTML? XML? JavaScript? Well, programming with React is programming in JavaScript. But React provides an HTML-like syntax for describing your UI called JSX. Before running your app, the JSX needs to be preprocessed to convert it into the actual JavaScript that creates the elements of your user interface. At first it seems a bit strange, mixing HTML with your JavaScript, but it turns out the convenience is a big plus. And once your code finally runs in the browser (or other environment), it really is just JavaScript. A package called *Babel* is almost always used to compile the code you write into the code that will run. You can find out more about Babel at https://babeljs.io.

This chapter offers only a high-level overview of React, so we won't explore JSX any further here. It's worth mentioning up front, though, because it's a widely used part of React development. In fact, in my opinion, React's JavaScriptiness is one of its appeals—*although other opinions are available*—and, for the most part, it doesn't introduce many constraints. While best practices have emerged and continue to do so, being a good JavaScript programmer and being a good React programmer are very similar skills.

So, say you've created the `TextToggle` component; what's next? With React, you can define new components made up of existing components. You can encapsulate the question card, showing the question and the answer, as its own `QuestionCard` component. And if you want to show multiple questions at once, your `Quiz` component UI could be made up of multiple `QuestionCard` components.

Figure 1.2 shows two `QuestionCard` components making up a `Quiz` component. The `Quiz` component is a container for the `QuestionCards` and has no visible presence apart from the cards it contains.

So, the `Quiz` component is made up of `QuestionCard` components, and they, in turn, are made up of `TextToggle` components, which are made up of standard HTML elements—an h2, a p, and a button, for example. Ultimately, the `Quiz` component comprises all native UI elements. Figure 1.3 shows the simple hierarchy for your `Quiz` component.

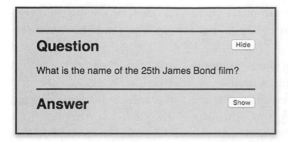
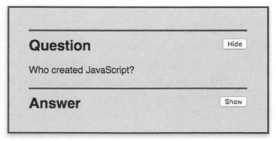

**Figure 1.2**  `Quiz` **component showing two** `QuestionCard` **components**

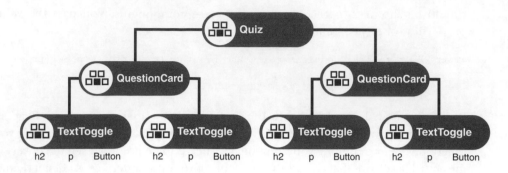

**Figure 1.3**  `Quiz` **component hierarchy**

React makes this component creation and composition much easier. And once you've crafted your components, you can reuse them and share them easily, too. Imagine a learning resource site with different pages for different topics. On each page, you could include your `Quiz` component, just passing it the quiz data for that topic.

Many React components are available to download in package management repositories like npm. There's no need to re-create common use cases, simple or complex, when well-used, well-tested examples of drop-down menus, date pickers, rich text editors, and probably quiz templates, also, are ready and waiting to be used.

React also provides mechanisms and patterns for passing your app's data to the components that need them. In fact, that synchronization, of state and UI, goes to the heart of what React is and what it does.

### 1.1.2  *Synchronizing state and UI*

React keeps an app's user interface synchronized with its data. The data held in your app at any moment is called the app's *state* and might include, for example, current posts, details about the logged-in user, whether comments are shown or hidden, or the content of a text input field. If new data arrives over the network or a user updates a value via a button or text input, React works out what changes need to be made to the display and efficiently updates it.

React intelligently schedules the order and timing of the updates to optimize the perceived performance of your app and improve the user experience. Figure 1.4 represents this idea, that React responds to a change in a component's state by re-rendering the user interface.

But updating state and re-rendering is not a one-off task. A visitor using your app is likely to cause a multitude of state changes, and React will need to repeatedly ask your components for the latest UI that represents those latest state values. It's your components' job to convert their state and props (the properties passed to them) into a description of their user interface. React then takes those UI descriptions and schedules updates to the browser's Document Object Model (DOM) where necessary.

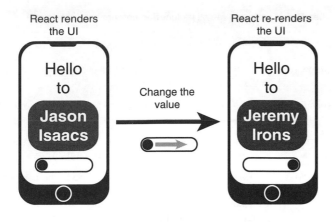

**Figure 1.4  When a value in a component's state changes, React re-renders the user interface.**

### CYCLE DIAGRAMS

To represent the ongoing cycle of state changes and UI updates, this book uses circular cycle diagrams to illustrate the interactions between your components and React. Figure 1.5 is a simple example, showing how React calls your component code when the component first appears and when a user updates a value.

The cycle diagrams are accompanied by tables, like table 1.1, describing the diagrams' steps in more detail. The diagram and table pair don't necessarily cover everything that is happening but pull out the key steps to help you understand the similarities and differences related to the way components work in different scenarios.

For example, this section's figure doesn't show *how* the event handler works with React to update the state; that detail is added in later diagrams when introducing the relevant React Hooks.

**Table 1.1  Some key steps when React calls and re-calls a function component**

| Step | What happens? | Discussion |
|------|---------------|------------|
| 1 | React calls the component. | To generate the UI for the page, React traverses the tree of components, calling each one. React will pass each component any props set as attributes in the JSX. |
| 2 | The component specifies an event handler. | The event handler may listen for user clicks, timers firing, or resources loading, for example. The handler will change the state when it runs later. React will hook up the handler to the DOM when it updates the DOM in step 4. |
| 3 | The component returns its UI. | The component uses the current state value to generate its user interface and returns it, finishing its work. |
| 4 | React updates the DOM. | React compares the description of the UI the component returns with the current description of the app's UI. It efficiently makes any necessary changes to the DOM and sets up or updates event handlers as necessary. |
| 5 | The event handler fires. | An event fires, and the handler runs. The handler changes the state. |

Table 1.1    Some key steps when React calls and re-calls a function component *(continued)*

| Step | What happens? | Discussion |
|---|---|---|
| 6 | React calls the component. | React knows the state value has changed so must recalculate the UI. |
| 7 | The component specifies an event handler. | This is a new version of the handler and may use the newly updated state value. |
| 8 | The component returns its UI. | The component uses the current state value to generate its user interface and returns it, finishing its work. |
| 9 | React updates the DOM. | React compares the description of the UI the component returns with the previous description of the app's UI. It efficiently makes any necessary changes to the DOM and sets up or updates event handlers as necessary. |

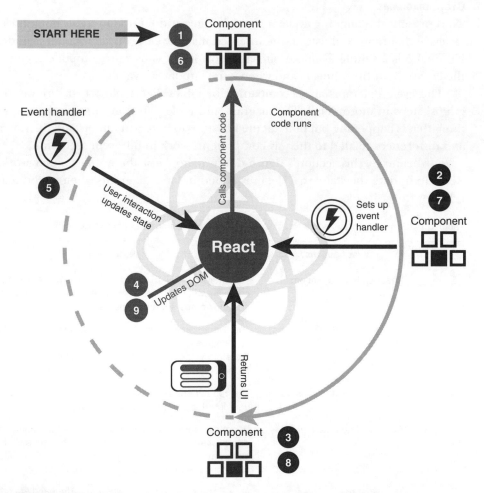

**Figure 1.5    React calls and re-calls your component to generate a description of its UI using the latest state.**

The illustrations also use consistent icons to represent key objects and actions discussed in the surrounding text, such as components, state values, event handlers, and UI.

### STATE IN THE QUIZ APP

Social media pages, like the one discussed at the start of the chapter, usually require a lot of state, with new posts being loaded and users liking posts, adding comments, and interacting with components in a variety of ways. Some of that state, like the current user, may be shared across many components, whereas other state, like a comment, may be local to a post.

In the Quiz app, you have a question-and-answer component, a `QuestionCard`, shown again in figure 1.6. Users can show and hide each question and answer and move to the next available question.

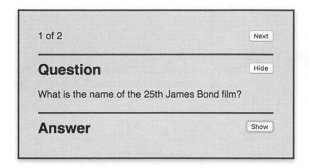

Figure 1.6    The question-and-answer component with the answer hidden

The `QuestionCard` component state includes the information needed to display the current question and answer:

- The question number
- The number of questions
- The question text
- The answer text
- Whether the question is hidden or shown
- Whether the answer is hidden or shown

Clicking the answer's Show button changes the state of the component. Maybe an `isAnswerShown` variable switches from `false` to `true`. React will notice that the state has changed, will update the displayed component to show the answer text, and toggle the button's text from Show to Hide (figure 1.7).

Clicking the Next button changes the question number. It will switch from question 1 to question 2, as shown in figure 1.8. If the questions and answers for the whole quiz are in memory, React can update the display straightaway. If they need to be loaded from a file or service, React can wait while the data is being fetched before updating the UI or, if the network is slow, show a loading indicator like a spinner.

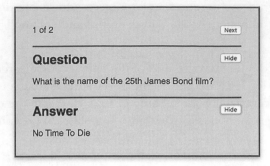

Figure 1.7   **The question-and-answer component with the answer shown**

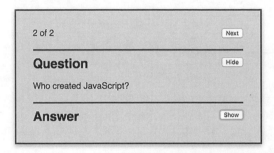

Figure 1.8   **The question-and-answer component showing the second question. The answer has been hidden.**

The simple Quiz app example doesn't need much state to perform its duties. Most real-world apps are more complicated. Deciding where state should live—whether a component should manage its own state, whether some components should share state, and whether some state should be globally shared—is an important part of building apps. React provides mechanisms for all three scenarios, and published packages, like Redux, MobX, React Query, and Apollo Client, for example, offer approaches to manage state via a data store outside your components.

In the past, whether or not your component managed some of its own state determined the method of component creation you would use; React provides two main methods: function components and class components, as discussed in the next section.

### 1.1.3   *Understanding component types*

To define a component, React lets you use two JavaScript structures: a function or a class. Before React Hooks, you would use a function when the component didn't need any local state (you would pass it all its data via props):

```
function MyComponent (props) {
  // Maybe work with the props in some way.
  // Return the UI incorporating prop values.
}
```

You would use a class when the component needed to manage its own state, perform side effects (like loading its data or getting hands-on with the DOM), or directly respond to events:

```
class MyComponent extends React.Component {
  constructor (props) {
    super(props);

    this.state = {                         Class components set up their
      // Set up state here.        ◁─┐    state in a constructor function.
    };
  }
                                                  Class components can include
  componentDidMount () {                           methods for various stages in
    // Perform a side effect like loading data.  ◁─  their life cycle.
  }
                                                  Class components have
  render () {                                     a render method that
    // Return the UI using prop values and state. ◁─ returns their UI.
  }
}
```

The addition of React Hooks means you can now use function components to manage state and side effects:

```
function MyComponent (props) {
  // Use local state.
  const [value, setValue] = useState(initialValue);      Use hooks to
  const [state, dispatch] = useReducer(reducer, initialState);  manage state.

  useEffect(() => {
    // Perform side effect.       ◁─┐ Use hooks to manage
  });                                 side effects.

  return (
    <p>{value} and {state.message}</p>  ◁─┐ Return UI directly
  );                                         from the function.
}
```

The React team recommends the use of functions for components in new projects (although there is no plan to remove class components, so no need for big rewrites of existing projects). Table 1.2 lists the component types and their descriptions.

**Table 1.2  Component types and their descriptions**

| Component type | Description |
| --- | --- |
| Stateless function component | A JavaScript function that is passed properties and returns UI |
| Function component | A JavaScript function that is passed properties and uses hooks to manage state and perform side effects, as well as returning UI |
| Class component | A JavaScript class that includes a render method that returns UI. It may also set up state in its constructor function and manage state and perform side effects in its life-cycle methods. |

Function components are just JavaScript functions that return a description of their user interface. When writing components, developers usually use JSX to specify the UI. The UI might depend on properties passed to the function. With stateless function components, that's where the story ends; they turn properties into UI. More generally, function components can now include state and work with side effects.

Class components are built using the JavaScript class syntax, extending from a `React.Component` or `React.PureComponent` base class. They have a constructor function, where state can be initialized, and methods that React calls as part of the component life cycle; for instance, when the DOM has been updated with the latest component UI or when the properties passed to the component change. They also have a `render` method that returns a description of the component's UI. Class components were *the* way to create stateful components that could cause side effects.

We'll see in section 1.3 how function components with hooks provide a better way of creating stateful components and managing side effects than classes. First, let's take a more general look at what's new in React and how the new features make working with React even better.

> ### Component side effects
>
> React components generally transform state into UI. When component code performs actions outside this main focus—perhaps fetching data like blog posts or stock prices from the network, setting up a subscription to an online service, or directly interacting with the DOM to focus form fields or measure element dimensions—we describe those actions as component *side effects*.
>
> We want our app and its components to behave predictably, so should make sure any necessary side effects are deliberate and visible. As you'll see in chapter 4, React provides the `useEffect` hook to help us set up and manage side effects in our functional components.

## 1.2   *What's new in React?*

React 16 included a rewrite of core functionality that has paved the way for a steady rollout of new library features and approaches. We'll explore several of the newest additions in the chapters that follow. The new features include the following:

- Stateful function components (`useState`, `useReducer`)
- Context API (`useContext`)
- Cleaner side-effect management (`useEffect`)
- Simple but powerful code reuse patterns (custom hooks)
- Code splitting (`lazy`)
- Faster initial loading and intelligent rendering (Concurrent Mode—experimental)
- Better feedback for loading states (`Suspense`, `useTransition`)
- Powerful debugging, inspection, and profiling (Development Tools and Profiler)
- Targeted error handling (error boundaries)

The words starting with *use*—useState, useReducer, useContext, useEffect, and useTransition—are examples of *React Hooks*. They are functions that you can call from React function components and that hook into key React functionality: state, life cycle, and context. React Hooks let you add state to function components, cleanly encapsulate side effects, and reuse code across your project. By using hooks, you do away with the need for classes, reducing and consolidating your code in an elegant way. Section 1.3 discusses React components and hooks in a little more detail.

Concurrent Mode and Suspense provide the means to be more deliberate about when code, data, and assets are loaded and to wrangle loading states and fallback content like spinners in a coordinated manner. The aim is to improve the user experience as applications load and states change and to improve the developer experience, making it easier to hook into these new behaviors. React can pause the rendering of expensive but nonurgent components and switch to urgent tasks, like reacting to user interactions, to keep your application responsive and to smooth the perceived path for user productivity.

The React documentation at https://reactjs.org is a great resource, providing clear, well-structured explanations of the philosophy, API, and recommended use of the library, as well as blog posts from the team and links to live code examples, conference talks on the new features, and other React-related resources. While this book will concentrate on hooks, Suspense, and Concurrent Mode, do check out the official docs to find out more about the other additions to React. In particular, take a look at the blog post on React 17 (https://reactjs.org/blog/2020/10/20/react-v17.html). The next major version of React was released in October 2020 but contains no new developer-facing features. Instead, it includes changes to make it easier to gradually upgrade React apps as well as further experimental development of Concurrent Mode and its APIs.

## 1.3 React Hooks can add state to function components

As discussed in section 1.1.2, one of React's core strengths is how it synchronizes application and component state with the UI. As the state changes, based on user interactions or data updates from the system or network, React intelligently and efficiently works out what changes should be made to the DOM in a browser or to the UI, more generally, in other environments.

The state could be local to a component, raised to a component higher in the tree, and shared among siblings via properties, or global and accessed via React's Context mechanism or higher-order components (functions that take a component as an argument and return a new component that wraps the passed-in component but that has extra functionality). For a component to have state, it used to be that you'd use a class component with the JavaScript class extending from React.Component. Now, with React Hooks, you can add state to function components.

### *1.3.1  Stateful function components: Less code, better organization*

Compared to classes, function components with hooks encourage cleaner, leaner code that can be easily tested, maintained, and reused. The *function component* is a JavaScript function that returns a description of its user interface. That UI depends on properties passed in and state managed or accessed by the component. Figure 1.9 shows a diagram representing a function component.

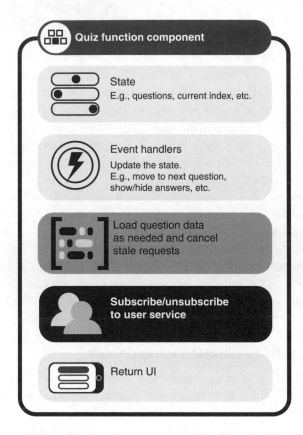

Figure 1.9   A `Quiz` function component with state and encapsulated code for loading data and managing a subscription to a service

The figure shows a `Quiz` component that performs a couple of side effects:

- It loads its own question data—both initial data and new questions when the user chooses a new question set.
- It subscribes to a user service—the service provides updates about other quiz users currently online so the user can join a team or challenge a rival.

In JavaScript, functions can contain other functions, so the component can contain event handlers that react to user interactions with the UI, for example, to show, hide, or submit answers, or to move to the next question. Within the component, you can easily encapsulate side effects, like fetching the question data or subscribing to the user service. You can also include cleanup code for those side effects to cancel any unfinished data fetching and unsubscribe from the user service. Using hooks, those features can even be extracted into their own functions outside the component, ready for reuse or sharing.

Here are some of the results of using the new function component approach rather than the older class-based approach:

- Less code
- Better code organization with related code kept together along with any cleanup code
- Extraction of features to external functions that can be reused and shared
- More easily testable components
- No need to call super() in a class constructor
- No need to work with this and bind handlers
- Simpler life-cycle model
- Local state in scope for handlers, side effect functions, and the returned UI

All of the items in this list facilitate writing code that's easier to understand and so easier to work with and maintain. That's not to say nuances might not trip up developers working with the new approaches for the first time, but I'll highlight those nuances as we delve more deeply into each concept and their connections throughout this book.

*React Hooks in Action* outlines the functional approach to component building, rather than using classes. But it's sometimes worth comparing the new methods with the old to motivate adoption and because it's interesting (and, in the case of hooks, a little cool!) to see the differences. If you're new to React and have never seen the code for class components, don't worry. Rest assured that the function components we'll be using for the rest of the book are the preferred approach going forward. The following discussion should still give you an idea of how this new approach simplifies and organizes the code needed to create React components.

The title of this section is "Stateful function components: Less code, better organization." Better than what? Well, with class components, state was set up in the constructor function, event handlers were bound to this, and side-effect code was split across multiple life-cycle methods (componentDidMount, componentWillUnmount, componentWillUpdate, and so on). It was common for code relating to different effects and features to sit side-by-side in a life-cycle method. You can see in figure 1.10 how the Quiz class component code for loading question data and subscribing to the user service is split across methods and how some methods include a mix of code for the two tasks.

Function components with hooks no longer need all the life-cycle methods because effects can be encapsulated into hooks. The change leads to neater, better organized

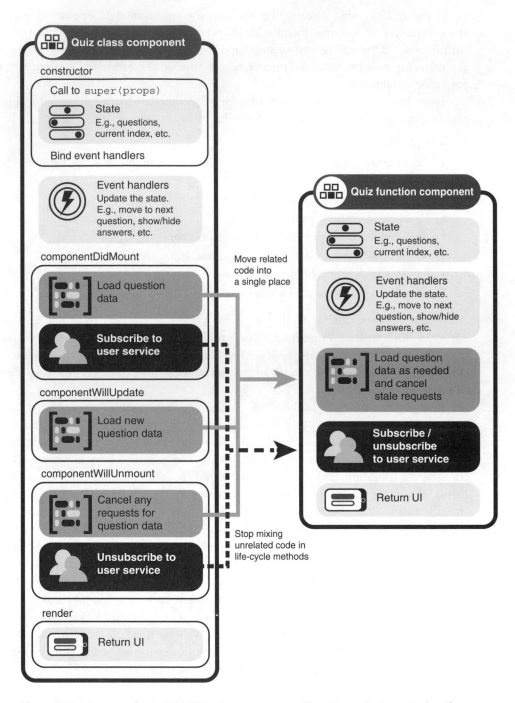

**Figure 1.10  A class component with code spread across life-cycle methods, and a function component with the same functionality but with less, better organized code**

code, as seen in the Quiz function component in figure 1.10. The code has been much more sensibly organized with the two side effects separated and their code consolidated in one place for each effect. The improved organization makes it easier to find the code for a particular effect, see how a component works, and maintain it in the future. In fact, keeping a feature or effect's code in one place makes it much easier to extract into an external function of its own, and that's what we'll discuss next.

### 1.3.2 Custom hooks: Easier code reuse

Function components with hooks encourage you to keep related side-effect logic in one place. If the side effect is a feature that many components will need, you can take the organization a step further and extract the code into its own external function; you can create what is called a *custom hook*.

Figure 1.11 shows how the question loading and user service subscription tasks for the Quiz function component could be moved into their own custom hooks. Any state that is used solely for those tasks can be moved into the corresponding hook.

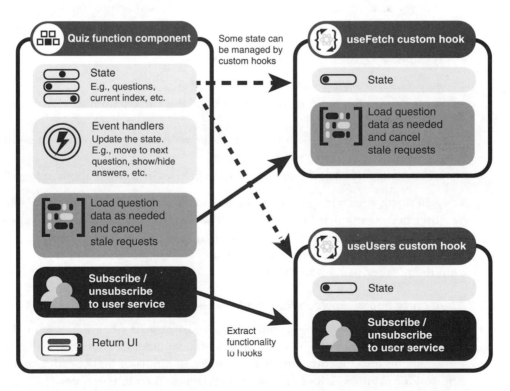

**Figure 1.11** The code for fetching question data and for subscribing to a user service can be extracted into custom hooks. The accompanying state can also be managed by the hooks.

There's no magic here; it's just how functions usually work in JavaScript: the function is extracted from the component and then called from the component. Once you have a custom hook, you aren't restricted to calling it from your original component. You can use it across many components, share it with your team, or publish it for others to use.

Figure 1.12 shows the new super-slim `Quiz` function component using the `useUsers` custom hook and the `useFetch` custom hook to carry out the user service subscription and question-fetching tasks that, previously, it carried out on its own. But now a second component, `Chat`, makes use of the `useUsers` custom hook too. Hooks make this kind of feature sharing much easier in React; custom hooks can be imported and used wherever they are needed in your portfolio of applications.

Each custom hook can maintain its own state, whatever it needs to perform its duties. And because hooks are just functions, if components need access to any of the hook's state, the hook can include the state in its return value. For example, a custom hook that fetches user info for a specified ID could store the fetched user data locally but return it to any components that call the hook. Each hook call encapsulates its own state, just like any other function.

To get a sense of the variety of common tasks that programmers have easily abstracted into custom hooks, take a look at the useHooks website at https://usehooks .com (figure 1.13).

It showcases easy-to-use recipes, including these:

- `useRouter`—Wraps the new hooks made available by React Router
- `useAuth`—Enables any component to get the current auth state and re-render if it changes
- `useEventListener`—Abstracts the process of adding and removing event listeners to components
- `useMedia`—Makes it easy to use media queries in your component logic

It's well worth researching on sites like useHooks or in package repositories like npm whether hooks exist that fit your use cases before rolling your own. If you already use libraries or frameworks for common scenarios like data fetching or state management, check the latest versions to see if they've introduced hooks to make working with them easier. We'll take a look at a few such packages in the next section.

### 1.3.3   *Third-party hooks provide ready-made, well-tested functionality*

Sharing functionality across components is not new; it's been an essential part of React development for some time. Hooks offer a much cleaner way of sharing code and hooking into functionality than the older methods of higher-order components and render props, which often lead to highly nested code ("wrapper hell") and false code hierarchies.

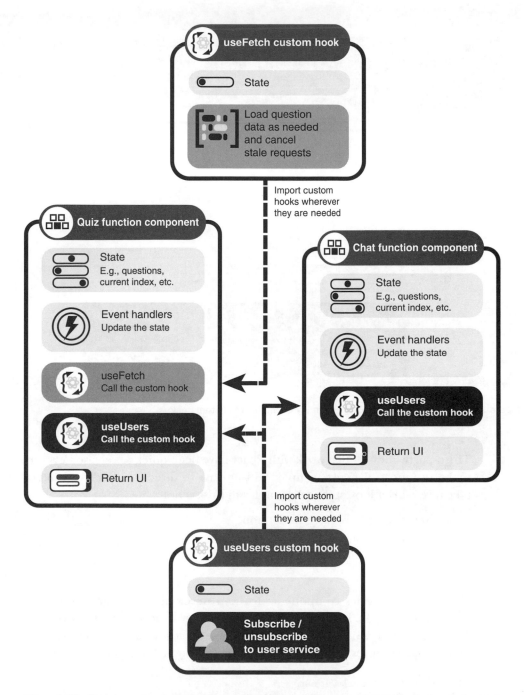

**Figure 1.12  You can extract code into custom hooks for reuse and sharing. The** `Quiz` **component calls both the** `useUsers` **and** `useFetch` **hooks. The** `Chat` **component calls the** `useUsers` **hook.**

**Figure 1.13   The useHooks website has many examples of custom hooks.**

Third-party libraries that work with React have been quick to release new versions that make the most of hooks' simpler API and more direct methods of integration. We take a very brief look at three examples in this section:

- React Router for page navigation
- Redux as an application data store
- React Spring for animation

### REACT ROUTER
*React Router* provides components to help developers manage navigation between pages in their apps. Its custom hooks make it easy to access common objects involved in navigation: useHistory, useLocation, useParams, and useRouteMatch. For example, useParams gives access to any parameters matched in a page's URL:

```
URL:     /quiz/:title/:qnum
Code:    const {title, qnum} = useParams();
```

### REDUX

For some applications, a separate store for state might be appropriate. *Redux* is a popular library for creating such stores and it is often combined with React via the React Redux library. Since version 7.1, React Redux offers hooks to make interacting with the store easier: useSelector, useDispatch, and useStore. For example, useDispatch lets you dispatch an action to update the state in the store. Say you have an application to build question sets for quizzes and you want to add a question:

```
const dispatch = useDispatch();
dispatch({type: "add question", payload: /* question data */});
```

The new custom hooks remove some of the boilerplate code that was associated with connecting a React application to a Redux store. React also has a built-in hook, useReducer, which might provide a simpler model for dispatching actions to update state and remove the perceived need for Redux in some cases.

### REACT SPRING

*React Spring* is a Spring-based animation library that currently provides five hooks to access its functionality: useSpring, useSprings, useTrail, useTransition, and useChain. For example, to animate between two values, you can opt for useSpring:

```
const props = useSpring({opacity: 1, from: {opacity: 0}});
```

React Hooks have made it easier for library authors to provide developers with simpler APIs that don't clutter their code with potentially deeply nested false component hierarchies. Similarly, a couple of other new React features, Concurrent Mode and Suspense, enable library authors and app developers to better manage asynchronous processes within their code and provide smoother, more responsive user experiences.

## 1.4　*Better UX with Concurrent Mode and Suspense*

We want to develop great experiences for our users that help them interact with our applications smoothly and enjoyably. That might mean them getting a job done in a productivity app, connecting with friends on a social platform, or capturing a crystal in a game. Whatever their goal, the interfaces we design and code should be a means to an end rather than a stumbling block. But our apps may need to load a lot of code, fetch a lot of data, and try to manipulate the data to provide the information the user needs, even as they switch quickly from view to view, scrolling and clicking and tapping as they go.

A large part of the motivation for the rewrites of React for versions 16 and 17 was to build the architecture to cope with the multiple demands put upon a user interface as it loads and manipulates data while users continue interacting with the application. Concurrent Mode is a core piece of that new architecture, and Suspense components fit the new mode naturally. But what problems do they solve?

Say you have an app that shows products in a long list and has a text box that users type in to filter the list. Your app updates the list as the user types. Each keystroke triggers the code to filter the list anew, requiring React to draw the updated list components to the screen. The expensive filtering process and recalculation and updating of the UI hogs the processing time, reducing the responsiveness of the text box. The experience for the user is one of a lagging, slow text box that doesn't show text as the user types. Figure 1.14, while obviously not being a perfect representation of how a browser might schedule code to run, does illustrate the point that long-running operations can slow updates to the screen, causing a poorer experience for users.

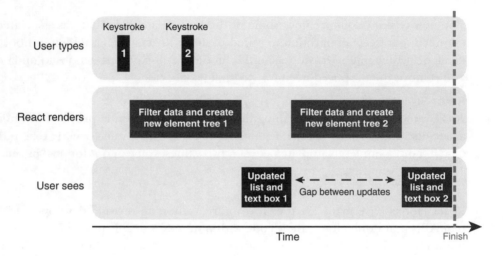

**Figure 1.14   Without Concurrent Mode, interactions like keystrokes are blocked by long-running updates.**

Wouldn't it be great if the app could prioritize the text box updates and keep the user experience smooth, pausing and restarting the filtering duties around the typing? Say hello to Concurrent Mode!

### 1.4.1   *Concurrent Mode*

With *Concurrent Mode*, React can schedule tasks in a more granular way, pausing its work building elements, checking for differences, and updating the DOM for previous state changes to make sure it responds to user interactions, for example. In the preceding filtering app example, React can pause rendering of the filtered list to make sure the text that the user is typing appears in the text box.

So how does Concurrent Mode enable this magic? The new React architecture breaks its tasks into smaller units of work, providing regular points for the browser or operating system to inform the application that a user is trying to interact with it. React's scheduler can then decide what jobs to do based on the priority of each. Reconciling and committing changes to one part of the component tree can be paused or

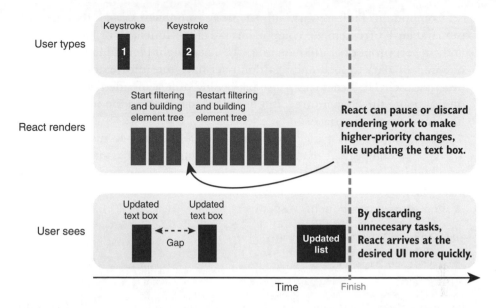

**Figure 1.15   In Concurrent Mode, React can pause longer-running updates to quickly react to user interactions.**

abandoned to make sure components with higher priority are updated first, as illustrated in figure 1.15.

It's not just user interactions that can benefit from this intelligent scheduling; responses to incoming data, lazily loaded components or media, or other asynchronous processes can also enjoy a smoother user-interface upgrade. React can continue to display a fully interactive existing UI (rather than a spinner) while it renders the UI for updated state in memory, switching to the new UI when enough of it is ready. Concurrent Mode enables a couple of new hooks, useTransition and useDeferredValue, that improve the user experience, smoothing the change from one view to another or one state to another. It also goes hand in hand with Suspense, both a component for rendering fallback content and a mechanism for specifying that a component is waiting for something, like loading data.

### 1.4.2   Suspense

As you have seen, React applications are built from components in a hierarchical tree. To display the current state of your app onscreen (using the DOM, for instance), React traverses your components and creates *element trees*, descriptions of the intended UI, in memory. It compares the latest tree with the previous one and intelligently decides what DOM updates need to be made to realize the intended UI. Concurrent mode lets React pause processing of parts of the element tree, either to work on higher-priority tasks or because the current component isn't ready to be processed.

Components built to work with `Suspense` can now *suspend* if they are not ready to return their UI (remember, components are either functions or have a render method and convert properties and state into UI). They might be waiting for component code or assets or data to load and just don't yet have the information they need to fully describe their UI. React can pause processing of a suspended component and carry on traversing the element tree. But how does that look on the screen? Will there be a hole in your user interface?

In addition to specifying a mechanism for components to suspend, React provides a `Suspense` component that you can use to plug holes that suspended components have left in your user interface. Wrap sections of your UI in `Suspense` components and use their `fallback` properties to let React know what content to show if one or more of the wrapped components suspends:

```
<Suspense fallback={<MySpinner />}>
   <MyFirstComponent />
   <MySecondComponent />
</Suspense>
```

`Suspense` allows the developer to deliberately manage loading states for multiple components, either showing fallbacks for individual components, groups of components, or the app as a whole. It provides a mechanism for library authors to update their APIs to work with the `Suspense` component, so their asynchronous features can make full use of the loading state management that `Suspense` provides.

## 1.5   *React's new publication channels*

To enable application developers and library authors to make the most of stable features in production but still prepare for upcoming features, the React team has started publishing code in separate channels:

- *Latest*—Stable semver release
- *Next*—Tracks the master branch of React development
- *Experimental*—Includes experimental APIs and features

For production, developers should stick with the Latest release; it's the one you get when installing React from npm (or another package manager). Much of Concurrent Mode and Suspense for data fetching are on the experimental channel at the time of writing. They are in the pipeline, but changes to the API may occur. The React and Relay (for data fetching) teams have been using many of the experimental features on the new Facebook website for some time. Such active use enables them to develop a strong understanding of the new approaches in context and at scale. By opening up the discussion of new features early and making them available in an experimental channel, the React team enables library authors to test integrations and new APIs, and application developers to start adapting to new mindsets and nuances.

## 1.6 Whom is this book for?

This book is for experienced JavaScript developers who want to learn about the latest features in React. It focuses on React Hooks, Concurrent Mode, and Suspense, using plenty of code examples to get you up to speed and ready to use these features in your own projects (although not necessarily in production yet for those features currently in React's Experimental channel). In addition to providing simple, practical examples, the book spends a little time probing a bit deeper into the reasoning behind some of the features and the nuances that developers would do well to be aware of.

This is not an introduction to React as a whole and won't cover the React ecosystem, build tools, styling, or testing in any detail. The reader should have a knowledge of basic React concepts and be able to create, build, and run a React application. The book will occasionally use class component examples as comparisons to the new function component approach but will not focus on teaching the class-based approach, higher-order components, or render props in any depth. (Don't worry if you don't know all those terms; you don't need to know about them to learn the new concepts.)

Readers should be comfortable with some of the more recent JavaScript syntax additions, like `const` and `let`, object and array destructuring, default parameters, the spread operator and array methods like `map`, `filter`, and `reduce`. Some of the comparisons with class components will obviously be using JavaScript's class syntax, so familiarity with that would be useful but is not essential.

## 1.7 Getting started

The code examples for the book's main example, a bookings app, are on GitHub at https://github.com/jrlarsen/react-hooks-in-action and are downloadable from the book's page at the Manning website (www.manning.com/books/react-hooks-in-action). Each step in the example apps development is on a separate Git branch, and the book's code listings include the name of the relevant branch. Smaller, standalone React examples are hosted on CodeSandbox (https://codesandbox.io), and a few simple vanilla JavaScript examples are on JS Bin (https://jsbin.com). Links to sandboxes and bins will accompany the book's listings.

### Summary

- Use React to create reusable components that make up an app by turning state into UI.
- Use JSX and props to describe the UI in an HTML-like syntax.
- Create function components that collocate related code and functionality.
- Use React Hooks to encapsulate and share functionality for components, performing side effects, and hooking into moments in the component's life cycle.
- Create your own custom hooks and use those provided by third-party libraries.
- Use `Suspense` components to provide fallbacks for components that take time to return their UI.

- Explore the experimental Concurrent Mode to work with multiple versions of the UI in memory, making it easier to transition smoothly from one interface to another in response to changes in state.
- Be aware of React's three publication channels: Latest, Next, and Experimental.
- Check out the React docs on https://reactjs.org.

# Managing component state with the useState hook

2

**This chapter covers**

- Asking React to manage component state values by calling `useState`
- Changing state values and triggering re-renders with an updater function
- Using the previous state to help generate new state values
- Managing multiple pieces of state
- Considering how React and components interact to persist and update state and synchronize state and UI

If you're building React apps, you're expecting the data your app uses to change over time. Whether it's fully server-rendered, a mobile app, or all in a browser, your application's user interface should represent the current data, or *state*, at the time of rendering. Sometimes multiple components throughout the app will use the data, and sometimes a component doesn't need to share its secrets and can manage its own state without the help of mammoth, application-wide, state-store behemoths. In this chapter, we keep it personal and concentrate on components taking care of themselves, without regard for other components around them.

Figure 2.1 is a very basic illustration of React's job: it should use the current state to render the UI. If the state changes, React should re-render the UI. The illustration shows a name in a friendly message. When the name value changes, React updates the UI to show the new name in its message. We usually want the state and UI to be in sync (although we might choose to delay synchronization during state transitions—when fetching the latest data, for example).

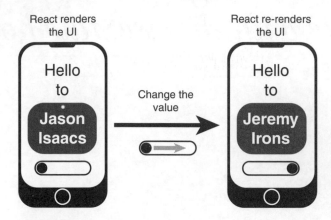

**Figure 2.1   When you change a value in a component, React should update the UI.**

React provides a small number of functions, or *hooks*, to enable it to track values in your components and keep the state and UI in sync. For single values, React gives us the useState hook, and that's the hook we explore in this chapter.

We'll look at how to call the hook, what it returns, and how to use it to update the state, triggering React to update the UI. Components often need more than one piece of state to do their jobs, so we'll see how to call useState multiple times to handle multiple values. It's not just a matter of documenting the useState API (you can go to the official React docs for that). We'll use the discussion of the useState hook to help you better understand what function components are and how they work. To that end, we'll finish the chapter with a review of the key concepts met as our code listings have evolved.

Talking of code listings, in this chapter, we'll start work on the app that will form the main example throughout this book. The example acts as a consistent context in which we use React Hooks to solve common coding problems. A little bit of house-keeping is required to set up the app, but once that's done, we'll be able to concentrate on a single component for the rest of the chapter.

## 2.1   Setting up the bookings manager app

Your fun but professional company has numerous resources that can be booked by staff: meeting rooms, AV equipment, technician time, table football, and even party supplies. One day, the boss asks you to set up the skeleton of an app for the company network that lets staff book the resources. The app should have three pages, for Bookings, Bookables, and Users, as shown in figure 2.2. (Technically, it's a single-page application, and the pages are really components, but we'll keep calling them *pages* because from the user's perspective, they're switching from page to page.)

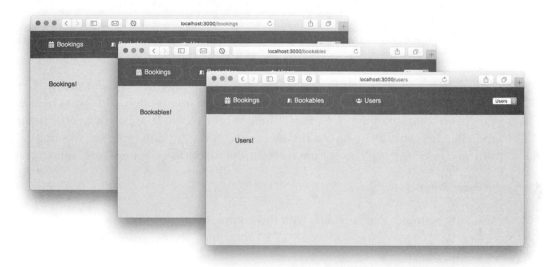

**Figure 2.2   The Bookings app has three pages: Bookings, Bookables, and Users.**

By the end of this section, you'll be able to display each page and use the links to navigate between them. The project folder at the end of the section will include public and src folders that look like those in figure 2.3.

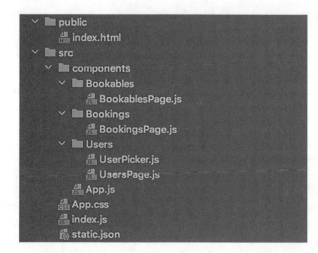

**Figure 2.3   The public and src folders after our initial setup**

You can see how the subfolders inside the components folder correspond to the three pages. We have six jobs to do to get the app into the shape shown in the figure:

1  Use `create-react-app` to generate the skeleton for our bookings app.
2  Remove the `create-react-app` generated files we won't be using.
3  Edit four of the files that are left in the public and src folders.
4  Install a few packages from npm.
5  Add a database file to give the app some data to display.
6  Create subfolders for each page and put the page components in them.

Alternatively, you can find the code examples for the ongoing bookings example app on GitHub at https://github.com/jrlarsen/react-hooks-in-action, with branches set up for each evolution of the code. Each listing for the example app includes the name of the branch to check out, linked (in the ebook) to the GitHub repo. For example, after you've cloned the repo, to get the code for the first branch, enter this command:

```
git checkout 0201-pages
```

Install the project dependencies with this command:

```
npm i
```

Run the project with this command:

```
npm start
```

You can then skip to section 2.2.

For those who want to get their hands dirty building most of the app from scratch, the first thing we need is a React app.

### 2.1.1   Generating the app skeleton with create-react-app

React's `create-react-app` utility generates projects with preset linting and compilation workflows set up. It also comes with a development server that's perfect for us as we work through the ever-evolving stages of our app. Let's use `create-react-app` to generate a new React project called `react-hooks-in-action`. We don't need to install `create-react-app` with npm before running it; we can run it from its repository by using the `npx` command:

```
npx create-react-app react-hooks-in-action
```

The command will take a little while to do its thing, and you should end up with a whole bunch of generated files in a react-hooks-in-action folder. When I ran the `create-react-app` command, my computer used npm to install the files. If you have Yarn installed, `create-react-app` will use that instead, and you'll get a yarn.lock file instead of package-lock.json. (npx is a handy command that's included when you install npm. Its author, Kat Marchán, explains the thinking behind it in the Medium article "Introducing npx" at http://mng.bz/RX2j.)

We don't need all of the installed files for our app, so let's quickly delete a few. From the public folder inside the react-hooks-in-action folder, remove all but index.html. From the src folder, remove all but App.css, App.js, and index.js. Figure 2.4 highlights the files to remove.

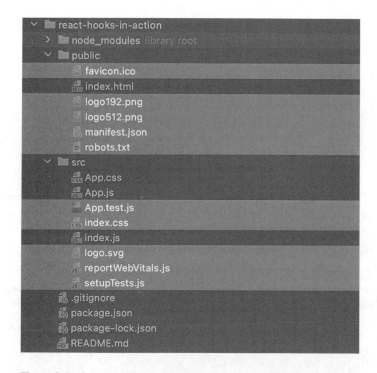

**Figure 2.4   Our project doesn't need many of the default files generated by `create-react-app`.**

Figure 2.5 shows the four main files left in the public and src folders. We use them to run our app, importing the components we build throughout the book.

The four files are set up for React's demo page, not our bookings app. It's time for a few tweaks.

### 2.1.2   Editing the four key files

Our little workhorse files will get the app up and running. Let me introduce you to:

- /public/index.html—The web page that contains the app
- /src/App.css—Some styles to organize elements on the page

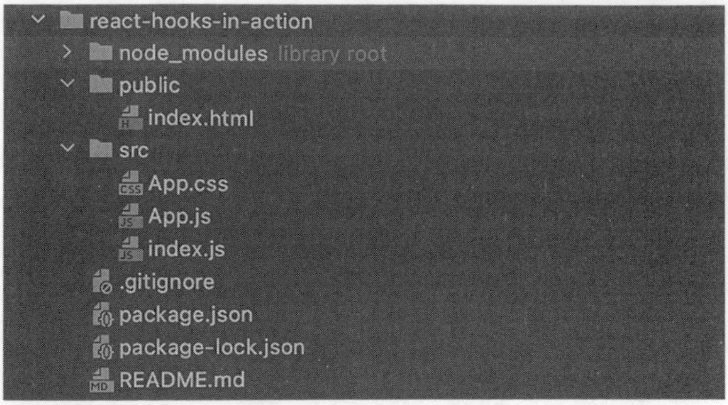

**Figure 2.5   The four files we need to set up in the public and src folders**

- /src/components/App.js—The root component that contains all the others
- /src/index.js—The file that imports the App component and renders it to the index.html page

## INDEX.HTML

Inside the public folder, edit the index.html file. A lot of the boilerplate generated by create-react-app can come out. The div element with an id of root must stay; it's the container element for the app. React will render the App component into that div. You can also set the title for the page, as shown in the following listing.

> **Branch**: 0201-pages, *File*: /public/index.html
>
> **Listing 2.1   The HTML skeleton for the bookings app**

```
<!DOCTYPE html>
<html lang="en">
  <head>
    <meta charset="utf-8" />
    <meta name="viewport" content="width=device-width, initial-scale=1" />
    <title>Bookings App</title>          ◁──┐  Set the title
  </head>                                      for the page.
  <body>
    <div id="root"></div>               ◁──  Make sure there is a
  </body>                                     div with an id of root.
</html>
```

That's all we need for the web page. The App component will appear in the div, and all our other components—for bookable items, bookings, users, and their separate pages—will be managed by the App component.

## APP.CSS

This book isn't here to teach you Cascading Style Sheets (CSS), so it doesn't focus on listings of styles. At times, CSS will be used in combination with events in components (when loading data, for example), and the relevant styles will be highlighted at those times. The stylesheet will develop over time, so, if you're interested, take a look in the repo. The initial styles can be found at *Branch:* 0201-pages, *File:* /src/App.css. (If you're not particularly interested in the evolution of the CSS throughout the project but want to code along with the JavaScript, just grab the App.css file from the finished project.)

The styles use CSS grid properties to position the main components on each page, and some CSS variables to define common colors for text and backgrounds.

### APP.JS

The App component is the root component for our application. It displays the header with its links and user-picker drop-down, as shown in figure 2.6.

**Figure 2.6   The header with three links and a drop-down list**

The App component also sets up routes to the three main pages, as shown in listing 2.2. The router shows the appropriate page to the user by matching the URL with a page component. The App.js file has been moved to a new components folder. It imports a number of components that we create later in the chapter.

> *Branch:* **0201-pages,** *File:* **/src/components/App.js**
>
> **Listing 2.2   The App component**

```
import {
  BrowserRouter as Router,          Import the routing
  Routes,                           elements from
  Route,                            react-router-dom.
  Link
} from "react-router-dom";

import "../App.css";                         Import the icons for
                                             the navigation links.

import {FaCalendarAlt, FaDoorOpen, FaUsers} from "react-icons/fa";

import BookablesPage from "./Bookables/BookablesPage";    Import the separate
import BookingsPage from "./Bookings/BookingsPage";       page components
import UsersPage from "./Users/UsersPage";                and the UserPicker.
import UserPicker from "./Users/UserPicker";

export default function App () {
  return (
    <Router>                          Wrap the app in a
      <div className="App">           Router component
        <header>                      to enable routing.
          <nav>
            <ul>
```

```
          <li>
            <Link to="/bookings" className="btn btn-header">
              <FaCalendarAlt/>
              <span>Bookings</span>
            </Link>
          </li>
          <li>
            <Link to="/bookables" className="btn btn-header">
              <FaDoorOpen/>
              <span>Bookables</span>
            </Link>
          </li>
          <li>
            <Link to="/users" className="btn btn-header">
              <FaUsers/>
              <span>Users</span>
            </Link>
          </li>
        </ul>
      </nav>

      <UserPicker/>
    </header>

    <Routes>
      <Route path="/bookings" element={<BookingsPage/>}/>
      <Route path="/bookables" element={<BookablesPage/>}/>
      <Route path="/users" element={<UsersPage/>}/>
    </Routes>
  </div>
  </Router>
  );
}
```

**Use Link components along with the Router.**

**Use the "to" attribute to specify where the link goes.**

**Use imported icons to decorate the links.**

**Place the UserPicker in the header.**

**Wrap the collection of Route components in a Routes component.**

**Use a Route for each path you want to match.**

**Match a path to display a particular page component.**

**Specify the component to display for the matched path.**

Notice that there is no import React from "react" at the top of the listing. React components used to need that line so they would work when the JSX in them was converted into regular JavaScript. But the tools that compile React, like create-react-app, can transform JSX in the latest versions of React without needing the import statement. Read about this change on the React blog (http://mng.bz/2ew8).

The app uses React Router version 6 to manage the display of its three pages. At the time of writing, React Router 6 is a beta release available via React Router's Next channel. Install it like this:

```
npm i history react-router-dom@next
```

Find out more about React Router on its GitHub page (https://github.com/React-Training/react-router). We use the Link component to display our page links in the header, and Route elements to conditionally display page components depending on the matched URL. For example, if the user visits /bookings, the BookingsPage component will be displayed:

```
<Route path="/bookings" element={<BookingsPage/>}/>
```

For now, you don't need to worry about React Router; it's just managing the links and the display of our page components. We'll make much more use of it in chapter 10, when we start to use some of the custom hooks it provides to access matched URLs and query string parameters.

As you can see in figure 2.7, we've decorated the header links with icons from Font Awesome (https://fontawesome.com).

**Figure 2.7   The header includes Font Awesome icons beside each link.**

The icons are available as part of the react-icons package, so we need to install the package:

```
npm i react-icons
```

The react-icons GitHub page (https://github.com/react-icons/react-icons) includes details of the icon sets available in the package, along with links to relevant licensing information.

The `App` component also imports the three page components—`BookablesPage`, `BookingsPage`, and `UsersPage`—and the `UserPicker` component. We create those in section 2.1.4.

### INDEX.JS

React needs a JavaScript file to act as a starting point for the application. In the src folder, edit the index.js file to look like the following listing. It imports the `App` component and renders it into the root `div` seen in the index.html file back in listing 2.1.

> Branch: 0201-pages, *File:* /src/index.js

> **Listing 2.3   The top-level JavaScript file**

```
import ReactDOM from "react-dom";
import App from "./components/App";        ◁──┐ Import the App
                                                component.

ReactDOM.render(
  <App />,                                 ◁──── Specify App as the
  document.getElementById("root")          ◁──   component to render.
);
                                                Specify where to render
                                                the App component.
```

And that's the four existing files tweaked! We still need to create the page components for the `App` component to import and the `UserPicker` drop-down for the header. First, the app will need some bookables and users to show. Let's give it some data.

### 2.1.3   Adding a database file for the application

Our application needs a few types of data, including users, bookables, and bookings. We start off by importing all of the data from a single JavaScript Object Notation (JSON) file, static.json. We just need some bookables and users to show in lists, so the initial data file isn't too complicated, as you can see in the following listing. (You can copy the data from the listing's branch on GitHub by visiting the specified file.)

**Branch**: 0201-pages, *File*: /src/static.json

**Listing 2.4    The bookings app data structure**

```json
{
  "bookables": [ /* array of bookable objects */ ],     ◁─┐   Assign an array of
                                                            bookables data to the
                                                            bookables property.
  "users": [ /* array of user objects */ ],        ◁──    Specify the users who
                                                          can use the app.
  "bookings": [],        ◁──┐   Leave the bookings
                             empty for now.
  "sessions": [     ◁──┐
    "Breakfast",        Configure the
    "Morning",          available sessions.
    "Lunch",
    "Afternoon",
    "Evening"
  ],

  "days": [        ◁──┐   Configure the days
    "Sunday",            of the week.
    "Monday",
    "Tuesday",
    "Wednesday",
    "Thursday",
    "Friday",
    "Saturday"
  ]
}
```

Each element in the array of bookables is an object that looks something like this:

```json
{
  "id": 3,
  "group": "Rooms",
  "title": "Games Room",
  "notes": "Table tennis, table football, pinball! Please tidy up!",
  "sessions": [0, 2, 4],
  "days": [0, 2, 3, 4, 5, 6]
}
```

The bookables are stored in an array of bookable objects, assigned to the `bookables` property. Each bookable has `id`, `group`, `title`, and `notes` properties. The data in the book's code repo has slightly longer notes, but the structure is the same. Each bookable also specifies the days and sessions for which it can be booked.

Users are also stored as objects, with this structure:

```
{
  "id": 1,
  "name": "Mark",
  "img": "user1.png",
  "title": "Envisioning Sculptor",
  "notes": "With the company for 15 years, Mark has consistently…"
}
```

The bookables will be listed by the `BookablesPage` component and the users by the `UsersPage` component. We'd better get those pages built!

### 2.1.4 *Creating page components and a UserPicker.js file*

As we add functionality to the app, we use components to encapsulate that functionality and to demonstrate techniques that working with hooks offers. We put our components in folders related to the page they're on. Create three new folders within the components folder and name them Bookables, Bookings, and Users. For the skeleton app, create three structurally identical placeholder pages like the one in the following listing. Call them `BookablesPage`, `BookingsPage`, and `UsersPage`.

---

*Branch*: 0201-pages, *File*: /src/components/Bookables/BookablesPage.js

**Listing 2.5   The `BookablesPage` component**

```
export default function BookablesPage () {
  return (
    <main className="bookables-page">          ◁─┐  Assign each page a class so
      <p>Bookables!</p>                           │  the CSS file can set out the
    </main>                                       │  page as appropriate.
  );
}
```

We finish off the app setup with a `UserPicker` component in the following listing. For now, it just shows the word *Users* in a drop-down list. We populate it with data later in the chapter.

---

*Branch*: 0201-pages, *File*: /src/components/Users/UserPicker.js

**Listing 2.6   The `UserPicker` component**

```
export default function UserPicker () {
  return (
    <select>
      <option>Users</option>
    </select>
  );
}
```

All the pieces are in place for our ongoing exploration of hooks in the context of the bookings app. Test that it's working by starting the `create-react-app` development server:

```
npm start
```

If all's well, you can navigate between the three pages, with each shouting its identity at you: Bookables! Bookings! Users! Let's calm down the Bookables page by displaying the bookables from the database.

## 2.2  *Storing, using, and setting values with useState*

Your React applications look after a certain state: values that are shown in the user interface or that help manage what's shown. The state may include posts on a forum, comments for those posts, and whether the comments are shown, for example. When users interact with the app, they change its state. They may load more posts, toggle whether comments are visible, or add their own comments. React is there to make sure state and UI are in sync. When the state changes, React needs to run the components that use that state. The components return their UI by using the latest state values. React compares the returned UI with the existing UI and efficiently updates the DOM as necessary.

Some state is shared across the application, some is shared by a few components, and some is managed locally by a component itself. If components are just functions, how can they persist their state across renders? Are their variables not lost when they finish executing? And how does React know when the variables change? If React is faithfully trying to match the state and the UI, it definitely needs to know about changes to the state, right?

The simplest way to persist state across calls to your components and keep React in the loop when you change a component's state is the `useState` hook. The `useState` hook is a function that enlists React's help to manage state values. When you call the `useState` hook, it returns both the latest state value *and* a function for updating the value. Using the updater function keeps React in the loop and lets it do its syncy business.

This section introduces the `useState` hook, covering why we need it and how it's used. In particular, we look at the following:

- Why just assigning values to variables doesn't let React do its job
- How `useState` returns both a value and a function for updating that value
- Setting an initial value for the state, both directly as a value and lazily as a function
- Using the updater function to let React know you want to change the state
- Making sure you have the latest state when you call the updater function and need to use an existing value to generate a new value

That list might seem a little scary, but the `useState` hook is very easy to use (and you'll be using it a lot!), so don't worry; we're just covering all the bases. Before we call useState for the first time, let's see what happens if we just try to manage the state ourselves.

### 2.2.1 Assigning new values to variables doesn't update the UI

Figure 2.8 shows what we want from our first attempt at the BookablesList component: a list of four bookable rooms with the Lecture Hall selected.

**Figure 2.8** The BookablesList component showing a list of rooms with the selected room highlighted

To display the list of rooms, the BookablesList component needs to get its hands on the data for the list. It imports the data from our static.json database file. The component also needs to track which bookable is currently selected. Listing 2.7 shows the code for the component, with a room selection hardcoded by setting bookableIndex to 1. (*Notice we're on a new Git branch; switch to it with the command* git checkout 0202-hard-coded.)

**Branch**: 0202-hard-coded, *File*: /src/components/Bookables/BookablesList.js

**Listing 2.7** The BookablesList component with hardcoded selection

```
import {bookables} from "../../static.json";        ◁─┐  Use object destructuring
                                                         to assign the bookables
export default function BookablesList () {                data to a local variable.

  const group = "Rooms";              ◁─┐  Set the group of bookables to be shown.

  const bookablesInGroup = bookables.filter(b => b.group === group);

  const bookableIndex = 1;            ◁──┐  Hardcode the index of
                                           the selected bookable.
  return (
    <ul className="bookables items-list-nav">
      {bookablesInGroup.map((b, i) => (        ◁──┐  Map over the bookables to
        <li                                         create a list item for each one.
          key={b.id}
          className={i === bookableIndex ? "selected" : null}    ◁────┐
        >
          <button                           Set the class by comparing the
            className="btn"                  current index to the selected index.
```

**Filter the bookables to just those in the group.**

```
          >
            {b.title}
          </button>
        </li>
      ))}
    </ul>
  );
}
```

The code assigns the array of bookables from the static.json file to a local variable called bookables. We could've taken an extra step:

```
import data from "../../static.json";

const {bookables} = data;
```

But we don't need the data for anything else, so we did our assignment to bookables directly inside the import:

```
import {bookables} from "../../static.json";
```

This *destructuring* approach is one we use often throughout the book.

With the array of bookables in hand, we filter it to get just those bookables in the specified group:

```
const group = "Rooms";

const bookablesInGroup = bookables.filter(b => b.group === group);
```

The filter method returns a new array, and we assign that to the bookablesInGroup variable. We then map over the bookablesInGroup array to generate the list of bookables for display. Within the map function, I use short variable names, b for bookable and i for index, because they're used right away, close to their assignment. I think their meaning is clear, but you may prefer more descriptive variable names.

To display our new component, we need to wire it into the BookablesPage component. The following listing shows the two changes needed.

---

**Branch: 0202-hard-coded, *File*: /src/components/Bookables/BookablesPage.js**

**Listing 2.8   The BookablesPage component showing the BookablesList**

```
import BookablesList from "./BookablesList";          ◁——  Import the new
                                                            component.
export default function BookablesPage () {
  return (
    <main className="bookables-page">
      <BookablesList/>                     ◁——  Replace the
    </main>                                      placeholder text with
  );                                             the component.
}
```

Have a go at changing the hardcoded index value in `BookablesList`. The component will always highlight the bookable with the specified index—so far, so good. But, it's all very well changing the code to change the highlighted room. What we really want is for the user to change it by clicking a bookable, so let's add an event handler to each list item button. Clicking a bookable should select it, and the UI should update to highlight the selected item. The following listing includes a `changeBookable` function and an `onClick` event handler that calls it.

**Branch**: 0203-direct-change, **File**: /src/components/Bookables/BookablesList.js

**Listing 2.9  Adding an event handler to the `BookablesList` component**

```
import {bookables} from "../../static.json";

export default function BookablesList () {
  const group = "Rooms";
  const bookablesInGroup = bookables.filter(b => b.group === group);

  let bookableIndex = 1;          ← Declare the variable with let because
                                    it will be assigned new values.

  function changeBookable (selectedIndex) {
    bookableIndex = selectedIndex;     Declare a function that assigns the
    console.log(selectedIndex);        index of the clicked bookable to
  }                                    the bookableIndex variable.

  return (
    <ul className="bookables items-list-nav">
      {bookablesInGroup.map((b, i) => (
        <li
          key={b.id}
          className={i === bookableIndex ? "selected" : null}
        >
          <button
            className="btn"
            onClick={() => changeBookable(i)}    ← Include an onClick handler
          >                                        that passes the index of
            {b.title}                              the clicked bookable to the
          </button>                                changeBookable function.
        </li>
      ))}
    </ul>
  );
}
```

Clicking one of the rooms now assigns that room's index to the `bookableIndex` variable. *Et voilà!* Oh. Hang on . . . If you run the code in listing 2.9 and try clicking different rooms, you'll see that the highlighting doesn't change. But, the code *does* update the `bookableIndex` value! You can check the console to see the index being logged. Why is the new selection not shown on the screen? Why has React not updated the UI? Why do people always ignore me?

It's okay, deep breaths. Remember, components are functions that return UI. React calls the functions to get a description of the UI. How does React know when to call the function and update the UI? Just because you change the value of a variable within your component function doesn't mean React will notice. If you want to get noticed, you can't just say "Hello, World!" to people in your head; you have to say it out loud. Figure 2.9 shows what happens when you directly change a value in a component: React doesn't notice. It's happy, whistling away, polishing its widgets—and the UI stays rock-solid, unchanged.

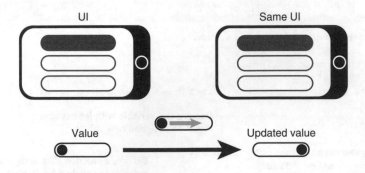

Figure 2.9    Directly changing a variable in our component code doesn't update the UI.

So how do we get React's attention and let it know it has work to do? We call the use-State hook.

### 2.2.2    *Calling useState returns a value and an updater function*

We want to alert React that a value used within a component has changed so it can rerun the component and update the UI. Just updating the variable directly won't do. We need a way of changing that value, some kind of updater function, that triggers React to call the component with the new value and get the updated UI, as shown in figure 2.10.

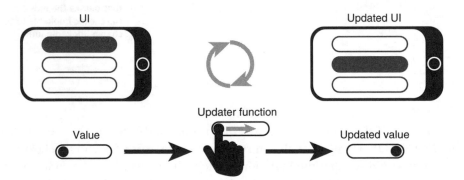

Figure 2.10    Rather than changing a value directly, we call an updater function. The updater function changes the value, and React updates the display with the recalculated UI from the component.

To avoid our component state value disappearing when the component code finishes running, we get React to manage the value for us. That's what the useState hook is for. Every time React calls our component to get ahold of its UI, the component can ask React for the latest state value and for a function to update the value. The component can use the value when generating its UI and use the updater function when changing the value, for example, in response to a user clicking an item in a list.

Calling useState returns a value and its updater function in an array with two elements, as shown in figure 2.11.

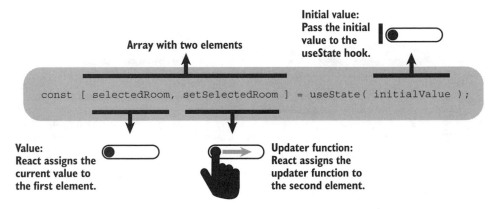

**Figure 2.11**  The useState function returns an array with two elements: a value and an updater function.

You could assign the returned array to a variable, and then access the two elements individually, by index, like this:

```
const selectedRoomArray = useState();          ←┐  The useState function returns an array.

const selectedRoom = selectedRoomArray[0];     ←───  The first element is the value.

const setSelectedRoom = selectedRoomArray[1];  ←┐  The second element is the
                                                 │  function for updating the value.
```

But it's more common to use array destructuring and assign the returned elements to variables in one step:

```
const [selectedRoom, setSelectedRoom] = useState();
```

Array destructuring lets us assign elements in an array to variables of our choosing. The names selectedRoom and setSelectedRoom are arbitrary and our choice, although it's common to start the variable name for the second element, the updater function, with set. The following would work just as well:

```
const [myRoom, updateMyRoom] = useState();
```

If you want to set an initial value for the variable, pass the initial value as an argument to the useState function. When React first runs your component, useState will return the two-element array as usual but will assign the initial value to the first element of the array, as shown in figure 2.12.

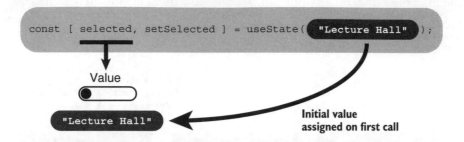

**Figure 2.12   When the component first runs, React assigns the initial value you pass to useState to the selected variable.**

The first time the following line of code is executed within a component, React returns the value Lecture Hall as the first element in the array. The code assigns that value to the selected variable:

```
const [selected, setSelected] = useState("Lecture Hall");
```

Let's update the BookablesList component to use the useState hook to ask React to manage the value of the selected item's index. We pass it 1 as the initial index. You should see the Lecture Hall highlighted when the BookablesList component first appears on the screen, as shown again in figure 2.13.

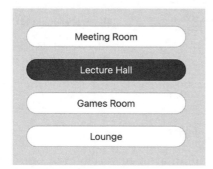

**Figure 2.13   The BookablesList component with Lecture Hall selected**

The following listing shows the updated code for the component. It includes an onClick event handler that uses the updater function assigned to setBookableIndex to change the selected index when a user clicks a bookable.

> *Branch:* 0204-set-index, *File:* /src/components/Bookables/BookablesList.js
>
> **Listing 2.10　Triggering a UI update when changing the selected room**

```
import {useState} from "react";                          ←┐  Import the
import {bookables} from "../../static.json";              ←┘  useState hook.

export default function BookablesList () {
  const group = "Rooms";
  const bookablesInGroup = bookables.filter(b => b.group === group);
  const [bookableIndex, setBookableIndex] = useState(1);    ←
                                                                Call useState and assign
                                                                the returned state value
                                                                and updater function to
                                                                variables.
  return (
    <ul className="bookables items-list-nav">
      {bookablesInGroup.map((b, i) => (
        <li
          key={b.id}
          className={i === bookableIndex ? "selected" : null}   ←  Use the state
        >                                                           value when
                                                                    generating
          <button                                                   the UI.
            className="btn"
            onClick={() => setBookableIndex(i)}   ←
          >                                           Use the updater
            {b.title}                               function to change
          </button>                                 the state value.
        </li>
      ))}
    </ul>
  );
}
```

React runs the BookablesList component code, returning the value for bookable-Index from the call to useState. The component uses that value when generating the UI to set the correct className attribute for each li element. When a user clicks a bookable, the onClick event handler uses the updater function, setBookableIndex, to tell React to update the value it's managing. If the value has changed, React knows it'll need a new version of the UI. React runs the BookablesList code again, assigning the updated state value to bookableIndex, letting the component generate the updated UI. React can then compare the newly generated UI to the old version and decide how to update the display efficiently.

With useState, React is now listening. I don't feel so lonely anymore. It's living up to its promise of keeping the state in sync with the UI. The BookablesList component describes the UI for a particular state and provides a way for users to change the state. React then does its magic, checking whether the new UI is different from the old (*diffing*), batching and scheduling updates, deciding on an efficient way to update DOM elements, and then doing the deed and reaching out to the DOM on our behalf. We fixate on the state; React does its diffing and updates the DOM.

**CHALLENGE 2.1**

Create a `UsersList` component that shows the list of users from the database. Enable the selection of a user and wire the component into the `UsersPage`. (Remember, if you haven't already, you can copy the full database file from the app's GitHub repo.)

**CHALLENGE 2.2**

Update the `UserPicker` drop-down list component so that it shows the users as options in the list. Don't worry about wiring up any event handlers for now. The challenge tasks are implemented in the 0205-user-lists branch.

In listing 2.10, we passed an initial value of 1 to `useState`. A user clicking a different bookable *replaces* that value with another number. What if we want to store something more complicated, like an object, as state? In that case, we need to be a bit more careful when updating the state. Let's see why.

### 2.2.3 *Calling the updater function replaces the previous state value*

If you're coming from the class-based approach to component building in React, you're used to state being an object with different properties for different state values. Moving to function components, you may try to replicate that state-as-an-object approach. It may feel more natural to have a single state object and have new state updates merge with the existing state.

But the `useState` hook is easy to use and easy to call multiple times, once for each state value you want React to monitor. It's worth getting used to separate calls to `useState` for each state property, as discussed further in section 2.4, rather than clinging to what's familiar. If you need to work with objects as state values or want to group some related values together (maybe a length and width, for example), you should be aware of how `setState` as a function component updater function is different from `this.setState` you use with a class component. In this section, we take a brief look at updating the state of an object in the two types of components.

#### THE CLASS COMPONENT APPROACH

With classes, you set up the state as an object in the constructor (or as a static property on the class):

```
class BookablesList extends React.Component {
  constructor (props) {
    super(props);

    this.state = {
      bookableIndex: 1,
      group: "Rooms"
    };
  }
}
```

To update the state (in an event handler, for example), you call `this.setState`, passing an object with any changes you want to make:

```
handleClick (index) {
  this.setState({
    bookableIndex: index
  });
}
```

React merges the object you passed to `setState` with the existing state. In the preceding example, it updates the `bookableIndex` property but leaves the `group` property alone, as shown in figure 2.14.

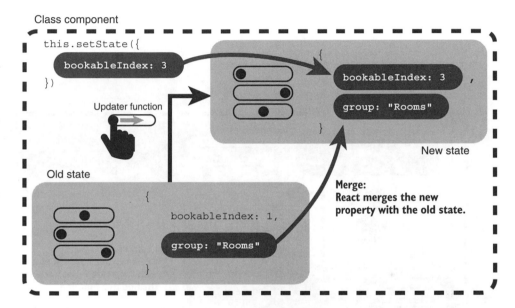

**Figure 2.14   In a class component, calling the updater function (`this.setState`) merges the new properties with the existing state object.**

### THE FUNCTION COMPONENT APPROACH

In contrast, for the new hooks approach, the updater function *replaces* the previous state value with the value you pass to the function. Now, that's straightforward if you have simple state values, like this:

```
const [bookableIndex, setBookableIndex] = useState(1);

setBookableIndex(3);  // React replaces the value 1 with 3.
```

But if you decide to store JavaScript objects in state, you need to tread carefully. The updater function will replace the old object entirely. Say you initialize the state like this:

```
function BookablesList () {
  const [state, setState] = useState({
    bookableIndex: 1,
```

```
    group: "Rooms"
  });
}
```

If you call the updater function, setState, with just the changed bookableIndex property, then you lose the group property:

```
function handleClick (index) {
  setState({
    bookableIndex: index
  });
}
```

The old state object is replaced by the new one, as shown in figure 2.15.

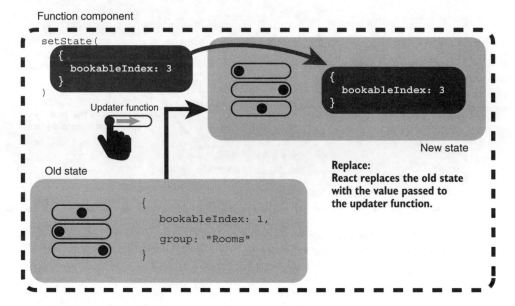

**Figure 2.15    In a function component, calling an updater function (returned by useState) replaces the old state value with whatever you pass to the updater function.**

So, if you really need to use an object with the useState hook, copy across all the properties from the old object when you set a new property value:

```
function handleClick (index) {
  setState({
    ...state,
    bookableIndex: index
  });
}
```

Notice how the spread operator, . . . `state`, is used in the preceding snippet to copy all of the properties from the old state to the new. In fact, to ensure that you have the latest state when setting new values based on old, you can pass a function as the argument to the updater function, like this:

```
function handleClick (index) {
  setState(state => {                    Pass a function
    return {                             to setState.
      ...state,
      bookableIndex: index               Use the old state value when
    };                                   setting the new one.
  });
}
```

React will pass in the latest state as the first argument. This function version of the updater function is discussed in more detail in section 2.2.5.

With that brief caveat about working with objects out of the way, there's one more feature of the `useState` hook API we need to mention before calling `useState` multiple times with abandon. Occasionally, you might need to hold off on calculating expensive initial values. There's a function for that.

## 2.2.4 *Passing a function to useState as the initial value*

Sometimes a component may need to do some work to calculate an initial value for a piece of state. Maybe the component is passed a tangled string of data from a legacy storage system and needs to extract a nugget of useful info from among the frayed knots. Unravelling the string may take a while, and you want to do the work only once. This approach is wasteful:

```
function untangle (aFrayedKnot) {
  // perform expensive untangling manoeuvers
  return nugget;
}


function ShinyComponent ({tangledWeb}) {
  const [shiny, setShiny] = useState(untangle(tangledWeb));

  // use shiny value and allow new shiny values to be set
}
```

Whenever `ShinyComponent` runs, maybe in response to setting another piece of state, the expensive `untangle` function runs as well. But `useState` uses its initial value argument on only the first call. After the first call, it won't use the value that `untangle` returns. Running the expensive `untangle` function again and again is a waste of time.

Luckily, the `useState` hook accepts a function as its argument, a *lazy initial state*, as shown in figure 2.16.

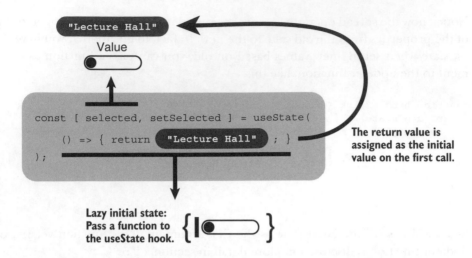

**Figure 2.16   You can pass a function to `useState` as the initial value. React will use the function's return value as the initial value.**

React executes the function only the first time the component is rendered. It uses the function's return value as the initial state:

```
function ShinyString ({tangledWeb}) {
  const [shiny, setShiny] = useState(() => untangle(tangledWeb));

  // use shiny value and allow new shiny values to be set
}
```

Use the lazy initial state if you need to undertake expensive work to generate an initial value for a piece of state.

### 2.2.5   *Using the previous state when setting the new state*

It would be great if users could more easily cycle through the bookables in the BookablesList component. Let's add a Next button that does the cycling, as shown in figure 2.17. If we move the focus to the Next button, users can activate it by using the keyboard.

The Next button needs to increment the bookableIndex state value, wrapping back around to 0 when it goes past the last bookable. The following listing shows the implementation of the Next button.

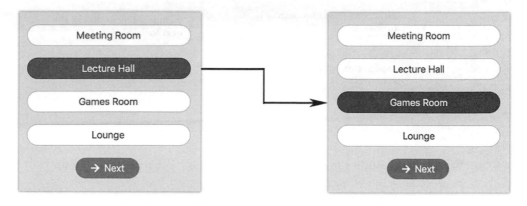

**Figure 2.17** Clicking the Next button selects the next bookable in the list.

> **Branch**: 0206-next-button, *File*: /src/components/Bookables/BookablesList.js
>
> **Listing 2.11** Passing a function to `setBookableIndex`

```
import {useState} from "react";
import {bookables} from "../../static.json";          Import a Font
import {FaArrowRight} from "react-icons/fa";     ◁    Awesome icon.

export default function BookablesList () {
  const group = "Rooms";                                            Create an
  const bookablesInGroup = bookables.filter(b => b.group === group);  event handler
  const [bookableIndex, setBookableIndex] = useState(1);            for the Next
                                                                    button.
  function nextBookable () {                              ◁
    setBookableIndex(i => (i + 1) % bookablesInGroup.length);    ◁
  }
                                                         Pass the updater
  return (                                              function a function to
    <div>                                               increment the index.
      <ul className="bookables items-list-nav">
        {bookablesInGroup.map((b, i) => (
          <li
            key={b.id}
            className={i === bookableIndex ? "selected" : null}
          >
            <button
              className="btn"
              onClick={() => setBookableIndex(i)}
            >
              {b.title}
            </button>
          </li>
        ))}
      </ul>
      <p>
        <button
          className="btn"
```

```
      onClick={nextBookable}
      autoFocus
   >
      <FaArrowRight/>
      <span>Next</span>
   </button>
  </p>
 </div>
);
}
```

Include a button to call the nextBookable function.

In the event handler for the Next button, nextBookable, we call the updater function, setBookableIndex, passing it a function:

```
setBookableIndex(i => (i + 1) % bookablesInGroup.length);
```

The function uses the % operator that gives the remainder when dividing. When i + 1 is the same as the number of bookables, bookablesInGroup.length, the remainder is 0, and the index cycles back to the start. But why not just use the state value for the index that we already have?

```
setBookableIndex((bookableIndex + 1) % bookablesInGroup.length);
```

By using hooks to hand over management of our state values to React, we don't just ask it to update values and trigger re-renders; we also give it permission to efficiently schedule when any updates take place. React can intelligently batch updates together and ignore redundant updates.

When we want to update a state value based on its previous value, as in our Next button example, instead of passing the updater function a value to set, we can pass it a function. React will pass that function the current state value and will use the return value of that function as the new state value. All the pieces are shown in figure 2.18.

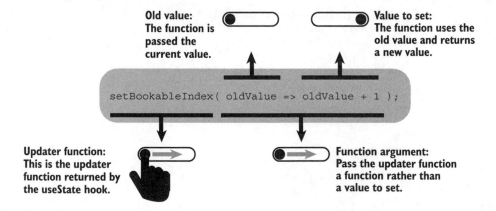

**Figure 2.18  Pass the updater function a function that uses the old state value and returns a new state value.**

By passing a function, we ensure that any new values that are based on old values have the latest information with which to work.

Listing 2.11 uses a separate function, `nextBookable`, for responding to clicks on the Next button but puts the handler for responding to clicks on bookables inline in the `onClick` attribute. This is just a personal choice; when a handler does more than call a simple updater function, I tend to put it in its own function rather than inline. In the case of listing 2.11, we could just as easily have the Next button handler inline or the bookable click handler in its own named function.

So, we can call `useState` to ask React to manage a value for us. But, surely, we'll need more than a single state value in our component. Let's see how to handle multiple state values as we give users the ability to choose groups in the `BookablesList` component.

## 2.3 *Calling useState multiple times to work with multiple values*

Having seen how `useState` works in some detail, it's time to get our money's worth. We're not limited to a solitary piece of information, or even a solitary object with many properties. If we're interested in multiple values to drive a component's UI, we can just keep calling that hook: `useState` for this, `useState` for that, `useState` for the other. We can `useState` all the things!

In this section, we add to the `BookablesList` component, first letting users switch between groups of bookables, and then displaying the details about the selected bookable. Remember, it's our job to fixate on the state, so we need to work with a few values:

- The selected group
- The selected bookable
- Whether the component has the bookable availability (days and sessions) showing

By the end of this section, we call `useState` for all three state values. We embed the values returned into our UI and use the updater functions to change the state when the user chooses a group or a bookable or toggles the display of details.

### 2.3.1 *Using a drop-down list to set state*

Let's start by updating the `BookablesList` component so that users can select a type of resource to book: Rooms or Kit. Two instances of the component are shown in figure 2.19, the first showing bookables in the Rooms group, and the second showing bookables in the Kit group.

We want the user to make two selections: the group to display, Rooms or Kit, and the bookable within the group. Changing either variable should update the display, so we want React to track them both. Should we create some kind of state object to pass to React via the `useState` hook? Well, no. The easiest approach is just to call `useState` twice:

```
const [group, setGroup] = useState("Kit");
const [bookableIndex, setBookableIndex] = useState(0);
```

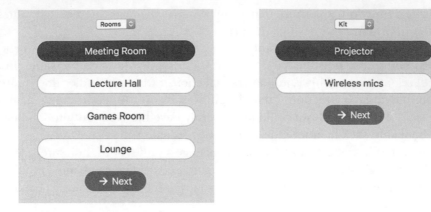

**Figure 2.19**   **Two views of the** `BookablesList` **component with a drop-down list for selecting the type of bookable: the first with Rooms selected and the second with Kit selected.**

React uses the order of the calls to determine which tracked variable is which. In the previous code snippet, every time React invokes the component code, the first call to useState assigns the first tracked value to the group variable, and the second call to useState assigns the second tracked value to the bookableIndex variable. setBookableIndex updates the second tracked value, and setGroup updates the first.

Your boss keeps glancing your way, so let's get the group-picking functionality implemented for the BookablesList component. The following listing shows the latest code.

---

*Branch*: **0207-groups**, *File*: **/src/components/Bookables/BookablesList.js**

**Listing 2.12**   **The** `BookablesList` **component with two** `useState` **calls**

```
import {useState} from "react";
import {bookables} from "../../static.json";
import {FaArrowRight} from "react-icons/fa";

export default function BookablesList () {
  const [group, setGroup] = useState("Kit");
  const bookablesInGroup = bookables.filter(b => b.group === group);
  const [bookableIndex, setBookableIndex] = useState(0);
  const groups = [...new Set(bookables.map(b => b.group))];

  function nextBookable () {
    setBookableIndex(i => (i + 1) % bookablesInGroup.length);
  }

  return (
    <div>
      <select
        value={group}
        onChange={(e) => setGroup(e.target.value)}
```

Use the first tracked state value to hold the selected group.

Use the second tracked state value to hold the selected bookable index.

Assign an array of unique group names to the groups variable.

Include an event handler to update the selected group.

```
      >
        {groups.map(g => <option value={g} key={g}>{g}</option>)}
      </select>

      <ul className="bookables items-list-nav">
        {bookablesInGroup.map((b, i) => (
          <li
            key={b.id}
            className={i === bookableIndex ? "selected" : null}
          >
            <button
              className="btn"
              onClick={() => setBookableIndex(i)}
            >
              {b.title}
            </button>
          </li>
        ))}
      </ul>
      <p>
        <button
          className="btn"
          onClick={nextBookable}
          autoFocus
        >
          <FaArrowRight/>
          <span>Next</span>
        </button>
      </p>
    </div>
  );
}
```

Create a drop-down list to show each group in the bookables data.

The code assigns the `group` variable the initial value of `Kit`, so the component starts off showing the list of bookables in the Kit group. When a user selects a new group from the drop-down list, the `setGroup` updater function lets React know the value has changed. To get the group names for the drop-down list, we put the bookables data through a few transformations. First, we create an array of just the group names:

```
bookables.map(b => b.group)  // array of group names
```

Then, we create a `Set` from the array of group names. Sets contain only unique values, so any duplicates will be discarded:

```
new Set(bookables.map(b => b.group))  // set of unique group names
```

Finally, we create a new array and spread the `Set` elements into it. The new array contains only unique group names. Exactly what we're after!

```
[...new Set(bookables.map(b => b.group))]  // array of unique group names
```

If the JS-Fu is a bit dense, you could always create a `getUniqueValues` utility function to make things more readable:

```
function getUniqueValues (array, property) {
  const propValues = array.map(element => element[property]);
  const uniqueValues = new Set(propValues);
  const uniqueValuesArray = [...uniqueValues];

  return uniqueValuesArray;
}

const groups = getUniqueValues(bookables, "group");
```

We'll stick with the terse version because it never changes.

I hope you agree, working with two pieces of state is pretty easy. We just call `use-State` twice. To update the state, we call the appropriate updater function. The user makes a selection, an event handler updates the state, and React does the diffing and tickles the DOM. Let's do it again!

### 2.3.2   *Using a check box to set state*

Our next job is to add a details section to the component to give our office colleagues a bit more info about each bookable. We make the display of each bookable's availability optional. Figure 2.20 shows the `BookablesList` component with the Show Details check box checked; the days and sessions for which the bookable is available are visible.

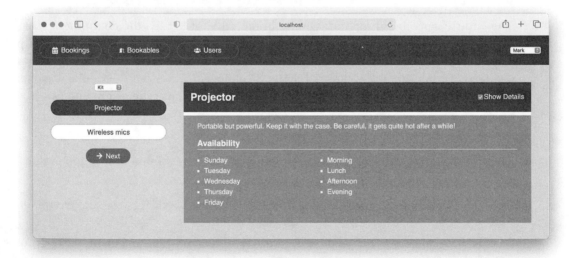

**Figure 2.20**   The `BookablesList` **component with the availability showing. The Show Details check box to the right of the title is checked.**

Figure 2.21 shows the component with the check box unchecked; the days and sessions are hidden.

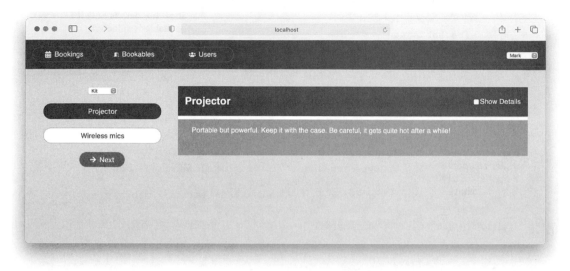

**Figure 2.21**　The `BookablesList` component with the availability hidden. The Show Details check box to the right of the title is not checked.

In addition to the selected group and the selected bookable index, we now have a third piece of state: we need to track whether the details for the selected bookable are displayed. The following listing shows the `BookablesList` component tracking our three variables via `useState` hook calls.

**Branch: 0208-bookable-details, *File*: /src/components/Bookables/BookablesList.js**
**Listing 2.13**　The `Bookables` component tracking three variables

```
import {useState, Fragment} from "react";               ◁──  Import
import {bookables, sessions, days} from "../../static.json";   React.Fragment
import {FaArrowRight} from "react-icons/fa";                  to wrap multiple
                                                              elements.
export default function BookablesList () {
  const [group, setGroup] = useState("Kit");
  const bookablesInGroup = bookables.filter(b => b.group === group);
  const [bookableIndex, setBookableIndex] = useState(0);
  const groups = [...new Set(bookables.map(b => b.group))];      Assign the currently
                                                                 selected bookable to
  const bookable = bookablesInGroup[bookableIndex];    ◁──┘     its own variable.

  const [hasDetails, setHasDetails] = useState(false);   ◁──  Use a third
                                                              tracked state
  function nextBookable () {                                  value to hold if
    setBookableIndex(i => (i + 1) % bookablesInGroup.length);  the details are
  }                                                           shown.
```

```
      return (
        <Fragment>
          <div>
            /* unchanged UI for list of bookables */
          </div>

          {bookable && (                              ◁──    Show the details only if a
            <div className="bookable-details">        ◁──    bookable is selected.
              <div className="item">
                <div className="item-header">                Include a new UI
                  <h2>                                        section for the selected
                    {bookable.title}                          bookable's details.
                  </h2>
                  <span className="controls">
                    <label>
                      <input                                Let users toggle the
                        type="checkbox"                     details with a check box.
                        checked={hasDetails}
                        onChange={() => setHasDetails(has => !has)}
                      />
                      Show Details
                    </label>
                  </span>
                </div>

                <p>{bookable.notes}</p>                  ◁──    Show the details only
                                                                if hasDetails is true.
                {hasDetails && (
                  <div className="item-details">
                    <h3>Availability</h3>
                    <div className="bookable-availability">
                      <ul>
                        {bookable.days
                          .sort()                               Display a list
                          .map(d => <li key={d}>{days[d]}</li>)  of available
                        }                                        days.
                      </ul>
                      <ul>
                        {bookable.sessions
                          .map(s => <li key={s}>{sessions[s]}</li>)
                        }
                      </ul>
                    </div>
                  </div>
                )}
              </div>
            </div>
          )}
        </Fragment>
      );
    }
```

Include an event handler to update if the details are shown.

Display a list of available sessions.

The component uses the current `bookableIndex` to access the selected bookable from the `bookablesInGroup` array:

```
const bookable = bookablesInGroup[bookablesIndex];
```

There's no need to call useState to store the bookable object itself because it can be derived from the index value already in state. The UI includes a new section to show the details of the selected bookable. But the component shows the section only if there's a bookable to display:

```
{bookable && (
  <div className="bookable-details">
    // details UI
  </div>
)}
```

Similarly, the extra info about the selected bookable is visible only if the hasDetails state value is true; in other words, the check box is checked:

```
{hasDetails && (
  <div className="item-details">
    // Bookable availability
  </div>
)}
```

It seems like our work on the BookablesList component is done. We have our list of bookables from the currently selected group and the ability to toggle the display of details for the selected bookable. But before you pat yourself on the back and book out the games room and party supplies, follow these three steps:

1 Select the Games Room; its details are then displayed.
2 Switch the group to Kit. The list of kit bookables is displayed with no bookable selected, and the details disappear. (Which bookable is selected?)
3 Click the Next button. The second item of Kit, Wireless Mics, is selected and its details appear.

There's a whiff of stale data in the air. Can you work out what's happening? We want user interactions to lead to predictable changes in state. Sometimes that means a single interaction should lead to multiple pieces of state changing. The next chapter investigates the problem and introduces *reducers*, a mechanism for orchestrating more complicated state changes and eliminating stale odors. But before we switch hooks, we'll review what building the BookablesList component has taught us about function components in general. And before that, here's a challenge!

### CHALLENGE 2.3

Update the UsersList component to show details for the selected user. Display the user's name, title, and notes. A possible approach is shown in figure 2.22, with code in the 0209-user-details branch of the book's GitHub repo.

**Figure 2.22   The `UsersList` component showing details for the selected user**

## 2.4   *Reviewing some function component concepts*

At this point, our `BookablesList` component is very simple. But some fundamental concepts are already at work, concepts that underpin our understanding of function components and React Hooks. Having a strong grasp of these concepts will make our future discussions throughout the book and your expert use of hooks much easier. In particular, here are five key concepts:

- Components are functions that accept props and return a description of their UI.
- React invokes the components. As functions, the components run their code and then end.
- Some variables may persist within closures created by event handlers. Others are destroyed when the function ends.
- We can use hooks to ask React to manage values for us. React can pass components the latest values and updater functions for those values.
- By using the updater functions, we let React know of changing values. It can rerun the components to get the latest description of the UI.

The component cycle diagram in figure 2.23 shows some of the steps involved when our `BookablesList` component runs and a user clicks a bookable. Table 2.1 discusses each step.

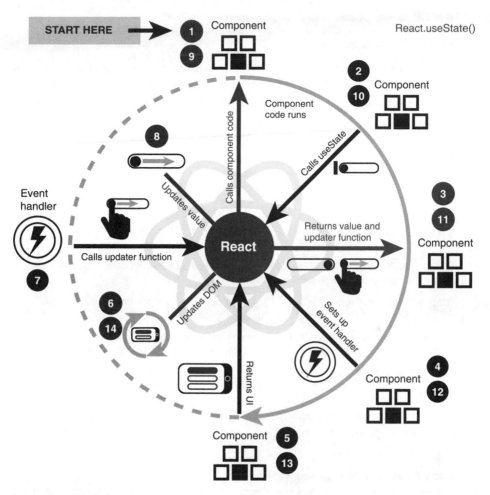

START HERE

1 Component

9

React.useState()

2 Component

10

Component code runs

Calls useState

Calls component code

8

Updates value

React

Returns value and updater function

3
11
Component

Event handler

Calls updater function

7

Updates DOM

6

14

Returns UI

Sets up event handler

4
12
Component

5
13
Component

**Figure 2.23   Stepping through the key moments when using** `useState`

**Table 2.1   Some key steps when using** `useState`

| Step | What happens? | Discussion |
|------|---------------|------------|
| 1 | React calls the component. | To generate the UI for the page, React traverses the tree of components, calling each one. React will pass each component any props set as attributes in the JSX. |
| 2 | The component calls `useState` for the first time. | The component passes the initial value to the `useState` function. React sets the current value for that `useState` call from that component. |
| 3 | React returns the current value and an updater function as an array. | The component code assigns the value and updater function to variables for later use. The second variable name often starts with `set` (for example, `value` and `setValue`). |
| 4 | The component sets up an event handler. | The event handler may listen for user clicks, for example. The handler will change the state when it runs later. React will hook up the handler to the DOM when it updates the DOM in step 6. |

**Table 2.1  Some key steps when using `useState` *(continued)***

| Step | What happens? | Discussion |
|------|--------------|------------|
| 5 | The component returns its UI. | The component uses the current state value to generate its user interface and returns it, finishing its work. |
| 6 | React updates the DOM. | React updates the DOM with any changes needed. |
| 7 | The event handler calls the updater function. | An event fires, and the handler runs. The handler uses the updater function to change the state value. |
| 8 | React updates the state value. | React replaces the state value with the value passed by the updater function. |
| 9 | React calls the component. | React knows that the state value has changed and so must recalculate the UI. |
| 10 | The component calls `useState` for the second time. | This time, React will ignore the initial value argument. |
| 11 | React returns the current state value and the updater function. | React has updated the state value. The component needs the latest value. |
| 12 | The component sets up an event handler. | This is a new version of the handler and may use the newly updated state value. |
| 13 | The component returns its UI. | The component uses the current state value to generate its user interface and returns it, finishing its work. |
| 14 | React updates the DOM. | React compares the newly returned UI with the old and efficiently updates the DOM with any changes needed. |

In order to discuss concepts with clarity and precision, from time to time we take stock of the keywords and objects we've encountered so far. Table 2.2 describes some of the terms we've come across.

**Table 2.2  Some of the key terms we've met**

| Icon | Term | Description |
|------|------|-------------|
| | Component | A function that accepts props and returns a description of its UI. |
| | Initial value | The component passes this value to `useState`. React sets the state value to this initial value when the component first runs. |
| | Updater function | The component calls this function to update the state value. |
| | Event handler | A function that runs in response to an event of some kind—for example, a user clicking a bookable. Event handlers often call updater functions to change the state. |
| | `UI` | A description of the elements that make up a user interface. The state values are often included somewhere in the UI. |

## Summary

- Call the `useState` hook when you want React to manage a value for a component. It returns an array with two elements: the state value and an updater function. You can pass in an initial value if required:

```
const [value, setValue] = useState(initialValue);
```

- If you need to perform an expensive calculation to generate the initial state, pass it to `useState` in a function. React will run the function to get this *lazy initial state* only when it first calls the component:

```
const [value, setValue] = useState(() => { return initialState; });
```

- Use the updater function that `useState` returns to set a new value. The new value *replaces* the old value. React will schedule a re-render if the value has changed:

```
setValue(newValue);
```

- If your state value is an object, make sure to copy over unchanged properties from the previous state when your updater function is updating only a subset of the properties:

```
setValue({
  ...state,
  property: newValue
});
```

- To be sure you're working with the latest state value when calling the updater function and setting a new value based on the old one, pass the updater function a function as its argument. React will assign the latest state value to the function argument:

```
setValue(value => { return newValue; });

setValue(state => {
  return {
    ...state,
    property: newValue
  };
});
```

- If you have multiple pieces of state, you can call `useState` multiple times. React uses the order of the calls to consistently assign values and updater functions to the correct variables:

```
const [index, setIndex] = useState(0);                        // call 1
const [name, setName] = useState("Jamal");                    // call 2
const [isPresenting, setIsPresenting] = useState(false);      // call 3
```

- Focus on the state and how events will update the state. React will do its job of synchronizing the state and the UI:

```
function Counter () {
  const [count, setCount] = useState(0);        ←┐  Consider what state the
                                                   component needs.

  return (                                          Display the state.
    <p>{count}                                 ←┐
      <button onClick={() => setCount(c => c + 1)}> + </button>    ←┐
    </p>
  );                                                                Update the state in
}                                                                   response to events.
```

# Managing
# component state with
# the useReducer hook

3

**This chapter covers**

- Asking React to manage multiple, related state values by calling useReducer
- Putting component state management logic in a single location
- Updating state and triggering re-renders by dispatching actions to a reducer
- Initializing state with initialization arguments and initialization functions

As your applications grow, it's natural for some components to handle more state, especially if they supply different parts of that state to multiple children. When you find you always need to update multiple state values together or your state update logic is so spread out that it's hard to follow, it might be time to define a function to manage state updates for you: a *reducer* function.

A simple, common example is for loading data. Say a component needs to load posts for a blog on things to do when stuck at home during a pandemic. You want to display loading UI when new posts are requested, error UI if a problem arises, and the posts themselves when they arrive. The component's state includes values for the following:

- *The loading state*—Are you in the process of loading new posts?
- *Any errors*—Has an error been returned from the server, or is the network down?
- *The posts*—A list of the posts retrieved.

When the component requests posts, you might set the loading state to `true`, the error state to `null`, and the posts to an empty array. One event causes changes to three pieces of state. When the posts are returned, you might set the loading state to `false` and the posts to those returned. One event causes changes to two pieces of state. You can definitely manage these state values with calls to the `useState` hook but, when you always respond to an event with calls to multiple updater functions (`setIsLoading`, `setError`, and `setPosts`, for example), React provides a cleaner alternative: the `useReducer` hook.

In this chapter, we start by addressing a problem with the `BookablesList` component in the bookings app: something is amiss with our state management. We then introduce reducers and the `useReducer` hook as a way of managing our state. Section 3.3 shows how to use a function to initialize the state for a reducer as we start work on a new component, the `WeekPicker`. We finish the chapter with a review of how the `useReducer` hook fits in with our understanding of function components.

Can you smell that? There's a definite whiff in the air. Something's been left out that should've been tidied up. Something stale. Let's purge that distracting pong!

## 3.1    *Updating multiple state values in response to a single event*

You're free to call `useState` as many times as you want, once for each piece of state you need React to manage. But a single component may need to hold many values in state, and often those pieces of state are related; you may want to update multiple pieces of state in response to a single user action. You don't want to leave some pieces of state unattended to when they should really be tidied up.

Our `BookablesList` component currently has a problem when users switch from one group to another. It's not a big problem, but in this section we discuss what the problem is, why it's a problem, and how we can solve it by using the `useState` hook. That sets us up for the `useReducer` hook in section 3.2.

### 3.1.1    *Taking users out of the movie with unpredictable state changes*

We don't want clunky, unpredictable interfaces preventing users from getting on with tasks. If the UI keeps pulling their attention away from their desired focus or makes them wait with no feedback or sends them off down dead ends, their thought process is interrupted, their work becomes more difficult, and their day is ruined.

It's like when you're watching a movie, and a strange camera movement, or frenzied editing, or blatant product placement, or Ed Sheeran pulls you out of the story.

Your train of thought is gone. You become overly aware that it's a movie, and something's not quite right. Or when you're reading a book on programming, and a tortured simile, a strained attempt at humor, perplexing asides, or meta jokes pull you out of the explanation. You become overly aware that you're reading a desperate author, and something's not quite right.

Okay, sorry. Back in the room. Let's see an example. At the end of section 2.3 in the preceding chapter, we diagnosed a mild case of jank in our `BookablesList` component's UI. Users are able to choose a group and then select a bookable from that group. The bookable's details are then displayed. But some combinations of bookable and group selection lead to UI updates that are a little bit off. If you follow these three steps, you should see the UI updates shown in figure 3.1:

1 Select the Games Room; its details are then displayed.
2 Switch the group to Kit. The list of Kit bookables is displayed with no bookable selected, and the details disappear.
3 Click the Next button. The second item of Kit, Wireless Mics, is selected, and its details appear.

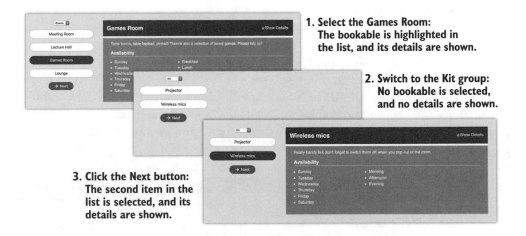

**Figure 3.1** Selecting a bookable, switching groups, and then clicking the Next button can lead to unpredictable state changes.

Switching from the Rooms group to the Kit group, the component seems to lose track of which bookable is selected. Clicking the Next button then selects the *second* item, skipping the first. It's not a huge problem—users can still select bookables—but it may be enough to jar the user out of their focused flow. What's going on?

It turns out that the selected bookable and the selected group aren't completely independent values in our state. When a user selects the Games Room, the `bookableIndex` state value is set to 2; it's the third item in the list. If they then switch to the Kit group, which has only two items, with indexes 0 and 1, the `bookableIndex` value no longer matches up with a bookable. The UI ends up with no bookable selected and no details displayed. We need to carefully consider the state we want the UI to be in after a user chooses a group. So, how do we fix our stale index problem and smooth the path for our users?

### 3.1.2  *Keeping users in the movie with predictable state changes*

Building a bookings app for our colleagues, we want to make its use as frictionless as possible. Say a colleague, Akiko, has clients visiting next week. She's organizing her schedule for the visit and needs to book the Meeting Room in the afternoon and then the Games Room after work. Akiko's focus is on her task: getting the schedule sorted and preparing for a great client visit. The bookings app should let her continue to focus on her task. She should be thinking, "I'll get those rooms booked and then order the catering," not "Um, hang on, which button? Did I click it? Has it frozen? Argh, *I hate computers*!"

It's like when you're watching a movie and you're completely invested in a character's plight. You don't notice the camera moves and the editing because they help to smoothly draw you into the story. You're no longer in the movie theater; you're in the world of the film. The artifice melts away, and the story is everything. Or when you're reading a book, and its quirky but relatable characters and propulsive plot pull you into the narrative. It's almost as if the book disappears, and you inhabit the characters' thoughts, feelings, locations, and actions. Eventually, you notice yourself, and realize you've read 100 pages and it's almost dark. . . .

Okay, sorry. Back in the room. Let's get back to the example. After the user selects a group, we want the UI to be in a predictable state. We don't want sudden deselections and skipped bookables. A simple and sensible approach is to always select the first bookable in the list when a user chooses a new group, as shown in figure 3.2.

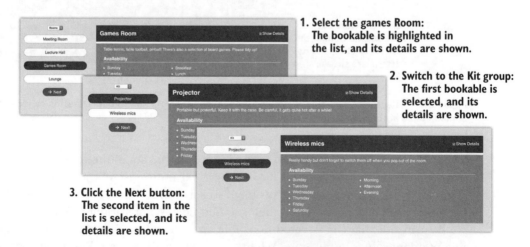

1. Select the games Room: The bookable is highlighted in the list, and its details are shown.

2. Switch to the Kit group: The first bookable is selected, and its details are shown.

3. Click the Next button: The second item in the list is selected, and its details are shown.

Figure 3.2  Selecting a bookable, switching groups, and then clicking the Next button leads to predictable state changes.

The group and bookableIndex state values are connected; when we change the group, we change the index as well. In step 2 of figure 3.2, notice that the first item in the list, Projector, is automatically selected when the group is switched. The following listing shows the changeGroup function setting bookableIndex to zero whenever a new group is set.

Branch: 0301-related-state, *File*: /src/components/Bookables/BookablesList.js

Listing 3.1 Automatically selecting a bookable when the group is changed

```
import {useState, Fragment} from "react";
import {bookables, sessions, days} from "../../static.json";
import {FaArrowRight} from "react-icons/fa";

export default function BookablesList () {
  const [group, setGroup] = useState("Kit");
  const bookablesInGroup = bookables.filter(b => b.group === group);
  const [bookableIndex, setBookableIndex] = useState(0);
  const groups = [...new Set(bookables.map(b => b.group))];
  const bookable = bookablesInGroup[bookableIndex];
  const [hasDetails, setHasDetails] = useState(false);

  function changeGroup (event) {              Create a handler function to
    setGroup(event.target.value);            respond to group selection.
    setBookableIndex(0);
  }                                          Select the first bookable
                                             in the new group.
  function nextBookable () {
    setBookableIndex(i => (i + 1) % bookablesInGroup.length);
  }

  return (
    <Fragment>
      <div>
        <select
          value={group}                      Specify the new function
          onChange={changeGroup}             as the onChange handler.
        >
          {groups.map(g => <option value={g} key={g}>{g}</option>)}
        </select>

        <ul className="bookables items-list-nav">
          /* unchanged list UI */
        </ul>
        <p>
          /* unchanged button UI */
        </p>
      </div>

      {bookable && (
        <div className="bookable-details">
          /* unchanged bookable details UI */
        </div>
      )}
```

Update the group.

```
    </Fragment>
  );
}
```

Whenever the group is changed, we set the bookable index to zero; when we call `setGroup`, we always follow it with a call to `setBookableIndex`:

```
setGroup(newGroup);
setBookableIndex(0);
```

This is a simple example of related state. When components start to get more complicated with multiple events causing multiple state changes, tracking those changes and making sure all related state values are updated together become more and more difficult.

When state values are related in such a way, either affecting each other or often being changed together, it can help to move the state update logic into a single place, rather than spreading the code that performs changes across event handler functions, whether inline or separately defined. React gives us the `useReducer` hook to help us manage this collocation of state update logic, and we look at that hook next.

## 3.2  *Managing more complicated state with useReducer*

As it stands, the `BookablesList` component example is simple enough that you could continue to use `useState` and just call the respective updater functions for each piece of state within the `changeGroup` event handler. But when you have multiple pieces of interrelated state, using a *reducer* can make it easier to make and understand state changes. In this section, we introduce the following topics:

- A reducer helps you to manage state changes in a centralized, well-defined way with clear actions that act on the state.
- A reducer uses actions to generate a new state from the previous state, making it easier to specify more complicated updates that may involve multiple pieces of interrelated state.
- React provides the `useReducer` hook to let your component specify initial state, access the current state, and dispatch actions to update the state and trigger a re-render.
- Dispatching well-defined actions makes it easier to follow state changes and to understand how your component interacts with the state in response to different events.

We start, in section 3.2.1, with a description of a reducer and a simple example of a reducer that manages incrementing and decrementing a counter. In section 3.2.2, we build a reducer for the `BookablesList` component that performs the necessary state changes like switching groups, selecting bookables, and toggling bookable details. Finally, in section 3.2.3, we incorporate our freshly minted reducer into the `BookablesList` component by using React's `useReducer` hook.

### 3.2.1　*Updating state using a reducer with a predefined set of actions*

A *reducer* is a function that accepts a state value and an action value. It generates a new state value based on the two values passed in. It then returns the new state value, as shown in figure 3.3.

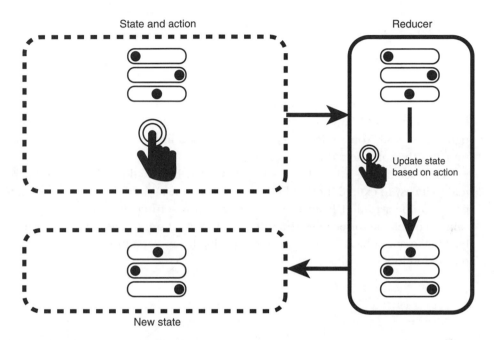

**Figure 3.3　A reducer takes a state and an action and returns a new state.**

The state and action can be simple, primitive values like numbers or strings, or more complicated objects. With a reducer, you keep all of the ways of updating the state in one place, which makes it easier to manage state changes, particularly when a single action affects multiple pieces of state.

We get back to the `BookablesList` component shortly, after a super-simple example. Say your state's just a counter and there are only two actions you can take: increment the counter or decrement the counter. The following listing shows a reducer that manages such a counter. The value of the `count` variable starts at 0 and changes to 1, to 2, and then back to 1.

> *Code on JS Bin:* https://jsbin.com/capogug/edit?js,console
>
> **Listing 3.2　A simple reducer for a counter**

```
let count = 0;

function reducer (state, action) {
```
**Create a reducer function that accepts the existing state and an action.**

```
  if (action === "inc") {
    return state + 1;
  }
  if (action === "dec") {
    return state - 1;
  }
  return state;
}

count = reducer(count, "inc");
count = reducer(count, "inc");
count = reducer(count, "dec");
```

**Check which action is specified and update state accordingly.**

**Handle missing or unrecognized actions.**

**Use the reducer to increment the counter.**

**Use the reducer to decrement the counter.**

The reducer handles the incrementing and decrementing actions and just returns the count unaltered for any other action specified. (Rather than silently ignoring unrecognized actions, you could throw an error, depending on the needs of your application and the role the reducer is playing.)

That seems like a bit of overkill for our two little actions, but having a reducer makes it easy to extend. Let's add three more actions, for adding and subtracting arbitrary numbers to and from the counter and for setting the counter to a specified value. To be able to specify extra values with our action, we need to beef it up a bit—let's make it an object with a type and a payload. Say we want to add 3 to the counter; our action looks like this:

```
{
  type: "add",
  payload: 3
}
```

The following listing shows the new reducer with its extra powers and calls to the reducer passing our beefed-up actions. The value of the count variable starts at 0 and changes to 3, to –7, to 41, and finally to 42.

---

*Code on JS Bin*: **https://jsbin.com/kokumux/edit?js,console**

**Listing 3.3   Adding more actions and specifying extra values**

```
let count = 0;

function reducer (state, action) {
  if (action.type === "inc") {
    return state + 1;
  }

  if (action.type === "dec") {
    return state - 1;
  }
```

**Now check the action type for the two original actions.**

```
  if (action.type === "add") {
    return state + action.payload;
  }

  if (action.type === "sub") {                    Use the action
    return state - action.payload;                payload to perform
  }                                               the new actions.

  if (action.type === "set") {
    return action.payload;
  }


  return state;
}
```

```
count = reducer(count, { type: "add", payload: 3 });      Pass an object
count = reducer(count, { type: "sub", payload: 10 });     to specify each
count = reducer(count, { type: "set", payload: 41 });     action.
count = reducer(count, { type: "inc" });
```

The last call to the reducer right at the end of listing 3.3 specifies the increment action. The increment action doesn't need any extra information. It always adds 1 to count, so the action doesn't include a payload property.

Let's put these ideas of state and actions with a type and payload into practice in the bookings app by building a reducer for our BookablesList component. Then we can see how to enlist React's help to use that reducer to manage the component's state.

### 3.2.2 *Building a reducer for the BookablesList component*

The BookablesList component has four pieces of state: group, bookableIndex, has-Details, and bookables (imported from static.json). The component also has four actions to perform on that state: set the group, set the index, toggle hasDetails, and move to the next bookable. To manage four pieces of state, we can use an object with four properties. It's common to represent both the state and the action as objects, as shown in figure 3.4.

The BookablesList component imports the bookables data from the static.json file. That data won't change while the BookablesList component is mounted, and we include it in the initial state for the reducer, using it to find the number of bookables in each group.

The following listing shows a reducer for the BookablesList component using objects for both the state and the actions. We export it from its own file, reducer.js, in the /src/components/Bookables folder.

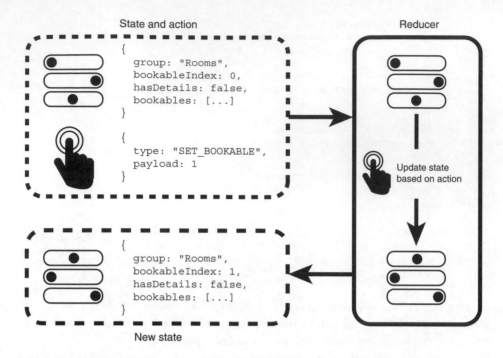

State and action

Reducer

```
{
  group: "Rooms",
  bookableIndex: 0,
  hasDetails: false,
  bookables: [...]
}

{
  type: "SET_BOOKABLE",
  payload: 1
}
```

Update state
based on action

```
{
  group: "Rooms",
  bookableIndex: 1,
  hasDetails: false,
  bookables: [...]
}
```

New state

Figure 3.4   **Pass the reducer a state object and an action object. The reducer updates the state based on the action type and payload. The reducer returns the new, updated state.**

*Branch:* **0302-reducer,** *File:* **/src/components/Bookables/reducer.js**

Listing 3.4    **A reducer for the** `BookablesList` **component**

```
export default function reducer (state, action) {
  switch (action.type) {

    case "SET_GROUP":
      return {
        ...state,
        group: action.payload,
        bookableIndex: 0
      };

    case "SET_BOOKABLE":
      return {
        ...state,
        bookableIndex: action.payload
      };

    case "TOGGLE_HAS_DETAILS":
      return {
        ...state,
        hasDetails: !state.hasDetails
      };
```

**Use a switch statement to organize the code for each action type.**

**Specify the action type as the comparison for each case.**

**Create a case block for each action type.**

**Update the group and set the bookableIndex to 0.**

**Use the spread operator to copy existing state properties.**

**Override existing state properties with any changes.**

```
case "NEXT_BOOKABLE":
  const count = state.bookables.filter(
    b => b.group === state.group
  ).length;
```

Count the bookables in
the current group.

```
  return {
    ...state,
    bookableIndex: (state.bookableIndex + 1) % count
  };
```

Use the count to
wrap from the last
index to the first.

```
  default:
    return state;
  }
}
```

Always include
a default case.

Each `case` block returns a new JavaScript object; the previous state is not mutated. The object spread operator is used to copy across properties from the old state to the new. You then set the property values that need updating on the object, overriding those from the previous state, like this:

```
return {
  ...state,
  group: action.payload,
  bookableIndex: 0
};
```

Spread the properties of the old
state object into the new one.

Override any properties
that need updating.

With only four properties in total in our state, we could have set them all explicitly:

```
return {
  group: action.payload,
  bookableIndex: 0,
  hasDetails: state.hasDetails,
  bookables: state.bookables
};
```

Copy across previous values
for unchanged properties.

Using the spread operator protects the code as it evolves; the state may gain new properties in the future, and they all need to be copied across.

Notice that the SET_GROUP action updates two properties. In addition to updating the group to be displayed, it sets the selected bookable index to 0. When switching to a new group, the action automatically selects the first bookable and, as long as the group has at least one bookable, the component shows the details for the first bookable if the Show Details toggle is checked.

The reducer also handles a NEXT_BOOKABLE action, removing from the Bookables component the onus for calculating indexes when moving from one bookable to the next. This is why including the bookables data in the reducer's state is helpful; we use the count of bookables in a group to wrap from the last bookable to the first when incrementing bookableIndex:

```
case "NEXT_BOOKABLE":
  const count = state.bookables.filter(
```

Use the bookables data to count the
bookables in the current group.

```
    b => b.group === state.group
).length;

return {
  ...state,
  bookableIndex: (state.bookableIndex + 1) % count
};
```

> Use the modulus operator to wrap from the last index to the first.

We have a reducer set up, but how do we fold it into our component? How do we access the state object and call the reducer with our actions? We need the useReducer hook.

### 3.2.3 Accessing component state and dispatching actions with useReducer

The useState hook lets us ask React to manage single values for our component. With the useReducer hook, we can give React a bit more help in managing values by passing it a reducer and the component's initial state. When events occur in our application, instead of giving React new values to set, we *dispatch* an *action*, and React uses the corresponding code in the reducer to generate a new state before calling the component for the latest UI.

When calling the useReducer hook, we pass it the reducer and an initial state. The hook returns the current state and a function for dispatching actions, as two elements in an array, as shown in figure 3.5.

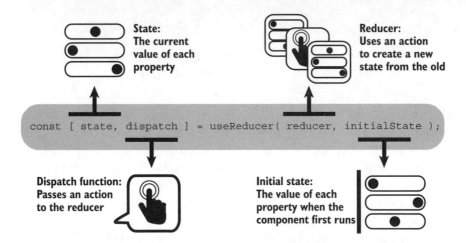

**State:**
The current value of each property

**Reducer:**
Uses an action to create a new state from the old

```
const [ state, dispatch ] = useReducer( reducer, initialState );
```

**Dispatch function:**
Passes an action to the reducer

**Initial state:**
The value of each property when the component first runs

Figure 3.5   Call useReducer with a reducer and an initial state. It returns the current state and a dispatch function. Use the dispatch function to dispatch actions to the reducer.

As we did with useState, here with useReducer we use array destructuring to assign the two elements of the returned array to two variables with names of our choosing.

The first element, the current state, we assign to a variable we call state, and the second element, the dispatch function, we assign to a variable we call dispatch:

```
const [state, dispatch] = useReducer(reducer, initialState);
```

React pays attention to only the arguments passed to useReducer (in our case, reducer and initialState) the first time React invokes the component. On subsequent invocations, it ignores the arguments but still returns the current state and the dispatch function for the reducer.

Let's get the useReducer hook up and running in the BookablesList component and start dispatching some actions! The following listing shows the changes.

Branch: 0302-reducer, File: /src/components/Bookables/BookablesList.js

Listing 3.5   The BookablesList component using a reducer

```
import {useReducer, Fragment} from "react";          ◁──── Import the
import {bookables, sessions, days} from "../../static.json";    useReducer hook.
import {FaArrowRight} from "react-icons/fa";

import reducer from "./reducer";       ◁──┐ Import the reducer
                                           from listing 3.4.

const initialState = {
  group: "Rooms",
  bookableIndex: 0,        Specify an
  hasDetails: true,        initial state.
  bookables
};
                                                           Call useReducer,
                                                           passing the
                                                           reducer and the
export default function BookablesList () {                  initial state.
  const [state, dispatch] = useReducer(reducer, initialState);  ◁──┘

  const {group, bookableIndex, bookables, hasDetails} = state;

  const bookablesInGroup = bookables.filter(b => b.group === group);
  const bookable = bookablesInGroup[bookableIndex];
  const groups = [...new Set(bookables.map(b => b.group))];

  function changeGroup (e) {
    dispatch({
      type: "SET_GROUP",         Dispatch an action
      payload: e.target.value    with a type and a
    });                          payload.
  }

  function changeBookable (selectedIndex) {
    dispatch({
      type: "SET_BOOKABLE",
      payload: selectedIndex
    });
  }
```

Assign state values to local variables.

```
function nextBookable () {
  dispatch({ type: "NEXT_BOOKABLE" });                ◁────  Dispatch an action
}                                                            that doesn't need
                                                            a payload.
function toggleDetails () {
  dispatch({ type: "TOGGLE_HAS_DETAILS" });
}

return (
  <Fragment>
    <div>
      // group picker

      <ul className="bookables items-list-nav">
        {bookablesInGroup.map((b, i) => (
          <li
            key={b.id}
            className={i === bookableIndex ? "selected" : null}
          >
            <button
              className="btn"
              onClick={() => changeBookable(i)}        ◁────  Call the new
            >                                                changeBookable
              {b.title}                                      function.
            </button>
          </li>
        ))}
      </ul>

      // Next button
    </div>

    {bookable && (
      <div className="bookable-details">
        <div className="item">
          <div className="item-header">
            <h2>
              {bookable.title}
            </h2>
            <span className="controls">
              <label>
                <input
                  type="checkbox"
                  checked={hasDetails}
                  onChange={toggleDetails}             ◁────  Call the new
                />                                             toggleDetails
                Show Details                                  function.
              </label>
            </span>
          </div>
          <p>{bookable.notes}</p>
          {hasDetails && (
            <div className="item-details">
              // details
            </div>
          )
```

```
        )}
      </div>
    </div>
  )}
</Fragment>
);
}
```

Listing 3.5 imports the reducer we created in listing 3.4, sets up an initial state object, and then, in the component code itself, passes the reducer and initial state to use-Reducer. Next, useReducer returns the current state and the dispatch function, and we assign them to variables, state and dispatch, using array destructuring. The listing uses an intermediate state variable and then destructures the state object into individual variables—group, bookableIndex, bookables, and hasDetails—but you could do the object destructuring directly inside the array destructuring:

```
const [
  {group, bookableIndex, bookables, hasDetails},
  dispatch
] = useReducer(reducer, initialState);
```

In the event handlers, the BookablesList component now dispatches actions rather than updating individual state values via useState. We use separate event handler functions (changeGroup, changeBookable, nextBookable, toggleDetails), but you could easily dispatch actions inline within the UI. For example, you could set up the Show Details check box like this:

```
<label>
  <input
    type="checkbox"
    checked={hasDetails}
    onChange={() => dispatch({ type: "TOGGLE_HAS_DETAILS" })}
  />
  Show Details
</label>
```

Either approach is fine, as long as you (and your team) find the code easy to read and understand.

Although the example is simple, you should appreciate how a reducer can help structure your code, your state mutations, and your understanding, particularly as the component state becomes more complex. If your state *is* complex and/or the initial state is expensive to set up or is generated by a function you'd like to reuse or import, the useReducer hook has a third argument you can use. Let's check it out.

## 3.3 *Generating the initial state with a function*

You saw in chapter 2 that we can generate the initial state for useState by passing a function to the hook. Similarly, with useReducer, as well as passing an initialization argument as the second argument, we can pass an initialization function as the third

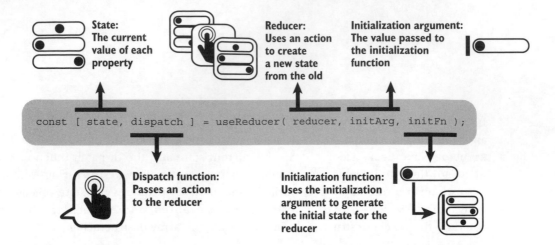

**Figure 3.6    The initialization function for `useReducer` uses the initialization argument to generate the reducer's initial state.**

argument. The initialization function uses the initialization argument to generate the initial state, as shown in figure 3.6.

As usual, `useReducer` returns an array with two elements: the state and a dispatch function. On the first call, the state is the return value of the initialization function. On subsequent calls, it is the state at the time of the call:

```
const [state, dispatch] = useReducer(reducer, initArgument, initFunction);
```

Use the dispatch function to dispatch actions to the reducer. For a particular call to `useReducer`, React will always return the same dispatch function. (Having an unchanging function is important when re-renders may depend on changing props or dependencies, as you'll see in later chapters.)

In this section, we put `useReducer`'s initialization function argument to use as we start work on a second component for the bookings app, the `WeekPicker` component. We split the work into five subsections:

- Introducing the `WeekPicker` component
- Creating utility functions to work with dates and weeks
- Building the reducer to manage dates for the component
- Creating `WeekPicker`, passing an initialization function to the `useReducer` hook
- Updating `BookingsPage` to use `WeekPicker`

### 3.3.1    Introducing the WeekPicker component

So far in the bookings app, we've been concentrating on the `BookablesList` component, displaying a list of bookables. To set the groundwork for actually booking a resource, we need to start thinking about calendars; in the finished app, our users will pick a date and session from a bookings grid calendar, as shown in figure 3.7.

| | Mon Jun 22 2020 | Tue Jun 23 2020 | Wed Jun 24 2020 | Thu Jun 25 2020 | Fri Jun 26 2020 |
|---|---|---|---|---|---|
| **Morning** | | | Movie Pitch! | | |
| **Lunch** | Onboarding | | | | New Employee Intro |
| **Afternoon** | | Project Update | | | |

Rooms / Meeting Room / Lecture Hall / Games Room / Lounge / → Next / ‹ Prev / Today / e.g. 2020-09-02 / Go / Next ›

**Figure 3.7    The bookings page will include a list of bookables, a bookings grid, and a week picker.**

Let's start small and just consider the interface for switching between one week and the next. Figure 3.8 shows a possible interface for picking the week to show in the bookings grid. It includes the following:

- The start and end dates for the selected week
- Buttons to move to the next and previous weeks
- A button to show the week containing today's date

‹ Prev    Today    Next ›

Sun Jun 07 2020 - Sat Jun 13 2020

**Figure 3.8    The `WeekPicker` component shows the start and end dates for the chosen week and has buttons to navigate between weeks.**

Later in the book, we'll add an input for jumping straight to a specific date. For now, we'll stick with our three buttons and week date text. To get the start and end dates for a specified week, we need a couple of utility functions to wrangle JavaScript's date object. Let's conjure those first.

### 3.3.2   *Creating utility functions to work with dates and weeks*

Our bookings grid will show one week at a time, running from Sunday to Saturday. On any particular date, we show the week that contains that date. Let's create objects that represent a week, with a particular date in the week and the dates for the start and end of the week:

```
week = {                JavaScript Date object
   date,    ◁           for a particular date
   start,   ◁                              Date object for the
   end      ◁                              start of the week
};           Date object for the           containing date
             end of the week
```

For example, take Wednesday, April 1, 2020. The start of the week was Sunday, March 29, 2020, and the end of the week was Saturday, April 4, 2020:

```
week = {
   date,    // 2020-04-01       Assign each property a
   start,   // 2020-03-29       JavaScript Date object
   end      // 2020-04-04       for the specified date.
};
```

The following listing shows a couple of utility functions: one to create a new date from an old date, offset by a number of days, and the second to generate the week objects. The file is called date-wrangler.js and is in a new /src/utils folder.

---

> *Branch:* 0303-week-picker, *File:* /src/utils/date-wrangler.js

##### Listing 3.6   Date-wrangling utility functions

```
export function addDays (date, daysToAdd) {
   const clone = new Date(date.getTime());              Shift the date by the
   clone.setDate(clone.getDate() + daysToAdd);  ◁       number of days specified.
   return clone;
}

export function getWeek (forDate, daysOffset = 0) {     Immediately
   const date = addDays(forDate, daysOffset);  ◁        shift the date.
   const day = date.getDay();           ◁
                                        Get the day index for the new
                                        date, for example, Tuesday = 2.
   return {
      date,
      start: addDays(date, -day),   ◁     For example, if it's Tuesday,
      end: addDays(date, 6 - day)         shift back by 2 days.
   };                            ◁
}                                   For example, if it's Tuesday,
                                    shift forward by 4 days.
```

The `getWeek` function uses the `getDay` method of JavaScript's `Date` object to get the day-of-the-week index of the specified date: Sunday is 0, Monday is 1, . . . , Saturday is

6. To get to the start of the week, the function subtracts the same number of days as the day index: for Sunday, it subtracts 0 days; for Monday, it subtracts 1 day; . . . ; for Saturday, it subtracts 6 days. The end of the week is 6 days after the start of the week, so to get the end of the week, the function performs the same subtraction as for the start of the week but also adds 6. We can use the `getWeek` function to generate a week object for a given date:

```
const today = new Date();              Get the week object for the
const week = getWeek(today);     ◁─┘   week containing today's date.
```

We can also specify an offset number of days as the second argument if we want the week object for a date relative to the date in the first argument:

```
const today = new Date();                 Get the week object for the week
const week = getWeek(today, 7);    ◁─┘    containing the date a week from today.
```

The `getWeek` function lets us generate week objects as we navigate from week to week in the bookings app. Let's use it to do just that in a reducer.

### 3.3.3 *Building the reducer to manage dates for the component*

A reducer helps us to centralize the state management logic for our `WeekPicker` component. In a single place, we can see all of the possible actions and how they update the state:

- Move to the next week by adding seven days to the current date.
- Move to the previous week by subtracting seven days from the current date.
- Move to today by setting the current date to today's date.
- Move to a specified date by setting the current date to the action's payload.

For each action, the reducer returns a week object as described in the previous section. Although we really need to track only a single date, we would need to generate the week object at some point, and abstracting the week object generation along with the reducer seems sensible to me. You can see how the possible state changes translate to a reducer in the following listing. We put the weekReducer.js file in the Bookings folder.

> **Branch: 0303-week-picker,** *File:* **/src/components/Bookings/weekReducer.js**
>
> **Listing 3.7  The reducer for** `WeekPicker`

```
import {getWeek} from "../../utils/date-wrangler";     ◁─┐  Import the
                                                          │  getWeek function.
export default function reducer (state, action) {
  switch (action.type) {
    case "NEXT_WEEK":
      return getWeek(state.date, 7);     ◁─┐  Return a week object
    case "PREV_WEEK":                        for 7 days ahead.
      return getWeek(state.date, -7);    ◁─┐  Return a week object
    case "TODAY":                            for 7 days before.
```

**Return a week object for today.**

```
      return getWeek(new Date());
    case "SET_DATE":
      return getWeek(new Date(action.payload));
    default:
      throw new Error(`Unknown action type: ${action.type}`)
  }
}
```

**Return a week object for a specified date.**

The reducer imports the getWeek function to generate the week object for each state change. Having the getWeek function available to import means we can also use it as an initialization function when we call the useReducer hook in the WeekPicker component.

### 3.3.4  *Passing an initialization function to the useReducer hook*

The WeekPicker component lets users navigate from week to week to book resources in the company. We set up the reducer in the preceding section; now it's time to use it. The reducer needs an initial state, a week object. The following listing shows how we can use the getWeek function to generate the initial week object from a date we pass to WeekPicker as a prop. The WeekPicker.js file is also in the Bookings folder.

> Branch: **0303-week-picker**, *File:* **/src/components/Bookings/WeekPicker.js**
>
> Listing 3.8   The `WeekPicker` component

```
import {useReducer} from "react";
import reducer from "./weekReducer";
import {getWeek} from "../../utils/date-wrangler";
import {FaChevronLeft, FaCalendarDay, FaChevronRight} from "react-icons/fa";
```

**Import the getWeek date-wrangler function.**

**Receive the initial date as a prop.**

```
export default function WeekPicker ({date}) {
  const [week, dispatch] = useReducer(reducer, date, getWeek);

  return (
    <div>
      <p className="date-picker">
        <button
          className="btn"
          onClick={() => dispatch({type: "PREV_WEEK"})}
        >
          <FaChevronLeft/>
          <span>Prev</span>
        </button>

        <button
          className="btn"
          onClick={() => dispatch({type: "TODAY"})}
        >
          <FaCalendarDay/>
          <span>Today</span>
        </button>

        <button
          className="btn"
          onClick={() => dispatch({type: "NEXT_WEEK"})}
```

**Generate the initial state, passing date to getWeek.**

**Dispatch actions to the reducer to switch weeks.**

```
          >
            <span>Next</span>
            <FaChevronRight/>
          </button>
        </p>
        <p>
          {week.start.toDateString()} - {week.end.toDateString()}    <──┐   Use the
        </p>                                                              current state
      </div>                                                              to display the
    );                                                                    date info.
  }
```

Our call to useReducer passes the specified date to the getWeek function. The getWeek function returns a week object that is set as the initial state. We assign the state that useReducer returns to a variable called week:

```
const [week, dispatch] = useReducer(reducer, date, getWeek);
```

In addition to letting us reuse the getWeek function to generate state (in the reducer and the WeekPicker component), the initialization function (useReducer's third argument) also allows us to run expensive state generation functions once only, on the initial call to useReducer.

At last, a new component! Let's hook it up to BookingsPage.

### 3.3.5   Updating BookingsPage to use WeekPicker

The following listing shows an updated BookingsPage component that imports and renders the WeekPicker component. The resulting page is shown in figure 3.9.

**Figure 3.9   The** BookingsPage **component with the** WeekPicker **component in place**

---

**Branch**: 0303-week-picker, *File*: /src/components/Bookings/BookingsPage.js

**Listing 3.9   The** `BookingsPage` **component using** `WeekPicker`

```
import WeekPicker from "./WeekPicker";          ⟵────  Import the WeekPicker
                                                        component.
export default function BookingsPage () {
  return (
    <main className="bookings-page">
      <p>Bookings!</p>
      <WeekPicker date={new Date()}/>           ⟵────  Include the WeekPicker
    </main>                                             in the UI, passing it the
  );                                                    current date.
}
```

`BookingsPage` passes the `WeekPicker` component the current date. The week picker first appears showing the start and end dates of the current week, from Sunday to Saturday. Have a go navigating from week to week and then click the Today button to jump back to the present week. It's a simple component but helps drive the bookings grid in chapters to come. And it provides an example of `useReducer`'s initialization function argument.

Before this chapter's formal Summary section, let's briefly recap some of the key concepts we've encountered, building your understanding of function components and hooks.

## 3.4    *Reviewing some useReducer concepts*

A bit more jargon has crept into this discussion, so just in case all the actions, reducers, and dispatch functions are causing some dizziness, table 3.1 describes the terms with examples. Take a breather!

**Table 3.1   Some of the key terms we've met**

| Icon | Term | Description | Example |
|------|------|-------------|---------|
| | Initial state | The values of variables and properties when the component first runs | `{`<br>`  group: "Rooms",`<br>`  bookableIndex: 0,`<br>`  hasDetails: false`<br>`}` |
| | Action | Information that the reducer uses to update the state | `{`<br>`  type: "SET_BOOKABLE",`<br>`  payload: 1`<br>`}` |

**Table 3.1  Some of the key terms we've met** *(continued)*

| Icon | Term | Description | Example |
|------|------|-------------|---------|
| | Reducer | A function React passes the current state and an action. It creates a new state from the current state, depending on the action. | `(state, action) => {`<br>`  // check action`<br><br>`  // update state based`<br>`  // on action type and`<br>`  // action payload`<br><br>`  // return new state`<br>`};` |
| | State | The values of variables and properties at a particular point in execution | `{`<br>`  group: "Rooms",`<br>`  bookableIndex: 1,`<br>`  hasDetails: false`<br>`}` |
| | Dispatch function | A function for dispatching actions to the reducer. Use it to tell the reducer what action to take. | `dispatch({`<br>`  type: "SET_BOOKABLE",`<br>`  payload: 1`<br>`});` |

Once we pass the reducer and initial state to React via our call to `useReducer`, it manages the state for us. We just have to dispatch actions, and React will use the reducer to update the state depending on which action it receives. Remember, our component code returns a description of its UI. Having updated the state, React knows it may need to update the UI, so it will call our component code again, passing it the latest state and the dispatcher function when the component calls `useReducer`. To reinforce the functional nature of our components, figure 3.10 illustrates each step when React first calls the `BookablesList` component and a user then fires an event by selecting a group, choosing a bookable, or toggling the Show Details check box.

Table 3.2 lists the steps from figure 3.10, describing what is happening and including short discussions of each one.

Each time it needs the UI, React invokes the component code. The component function runs to completion, and local variables are created during execution, and destroyed or referenced in closures when the function ends. The function returns a description of the UI for the component. The component uses hooks, like `useState` and `useReducer`, to persist state across invocations and to receive updater and dispatch functions. Event handlers call the updater functions or dispatch actions in response to user actions, and React can update the state and call the component code again, restarting the cycle.

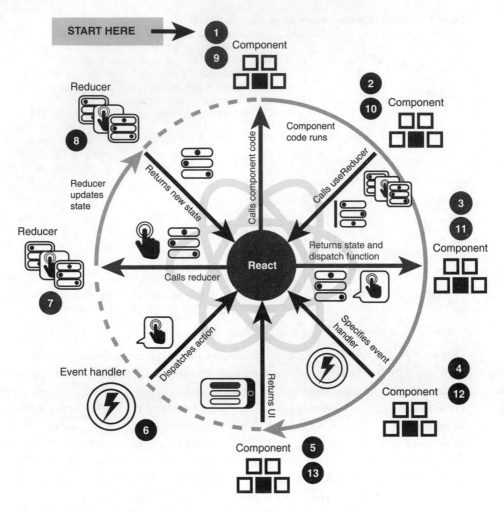

**Figure 3.10   Stepping through the key moments when using `useReducer`**

**Table 3.2   Some key steps when using useReducer**

| Step | What happens? | Discussion |
|------|---------------|------------|
| 1 | React calls the component. | To generate the UI for the page, React traverses the tree of components, calling each one. React will pass each component any props set as attributes in the JSX. |
| 2 | The component calls `useReducer` for the first time. | The component passes the initial state and the reducer to the `useReducer` function. React sets the current state for the reducer as the initial state. |

**Table 3.2  Some key steps when using useReducer (continued)**

| Step | What happens? | Discussion |
|------|---------------|------------|
| 3 | React returns the current state and the dispatch function as an array. | The component code assigns the state and dispatch function to variables for later use. The variables are often called `state` and `dispatch`, or we might destructure the state into further variables. |
| 4 | The component sets up an event handler. | The event handler may listen for user clicks, timers firing, or resources loading, for example. The handler will dispatch an action to change the state. |
| 5 | The component returns its UI. | The component uses the current state to generate its user interface and returns it, finishing its work. React compares the new UI to the old and updates the DOM. |
| 6 | The event handler dispatches an action. | An event fires, and the handler runs. The handler uses the dispatch function to dispatch an action. |
| 7 | React calls the reducer. | React passes the current state and the dispatched action to the reducer. |
| 8 | The reducer returns the new state. | The reducer uses the action to update the state and returns the new version. |
| 9 | React calls the component. | React knows the state has changed and so must recalculate the UI. |
| 10 | The component calls `use-Reducer` for the second time. | This time, React will ignore the arguments. |
| 11 | React returns the current state and the dispatch function. | The state has been updated by the reducer, and the component needs the latest values. The dispatch function is the exact same function as React returned for the previous call to `useReducer`. |
| 12 | The component sets up an event handler. | This is a new version of the handler and may use some of the newly updated state values. |
| 13 | The component returns its UI. | The component uses the current state to generate its user interface and returns it, finishing its work. React compares the new UI to the old and updates the DOM. |

## *Summary*

- If you have multiple pieces of interrelated state, consider using a reducer to clearly define the actions that can change the state. A reducer is a function to which you pass the current state and an action. It uses the action to generate a new state. It returns the new state:

```
function reducer (state, action) {
  // use the action to generate a new state from the old state.
  // return newState.
}
```

- Call the `useReducer` hook when you want React to manage the state and reducer for a component. Pass it the reducer and an initial state. It returns an array with two elements, the state and a dispatch function:

```
const [state, dispatch] = useReducer(reducer, initialState);
```

- Call the `useReducer` hook with an initialization argument and an initialization function to generate the initial state when the hook is first called. The hook automatically passes the initialization argument to the initialization function. The initialization function returns the initial state for the reducer. This is useful when initialization is expensive or when you want to use an existing function to initialize the state:

```
const [state, dispatch] = useReducer(reducer, initArg, initFunc);
```

- Use the `dispatch` function to dispatch an action. React will pass the current state and the action to the reducer. It will replace the state with the new state generated by the reducer. It will re-render if the state has changed:

```
dispatch(action);
```

- For anything more than the most basic actions, consider following common practice and specify the action as a JavaScript object with `type` and `payload` properties:

```
dispatch({ type: "SET_NAME", payload: "Jamal" });
```

- React always returns the same `dispatch` function for a particular call to `useReducer` within a component. (If the `dispatch` function changed between calls, it could cause unnecessary re-renders when passed as a prop or included as a dependency for other hooks.)
- In the reducer, use `if` or `switch` statements to check for the type of action dispatched:

```
function reducer (state, action) {
  switch (action.type) {
    case "SET_NAME":
      return {
        ...state,
        name: action.payload
      }
    default:
      return state;
```

```
        // or return new Error(`Unknown action type: ${action.type}`)
  }
}
```

In the `default` case, either return the unchanged state (if the reducer will be combined with other reducers, for example) or throw an error (if the reducer should never receive an unknown action type).

# Working with side effects

**This chapter covers**

- Recognizing types of side effects in components
- Wrapping side effects with the `useEffect` hook
- Controlling when an effect runs by specifying a dependency list
- Returning a cleanup function from an effect
- Using an effect to fetch data for a component

React transforms our data into UI. Each component plays its part, returning its contribution to the overall user interface. React builds the tree of elements, compares it with what's already rendered, and commits any necessary changes to the DOM. When the state changes, React goes through the process again to update the UI. React is really good at efficiently deciding what should update and scheduling any changes.

Sometimes, however, we need our components to reach outside this data-flow process and directly interact with other APIs. An action that impinges on the outside world in some way is called a *side effect*. Common side effects include the following:

- Setting the page title imperatively
- Working with timers like `setInterval` or `setTimeout`

- Measuring the width, height, or position of elements in the DOM
- Logging messages to the console or other service
- Setting or getting values in local storage
- Fetching data or subscribing and unsubscribing to services

Whatever our components are trying to achieve, it would be risky for them to simply ignore React and try to perform their tasks blindly. It's much better to enlist React's help to schedule such side effects effectively, considering when and how often they should run, even as React does its job of rendering each component and committing changes to the screen. React provides the useEffect hook so that we can better control side effects and integrate them into the life cycles of our components.

In this chapter, we come to grips with how the useEffect hook works. We start, in section 4.1, by trying out simple examples that highlight calling the hook, controlling when it runs, and specifying how to clean up any effects when a component unmounts. In section 4.2, we set up a simple server for data in the bookings app example and create components to practice fetching that data. Finally, in section 4.3, we switch our bookings app over from importing database files to fetching data from a server.

The useEffect hook is our gateway to safe interactions with the outside world. Let's take our first steps on the path.

## 4.1 Exploring the useEffect API with simple examples

Some of our React components are super friendly, reaching out to say "hi" to APIs and services outside React. Although these components are eternally optimistic and like to think the best of all those they meet, there are some safeguards to be followed. In this section, we look at setting up side effects in ways that won't get out of hand. In particular, we explore these four scenarios:

- Running side effects after every render
- Running an effect only when a component mounts
- Cleaning up side effects by returning a function
- Controlling when an effect runs by specifying dependencies

To focus on the API, we'll create some super-simple component examples, rather than jumping straight into the bookings app as a context. First up, let's say, "Bonjour, les side-effects."

### 4.1.1 Running side effects after every render

Say you want to add a random greeting to the page's title in the browser. Clicking your friendly component's Say Hi button should generate a new greeting and update the title. Three such greetings are shown in figure 4.1.

The document title isn't part of the document body and isn't rendered by React. But the title is accessible via the document property of the window. You can set the title like this:

```
document.title = "Bonjour";
```

**Figure 4.1   Clicking the Say Hi button updates the page title with a random greeting.**

Reaching out to a browser API in this way is considered a side effect. We can make that explicit by wrapping the code in the useEffect hook:

```
useEffect(() => {
  document.title = "Bonjour";
});
```

The following listing shows a SayHello component that updates the page title with a random greeting whenever the user clicks the Say Hi button.

*Live*: https://jhijd.csb.app, *Code*: https://codesandbox.io/s/sayhello-jhijd

Listing 4.1    Updating the browser title

```
import React, { useState, useEffect } from "react";        ◁—  Import the
                                                               useEffect hook.
export default function SayHello () {
  const greetings = ["Hello", "Ciao", "Hola", "こんにちは"];

  const [index, setIndex] = useState(0);

                                             Pass the useEffect hook
  useEffect(() => {                      ◁—  a function, the effect.
    document.title = greetings[index];       ◁—  Update the browser title
  });                                              from inside the effect.

  function updateGreeting () {
    setIndex(Math.floor(Math.random() * greetings.length));
  }

  return <button onClick={updateGreeting}>Say Hi</button>
}
```

The component uses a randomly generated index to pick a greeting from an array. Whenever the updateGreeting function calls setIndex, React re-renders the component (unless the index value doesn't change).

React runs the effect function within the useEffect hook *after* every render, once the browser has repainted the page, updating the page title as required. Notice that the effect function has access to the variables within the component because it's in the same scope. In particular, it uses the values of the greetings and index variables. Figure 4.2 shows how you pass an effect function as the first argument to the useEffect hook.

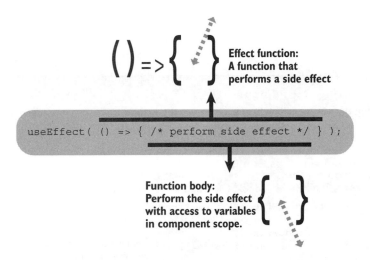

**Figure 4.2   Passing an effect function to the useEffect hook**

When you call the useEffect hook in this way, without a second argument, React runs the effect after every render. But what if you want to run an effect only when a component mounts?

### 4.1.2   *Running an effect only when a component mounts*

Say you want to use the width and height of the browser window, maybe for a groovy animation effect. To test out reading the dimensions, you create a little component that displays the current width and height, just as in figure 4.3.

The following listing shows the code for the component. It reaches out to read the innerWidth and innerHeight properties of the window object, so, once again, we use the useEffect hook.

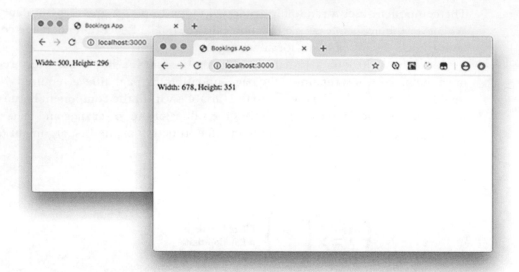

**Figure 4.3   Displaying the width and height of a window as it's resized**

*Live:* https://gn80v.csb.app/, *Code:* https://codesandbox.io/s/windowsize-gn80v

**Listing 4.2   Resizing the window**

```
import React, { useState, useEffect } from "react";

export default function WindowSize () {
  const [size, setSize] = useState(getSize());

  function getSize () {
    return {
      width: window.innerWidth,
      height: window.innerHeight
    };
  }

  useEffect(() => {
    function handleResize () {
      setSize(getSize());
    }

    window.addEventListener('resize', handleResize);
  }, []);

  return <p>Width: {size.width}, Height: {size.height}</p>
}
```

**Define a function that returns the dimensions of the window.**

**Read the dimensions from the window object.**

**Update the state, triggering a re-render.**

**Pass an empty array as the dependency argument.**

**Register an event listener for the resize event.**

Within `useEffect`, the component registers an event listener for resize events:

```
window.addEventListener('resize', handleResize);
```

Whenever the user resizes the browser, the handler, `handleResize`, updates the state with the new dimensions by calling `setSize`:

```
function handleResize () {
  setSize(getSize());
}
```

By calling the updater function, the component kicks off a re-render. We don't want to keep reregistering the event listener every time React calls the component. So how do we prevent the effect from running after every render? The trick is the empty array passed as the second argument to `useEffect`, as illustrated in figure 4.4.

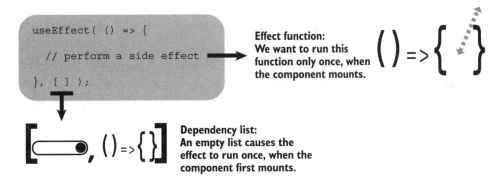

**Figure 4.4   Passing an empty dependency array causes the effect function to run once, when the component mounts.**

As we see in section 4.1.4, the second argument is for a list of dependencies. React determines whether to run an effect by checking if the values in the list have changed since the last time the component called the effect. By setting the list to an empty array, the list will never change, and we cause the effect to run only once, when the component first mounts.

But hang on a second; alarm bells should be ringing. We registered an event listener . . . we shouldn't just leave that listener listening away, like a zombie shambling in a crypt for all eternity. We need to perform some cleaning up and unregister the listener. Let's wrangle those zombies.

### 4.1.3   *Cleaning up side effects by returning a function*

We have to be careful not to make a mess when we set up long-running side effects like subscriptions, data requests, timers, and event listeners. To avoid zombies eating our brains so our memories start to leak, or ghosts shifting the furniture unexpectedly, we should carefully undo any effects that may cause undead echoes of our actions to live on.

The useEffect hook incorporates a simple mechanism for cleaning up our effects. Just return a function from the effect. React runs the returned function when it's time to tidy up. The following listing updates our window-measuring app to remove the resize listener when it's no longer needed.

*Live:* **https://b8wii.csb.app/,** *Code:* **https://codesandbox.io/s/windowsizecleanup-b8wii**

Listing 4.3   **Returning a cleanup function to remove a listener**

```
import React, { useState, useEffect } from "react";

export default function WindowSize () {
  const [size, setSize] = useState(getSize());

  function getSize () {
    return {
      width: window.innerWidth,
      height: window.innerHeight
    };
  }

  useEffect(() => {
    function handleResize () {
      setSize(getSize());
    }

    window.addEventListener('resize', handleResize);

    return () => window.removeEventListener('resize', handleResize);
  }, []);


  return <p>Width: {size.width}, Height: {size.height}</p>
}
```

Return a cleanup function from the effect.

Because the code passes useEffect an empty array as the second argument, the effect will run only once. When the effect runs, it registers an event listener. React keeps ahold of the function the effect returns and calls it when it's time to clean up. In listing 4.3, the returned function removes the event listener. Our memory won't leak. Our brains are safe from zombie effects.

Figure 4.5 shows this latest step in our evolving knowledge of the useEffect hook: returning a cleanup function.

Because the cleanup function is defined within the effect, it has access to the variables within the effect's scope. In listing 4.3, the cleanup function can remove the handleResize function because handleResize was also defined within the same effect:

```
useEffect(() => {
  function handleResize () {
    setSize(getSize());
  }
```

Define the handleResize function.

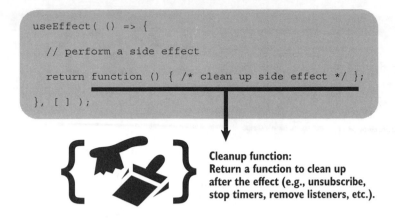

```
useEffect( () => {

  // perform a side effect

  return function () { /* clean up side effect */ };

}, [ ] );
```

**Cleanup function:**
**Return a function to clean up**
**after the effect (e.g., unsubscribe,**
**stop timers, remove listeners, etc.).**

**Figure 4.5**  Return a function from the effect. React will run the function to clean up after the effect.

```
window.addEventListener('resize', handleResize);

  return () => window.removeEventListener('resize', handleResize);    ⟵
}, []);
```
**Reference the handleResize function**
**from the cleanup function.**

The React Hooks approach, in which components and hooks are just functions, makes good use of the inherent nature of JavaScript, rather than too heavily relying on a layer of idiosyncratic APIs conceptually divorced from the underlying language. That does mean, however, that you need a good grasp of scope and closures to best understand where to put your variables and functions.

React runs the cleanup function when it unmounts the component. But that's not the only time it runs it. Whenever the component re-renders, React calls the cleanup function before running the effect function, *if the effect runs again.* If multiple effects need to run again, React calls all of the cleanup functions for those effects. Once the cleanup is finished, React reruns the effect functions as needed.

We've seen the two extremes: running an effect only once and running an effect after every render. What if we want more control over when an effect runs? There's one more case to cover. Let's populate that dependency array.

### 4.1.4  *Controlling when an effect runs by specifying dependencies*

Figure 4.6 is our final illustration of the useEffect API, including dependency values in the array we pass as the second argument.

Each time React calls a component, it keeps a record of the values in the dependency arrays for calls to useEffect. If the array of values has changed since the last call, React runs the effect. If the values are unchanged, React skips the effect. This

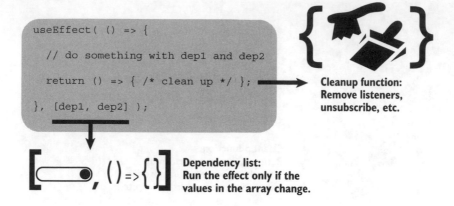

**Figure 4.6    When calling** `useEffect`**, you can specify a list of dependencies and return a cleanup function.**

saves the effect from running when the values it depends on are unchanged and so the outcome of its task will be unchanged.

Let's look at an example. Say you have a user picker that lets you select a user from a drop-down menu. You want to store the selected user in the browser's local storage so that the page remembers the selected user from visit to visit, as shown in figure 4.7.

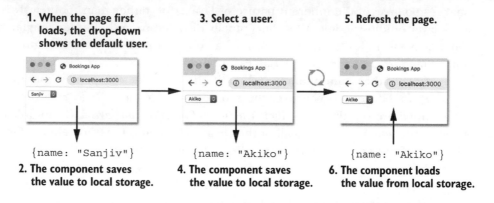

**Figure 4.7    Once you select a user, refreshing the page automatically reselects the same user.**

The following listing shows the code to achieve the desired effect. It includes two calls to `useEffect`, one to get any stored user from local storage, and one to save the selected user whenever that value changes.

**Listing 4.4    Using local storage**

```
import React, { useState, useEffect } from "react";

export default function UserStorage () {
  const [user, setUser] = useState("Sanjiv");

  useEffect(() => {
    const storedUser = window.localStorage.getItem("user");

    if (storedUser) {
      setUser(storedUser);
    }
  }, []);

  useEffect(() => {
    window.localStorage.setItem("user", user);
  }, [user]);

  return (
    <select value={user} onChange={e => setUser(e.target.value)}>
      <option>Jason</option>
      <option>Akiko</option>
      <option>Clarisse</option>
      <option>Sanjiv</option>
    </select>
  );
}
```

Annotations:
- **Read the user from local storage.** → `const storedUser = window.localStorage.getItem("user");`
- **Run this effect only when the component first mounts.** → `}, []);`
- **Specify a second effect.** → `useEffect(() => {`
- **Save the user to local storage.** → `window.localStorage.setItem("user", user);`
- **Run this effect whenever the user changes.** → `}, [user]);`

The component works as expected, saving changes to local storage and automatically selecting the saved user when the page is reloaded.

But to get a better feel for how the function component and its hooks manage all the pieces, let's run through the steps for the component as it renders and re-renders and a visitor to the page selects a user from the list. We look at two key scenarios:

1   The visitor first loads the page. There is no user value in local storage. The visitor selects a user from the list.

2   The visitor refreshes the page. There is a user value in local storage.

As we go through the steps, notice how the dependency lists for the two effects determine when the effect functions run.

**THE VISITOR FIRST LOADS THE PAGE**

When the component first runs, it renders the drop-down list of users with Sanjiv selected. Then the first effect runs. No user is in local storage, so nothing happens. Then the second effect runs. It saves Sanjiv to local storage. Here are the steps:

1   The user loads the page.

2   React calls the component.

3 The useState call sets the value of user to Sanjiv. (It's the first time the component has called useState, so the initial value is used.)

4 React renders the list of users with Sanjiv selected.

5 Effect 1 runs, but there is no stored user.

6 Effect 2 runs, saving Sanjiv to local storage.

React calls the effect functions in the order they appear in the component code. When the effects run, React keeps a record of the values in the dependency lists, [] and ["Sanjiv"] in this case.

When the visitor selects a new user (say, Akiko), the onChange handler calls the setUser updater function. React updates the state and calls the component again. This time, effect 1 doesn't run because its dependency list hasn't changed; it's still []. But the dependency list for effect 2 has changed from ["Sanjiv"] to ["Akiko"], so effect 2 runs again, updating the value in local storage. The steps continue as follows:

7 The user selects Akiko.

8 The updater function sets the user state to Akiko.

9 React calls the component.

10 The useState call sets the value of user to Akiko. (It's the second time the component has called useState, so the latest value, set in step 8, is used.)

11 React renders the list of users with Akiko selected.

12 Effect 1 doesn't run ([] = []).

13 Effect 2 runs (["Sanjiv"] != ["Akiko"]), saving Akiko to local storage.

### THE VISITOR REFRESHES THE PAGE

With local storage set to Akiko, if the user reloads the page, effect 1 will set the user state to the stored value, Akiko, as we saw in figure 4.7. But before React calls the component with the new state value, effect 2 still has to run with the old value. Here are the steps:

1 The user refreshes the page.

2 React calls the component.

3 The useState call sets the value of user to Sanjiv. (It's the first time the component has called useState, so the initial value is used.)

4 React renders the list of users with Sanjiv selected.

5 Effect 1 runs, loading Akiko from local storage and calling setUser.

6 Effect 2 runs, saving Sanjiv to local storage.

7 React calls the component (because effect 1 called setUser, changing the state).

8 The useState call sets the value of user to Akiko.

9 React renders the list of users with Akiko selected.

10 Effect 1 doesn't run ([] = []).

11 Effect 2 runs (["Sanjiv"] != ["Akiko"]), saving Akiko to local storage.

In step 6, effect 2 was defined as part of the initial render, so it still uses the initial `user` value, `Sanjiv`.

By including `user` in the list of dependencies for effect 2, we're able to control when effect 2 runs: only when the value of `user` changes.

### 4.1.5 *Summarizing the ways to call the useEffect hook*

Table 4.1 collects the various use cases for the `useEffect` hook into one place, showing how the different code patterns lead to different execution patterns.

**Table 4.1**　**The various use cases for the `useEffect` hook**

| Call pattern | Code pattern | Execution pattern |
|---|---|---|
| No second argument | `useEffect(() => {`<br>`  // perform effect`<br>`});` | Run after every render. |
| Empty array as second argument | `useEffect(() => {`<br>`  // perform effect`<br>`}, []);` | Run once, when the component mounts. |
| Dependency array as second argument | `useEffect(() => {`<br>`  // perform effect`<br>`  // that uses dep1 and dep2`<br>`}, [dep1, dep2]);` | Run whenever a value in the dependency array changes. |
| Return a function | `useEffect(() => {`<br>`  // perform effect`<br>`  return () => {/* clean-up */};`<br>`}, [dep1, dep2]);` | React will run the cleanup function when the component unmounts and before rerunning the effect. |

**CHALLENGE 4.1**

On CodeSandbox (or anywhere you prefer), create an app that updates the document title as the window is resized. It should say "Small" or "Medium" or "Large," depending on the size of the window.

### 4.1.6 *Calling useLayoutEffect to run an effect before the browser repaints*

Most of the time, we synchronize side effects with state by calling `useEffect`. React runs the effects after the component has rendered and the browser has repainted the screen. Occasionally, we might want to make further changes to state after React has updated the DOM but before the browser has repainted. We might want to use the dimensions of DOM elements to set state in some way, for example. Making changes in `useEffect` will show users an intermediate state that'll immediately be updated.

We can avoid such flashes of changing state by calling the `useLayoutEffect` hook instead of `useEffect`. This hook has the same API as `useEffect` but runs synchronously after React updates the DOM and before the browser repaints. If the effect makes further updates to the state, the intermediate state isn't painted to the screen.

You generally won't need useLayoutEffect, but if you come across problems (maybe with an element flickering between states), you could try switching from useEffect for the suspect effect.

Now that we've seen what the useEffect hook can do, it's time to fetch some data. Let's make our app data available via a server rather than as a file import.

## 4.2   Fetching data

So far in this book, we've been importing data for the bookings app example from the static.json file. But it's more common to fetch data from a server. To make our examples a little more realistic, let's start doing just that. Rather than reach out to a public server, we'll run a JSON server locally, using a new db.json file outside the src folder. We'll then create a component that fetches data from that server. We cover the following:

- Creating the new db.json file
- Setting up a JSON server using the json-server package
- Building a component to fetch data from our server, displaying a list of users
- Taking care when using async and await within an effect

### 4.2.1   Creating the new db.json file

In chapters 2 and 3, we imported data from the static.json file. For our server, copy across the bookings, users, and bookables data to a new db.json file in the root of the project. Don't copy the days and sessions arrays in static.json; we treat that as config information and continue to import it. (We'll remove the duplicated data from static.json after we've updated the components that are currently using it.)

```
// db.json
{
  bookings: [/* empty */],
  users: [/* user objects */],
  bookables: [/* bookable objects */]
}

// static.json
{
  days: [/* names of days */],
  sessions: [/* session names */]
}
```

In later chapters, we'll start updating the database file by sending POST and PUT requests. The create-react-app development server restarts whenever files within the src folder change. Having the db.json file outside src avoids unnecessary restarts as we test adding new bookables and making bookings.

### 4.2.2 Setting up a JSON server

Until now, we've been *importing* data for the `BookablesList`, `UsersList`, and `User-Picker` components from a JSON file, static.json:

```
import {bookables} from "../../static.json";
import {users} from "../../static.json";
```

To better exemplify the kinds of data-fetching tasks we perform in a real application, we want to make our data available via HTTP. Luckily, we don't need to spin up a real database for our data. We can instead use the `json-server` npm package. This package is a really handy, easy way of serving up JSON data as a mock REST API. There's a user guide at https://github.com/typicode/json-server, where you can see just how flexible the package is. To install the package globally using npm, enter this command:

```
npm install -g json-server
```

Then, from within the root of our project, start the server with this command:

```
json-server --watch db.json --port 3001
```

You should be able to query our database on `localhost:3001`. Figure 4.8 shows the terminal output on my machine when I start up the server.

We've made our db.json file JSON data available over HTTP via URL endpoints. Comparing the data from the file to figure 4.8, you can see that the server has turned

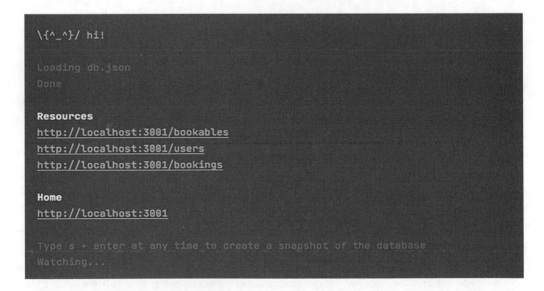

**Figure 4.8   The output when running** `json-server`**. Properties from within the db.json file have been turned into endpoints for fetchable resources.**

each property from the JSON object into an endpoint. For example, to get the list of users, navigate to `localhost:3001/users`; and to get the user with an ID of 1, navigate to `localhost:3001/users/1`. Nice!

You can test out the requests in a browser. The results of the two requests just mentioned are shown in figure 4.9: first, the list of user objects in an array, and second, the user object with an ID of 1.

**Figure 4.9   Two browser responses showing our bookings app data is now available via HTTP**

Let's try out our server and fetch some data from within a `useEffect` hook.

### 4.2.3   *Fetching data within a useEffect hook*

To introduce data fetching from within a `useEffect` hook, we update the `UserPicker` component to fetch the users from our JSON database. Figure 4.10 shows the expanded drop-down list with the four users.

**Figure 4.10   Displaying a list of users fetched from the database**

Remember, React calls effect functions *after* rendering, so the data won't be available for the first render; we set an empty list of users as the initial value and return alternative UI, a new `Spinner` component, for the loading state. The following listing shows the code to fetch the list of users and display it in the drop-down.

Branch: 0401-user-picker, *File*: /src/components/Users/UserPicker.js

Listing 4.5   The `UserPicker` component fetching data

```
import {useState, useEffect} from "react";
import Spinner from "../UI/Spinner";
                                                    Fetch the data from
                                                    inside an effect function.
export default function UserPicker () {
  const [users, setUsers] = useState(null);

  useEffect(() => {                   ◁────────────  Make the request to the
                                                     database by using the
                                                     browser's fetch API.
    fetch("http://localhost:3001/users")  ◁──────
      .then(resp => resp.json())      ◁─────────── Convert the JSON string returned
      .then(data => setUsers(data));              into a JavaScript object.

  }, []);     ◁───────────  Include an empty dependency
                            array to load the data once,
  if (users === null) {     when the component is first
    return <Spinner/>       mounted.
  }

  return (
    <select>
      {users.map(u => (
        <option key={u.id}>{u.name}</option>
      ))}
    </select>
  );
}
```

Update the state with the loaded users.

Return alternative UI while the users load.

The `UserPicker` code uses the browser's fetch API to retrieve the list of users from the database, parses the response as JSON by using the `resp.json` method, and calls `setUsers` to update the local state with the result. The component initially renders a `Spinner` placeholder (from the new /src/components/UI folder in the repo), before replacing it with the list of users. If you want to add latency to the fetch calls, to better see any loading states, start the JSON server with a `delay` flag. This snippet delays responses for 3000 milliseconds, or 3 seconds:

```
json-server --watch db.json --port 3001 --delay 3000
```

The effect in listing 4.5 runs only once, when the component mounts. We're not expecting the list of users to change, so there's no need to manage the reloading of the list. The following list shows the sequence of steps for fetching data from an effect in this way:

1 React calls the component.
2 The useState call sets the users variable to null.
3 The useEffect call registers the data-fetching effect function with React.
4 The users variable is null, so the component returns the spinner icon.
5 React runs the effect, requesting data from the server.

6   The data arrives, and the effect calls the `setUsers` updater function, triggering a re-render.

7   React calls the component.

8   The `useState` call sets the `users` variable to the returned list of users.

9   The empty dependency array, `[]`, for `useEffect` is unchanged, so the hook call does not reregister the effect.

10  The `users` array has four elements (it's not `null`), so the component returns the drop-down UI.

This method of fetching data, in which the component renders before it kicks off a request for data, is called *fetch on render*. Other methods can sometimes offer a smoother experience for your users, and we'll take a look at some of those in part 2. But depending on the complexity and stability of the data source and your application's needs, the simplicity of fetching within a call to the `useEffect` hook might be perfectly adequate and quite appealing.

### CHALLENGE 4.2

Update the `UsersList` component on the `UsersPage` to fetch the users data from the server. The 0402-users-list branch has the challenge solution code for the updated component.

### 4.2.4  *Working with async and await*

The `fetch` call in listing 4.5 returns a promise, and the listing uses the promise's `then` method to process the response:

```
fetch("http://localhost:3001/users")
  .then(resp => resp.json())
  .then(data => setUsers(data));
```

JavaScript also offers `async` functions and the `await` keyword for working with asynchronous responses, but there are some caveats when combining them with the `useEffect` hook. As an initial attempt to convert our data-fetching to async-await, we might try this:

```
useEffect(async () => {
  const resp = await fetch("http://localhost:3001/users");
  const data = await (resp.json());
  setUsers(data);
}, []);
```

But that approach provokes React to show a warning on the console, as shown in figure 4.11.

The key message from the browser is as follows:

- Effect callbacks are synchronous to prevent race conditions. Put the async function inside.

```
⚠ ▸ src/components/Users/UserPicker.js                    webpackHotDevClient.js:138
    Line 15:13:  Effect callbacks are synchronous to prevent race conditions. Put the async function
  inside:

  useEffect(() => {
    async function fetchData() {
      // You can await here
      const response = await MyAPI.getData(someId);
      // ...
    }
    fetchData();
  }, [someId]); // Or [] if effect doesn't need props or state

  Learn more about data fetching with Hooks: https://reactjs.org/link/hooks-data-fetching  react-
  hooks/exhaustive-deps
```

**Figure 4.11   Our async-await data-fetching effect causes React to issue some warnings.**

async functions return a promise by default. Setting the effect function as `async` will cause trouble because React is looking for the return value of an effect to be a cleanup function. To solve the issues, remember to put the `async` function inside the effect function, rather than making the effect function `async` itself:

```
useEffect(() => {
  async function getUsers() {            Define an async function.
    const resp = await fetch(url);
    const data = await (resp.json());    Wait for asynchronous
    setUsers(data);                      results.
  }
  getUsers();                            Call the async
}, []);                                  function.
```

Now that we've set up the JSON server, tried an example of the fetch-on-render data-fetching method with the `useEffect` hook, and taken a moment to consider async-await syntax, we're ready to update the bookings app to fetch data for the `BookablesList` component.

## 4.3   *Fetching data for the BookablesList component*

In the preceding section, we saw how a component can load data after its initial render by including the fetching code within a call to the `useEffect` hook. More-complicated applications consist of many components and multiple queries for data that could use multiple endpoints. You might try to smooth that complexity by moving the state and its associated data-fetching actions into a separate data store and then connecting components to the store. But situating the data fetching within the components that consume the data may be a more direct and understandable approach for your app. We'll consider different approaches in chapter 9, when we look at custom hooks, and in part 2, when we look at models for data fetching.

For now, we'll keep things simple and get the `BookablesList` component to load its own data. We'll develop its data-fetching capability over four steps:

- Examining the data-loading process
- Updating the reducer to manage loading and error states
- Creating a helper function to load data
- Loading the bookables

### 4.3.1   *Examining the data-loading process*

The `UserPicker` component, in section 4.2, used the fetch API to load the list of users from the JSON database server. For the `BookablesList` component, we consider loading and error states as well as the bookables themselves. What exactly do we want the updated component to do?

After the component first renders, it will fire off a request for the data it needs. At this point, before any data has loaded, we have no bookables or groups to display, so the component will show a loading indicator, as shown in figure 4.12.

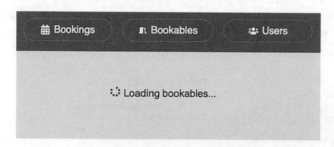

**Figure 4.12   The `BookablesList` component shows a loading indicator while the data is loading.**

If a problem loading the data occurs—maybe network, server, authorization, or missing file issues—the component will display an error message like the one in figure 4.13.

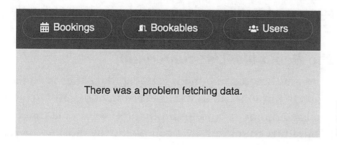

**Figure 4.13   The `BookablesList` component shows an error message if there was a problem loading data.**

If everything goes well and the data arrives, it'll be displayed in the UI we developed in chapters 2 and 3. The Meeting Room bookable from the Rooms group is selected, and its details are showing. Figure 4.14 shows the expected result.

At this point, the user will be able to interact with the app, selecting groups and bookables, cycling through the bookables with the Next button, and toggling bookable details with the Show Details check box.

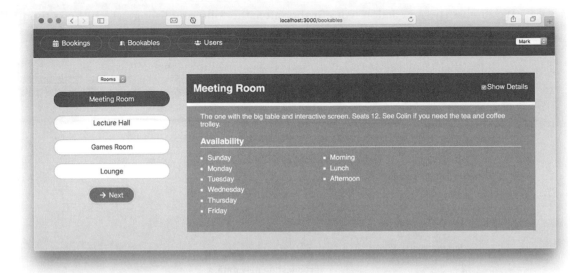

**Figure 4.14** The `BookablesList` component shows the list of bookables after the data has loaded.

In chapter 3, we created a reducer to help manage the `BookablesList` component's state. How should we update the reducer to cope with the new functionality?

### 4.3.2 Updating the reducer to manage loading and error states

We've seen what we're trying to achieve. Now we must consider the component state needed to drive such an interface. To enable the loading indicator and the error message, we add two more properties to the state: `isLoading` and `error`. We also set the bookables as an empty array. The full initial state now looks like this:

```
{
    group: "Rooms",
    bookableIndex: 0,
    hasDetails: true,
    bookables: [],
    isLoading: true,
    error: false
}
```

The component will start loading data *after* the first render, so we set `isLoading` to `true` right from the start. Our initial UI will be the loading indicator.

To change the state in response to data-fetching events, we add three new action types to the reducer:

- `FETCH_BOOKABLES_REQUEST`—The component initiates the request.
- `FETCH_BOOKABLES_SUCCESS`—The bookables arrive from the server.
- `FETCH_BOOKABLES_ERROR`—Something went wrong.

We discuss the new action types further after the following listing, which shows them in our updated reducer.

*Branch:* 0403-bookables-list, *File:* /src/components/Bookables/reducer.js

**Listing 4.6   Managing loading and error states in the reducer**

```
export default function reducer (state, action) {
  switch (action.type) {
    case "SET_GROUP": return { /* unchanged */ }
    case "SET_BOOKABLE": return { /* unchanged */ }
    case "TOGGLE_HAS_DETAILS": return { /* unchanged */ }
    case "NEXT_BOOKABLE": return { /* unchanged */ }

    case "FETCH_BOOKABLES_REQUEST":
      return {
        ...state,
        isLoading: true,
        error: false,
        bookables: []            ◁—— Clear the bookables when
      };                             requesting new data.

    case "FETCH_BOOKABLES_SUCCESS":
      return {
        ...state,                    Pass the loaded
        isLoading: false,            bookables to the
        bookables: action.payload  ◁—— reducer via the payload.
      };

    case "FETCH_BOOKABLES_ERROR":
      return {
        ...state,
        isLoading: false,          Pass the error to the
        error: action.payload    ◁—— reducer via the payload.
      };

    default:
      return state;
  }
}
```

**FETCH_BOOKABLES_REQUEST**

When the component sends off its request for the bookables data, we want to show the loading indicator in the UI. In addition to setting isLoading to true, we make sure there are no existing bookables and clear out any error message.

**FETCH_BOOKABLES_SUCCESS**

Woo-hoo! The bookables have arrived and are in the action's payload. We want to display them, so set isLoading to false and assign the payload to the bookables state property.

**FETCH_BOOKABLES_ERROR**

Boo! Something went wrong, and the error message is in the action's payload. We want to display the error message, so set isLoading to false and assign the payload to the error state property.

You can see that a lot of interrelated state changes are going on for each action; having a reducer to group and centralize those changes is really helpful.

### 4.3.3 *Creating a helper function to load data*

When the UserPicker component fetched its data, it didn't worry about loading states or error messages; it just went right ahead and called fetch from within a useEffect hook. Now that we're doing a bit more to give users some feedback while data is loading, it might be better to create some dedicated data-fetching functions. We want our data code to perform three key tasks:

- Send the request
- Check the response for errors
- Convert the response to a JavaScript object

The getData function in the following listing performs the three tasks, as required. We discuss each task in more detail after the listing. The file api.js has been added in the utils folder.

---

*Branch*: 0403-bookables-list, *File*: /src/utils/api.js

**Listing 4.7   A function for fetching data**

```
export default function getData (url) {          ◁── Accept a URL argument.

    return fetch(url)                            ◁── Pass the URL on to the
       .then(resp => {                              browser's fetch function.

         if (!resp.ok) {                         Check if there is a problem with the response.
            throw Error("There was a problem fetching data.");   ◁── Throw an error for any problems.
         }

         return resp.json();          ◁── Convert the response JSON
      });                                string into a JavaScript object.
}
```

**SEND THE REQUEST**

The getData function accepts one argument, the url, and passes it on to the fetch function. (The fetch function also accepts a second argument, an init object, but we won't be using that for now.) You can find out more about the fetch API on MDN: http://mng.bz/1r81. fetch returns a promise that should resolve to a response object from which we can get our data.

### CHECK THE RESPONSE FOR ERRORS

We call then on the promise that fetch returns, setting up a function to do some initial processing of the response:

```
return fetch(url)
  .then(resp => {
    // do some initial processing of the response
  });
```

First, we check the status of the response and throw an error if it's not ok (the HTTP status code is not in the range 200 to 299):

```
if (!resp.ok) {
  throw Error("There was a problem fetching data.");
}
```

Responses with status codes outside the 200 to 299 range are valid, and fetch doesn't automatically throw any errors for them. We do our own check and throw an error if necessary. We don't catch any errors here; the calling code should set up any catch blocks it needs.

### CONVERT THE RESPONSE TO A JAVASCRIPT OBJECT

If the response passes muster, we convert the JSON string the server has returned into a JavaScript object by calling the response's json method. The json method returns a promise that resolves to our data object, and we return that promise from the function:

```
return resp.json();
```

The getData function does some preprocessing of the response from fetch, a little like a piece of middleware. Components that use getData won't need to make these preprocessing checks and changes themselves. Let's see how the BookablesList component can use our data-fetching function to load the bookables for display.

### 4.3.4   *Loading the bookables*

It's time to reap the benefits of all those preparations. Listing 4.8 shows the latest BookablesList component file. The code imports our new getData function and uses it within a useEffect hook that runs once, when the component first mounts. It also includes the isLoading and error state values and some associated UI for when data is loading or there is an error message to display.

> Branch: 0403-bookables-list, *File:* /src/components/Bookables/BookablesList.js

**Listing 4.8   The BookablesList component loading its own data**

```
import {useReducer, useEffect, Fragment} from "react";
import {sessions, days} from "../../static.json";        ⟵  No longer import
import {FaArrowRight} from "react-icons/fa";                  bookables.
```

```
import Spinner from "../UI/Spinner";
import reducer from "./reducer";

import getData from "../../utils/api";          ⟵──┐  Import the
                                                        getData function.

const initialState = {
  group: "Rooms",
  bookableIndex: 0,              Set bookables to
  hasDetails: true,             an empty array.
  bookables: [],        ⟵──┐
  isLoading: true,             Add the new properties
  error: false                 to the initial state.
};

export default function BookablesList () {
  const [state, dispatch] = useReducer(reducer, initialState);

  const {group, bookableIndex, bookables} = state;          Destructure the new
  const {hasDetails, isLoading, error} = state;    ⟵──┐    properties from state.

  const bookablesInGroup = bookables.filter(b => b.group === group);
  const bookable = bookablesInGroup[bookableIndex];
  const groups = [...new Set(bookables.map(b => b.group))];

  useEffect(() => {
                                                     Dispatch an action for the
    dispatch({type: "FETCH_BOOKABLES_REQUEST"});  ⟵── start of the data fetching.

    getData("http://localhost:3001/bookables")   ⟵──┐  Fetch the data.

      .then(bookables => dispatch({
        type: "FETCH_BOOKABLES_SUCCESS",          Save the loaded
        payload: bookables                        bookables in state.
      }))

      .catch(error => dispatch({
        type: "FETCH_BOOKABLES_ERROR",            Update state
        payload: error                            with any error.
      }));

  }, []);

  function changeGroup (e) {}
  function changeBookable (selectedIndex) {}
  function nextBookable () {}
  function toggleDetails () {}

  if (error) {                                    Return some
    return <p>{error.message}</p>                 simple error UI if
  }                                               there's an error.

  if (isLoading) {                                Return some simple
    return <p><Spinner/> Loading bookables...</p>  loading UI while
  }                                               waiting for data.
```

```
    return ( /* unchanged UI for bookables and details */ );
}
```

The call to getData is in the effect function. In section 4.3.3, we saw how getData returns a promise and can throw an error. So, in listing 4.8, we use both a then and a catch method, dispatching the appropriate actions, discussed in section 4.3.2, from each. Finally, we use if statements to return UI for loading and error conditions. If there's no error and isLoading is false, we return our existing UI for the list of bookables and bookable details.

### CHALLENGE 4.3

Update the UsersList component to use the getData function and to manage loading and error states. Possible solution code is on the 0404-users-errors branch.

We'll return to data fetching in chapter 6, when we expand our roster of components in the bookings app. Before that, in the next chapter, we'll investigate another way of managing state in components: the useRef hook.

## Summary

- Sometimes our components reach outside the React data-flow process and directly interact with other APIs, most commonly in the browser. An action that impinges on the outside world in some way is called a *side effect*.
- Common side effects include setting the page title imperatively, working with timers like setInterval or setTimeout, measuring the width or height or position of elements in the DOM, logging messages to the console, setting or getting values in local storage, and fetching data or subscribing and unsubscribing to services.
- Wrap side effects inside an effect function as the first argument to the use-Effect hook:

```
useEffect(() => {
  // perform effect
});
```

  React runs the effect function after every render.
- To manage when an effect function runs, pass a dependencies array as the second argument to the useEffect hook.
- Pass an empty dependencies array to make React run the effect function once, when the component mounts:

```
useEffect(() => {
  // perform effect
}, []);
```

- Include all of the effect function's dependencies in the dependencies array to make React run the effect function whenever the values of the specified dependencies change:

```
useEffect(() => {
  // perform effect
  // that uses dep1 and dep2
}, [dep1, dep2]);
```

- Return a cleanup function from the effect that React will run before rerunning the effect function and when the component unmounts:

```
useEffect(() => {
  // perform effect
  return () => {/* clean-up */};
}, [dep1, dep2]);
```

- Fetch data from within an effect if you're using the fetch-on-render approach. React will render the component and then fire the data-fetching code. It will re-render the component when the data arrives:

```
useEffect(() => {
  fetch("http://localhost:3001/users")
    .then(resp => resp.json())
    .then(data => setUsers(data));
}, []);
```

- To avoid race conditions and to follow the convention of returning nothing or a cleanup function from the effect function, put async functions inside the effect function. You can call them immediately, as necessary:

```
useEffect(() => {
  async function getUsers() {
    const resp = await fetch(url);
    const data = await (resp.json());
    setUsers(data);
  }
  getUsers();
}, []);
```

- Put separate side effects into separate calls to useEffect. It will be easier to understand what each effect does, easier to control when the effects run by using separate dependencies lists, and easier to extract the effects into custom hooks.
- If, on re-render, multiple effects are going to run, React will call all of the cleanup functions for the rerunning effects before it runs any effects themselves.

# Managing component state with the useRef hook

**This chapter covers**

- Calling the `useRef` hook to obtain a ref
- Updating a ref by assigning values to its `current` property
- Updating state without triggering re-renders
- Setting the `ref` attribute in JSX to assign DOM element references to a ref
- Accessing DOM element properties and methods via a ref

While most of the values stored by your component will be directly represented in the user interface of your application, sometimes you'll use a variable only for the mechanics of your app rather than for consumption by users. You may want to use `setTimeout` or `setInterval` as part of an animation, so you need to keep hold of the IDs they return. Or you may want to work with DOM form elements as uncontrolled inputs, so you need to keep hold of references to those elements. Either way, you may not need to display these values to the user, and so changing them shouldn't automatically trigger a re-render.

This chapter starts with two examples that explore changing state without updating the UI: first a comparison of managing state with useState and useRef, then a longer example as we manage timers for the BookablesList component's new Presentation Mode. The second half of the chapter has two more examples, this time exploring references to DOM elements: automatically setting focus in the Bookables-List component and reading the date from a text box for the WeekPicker component. The mix of examples will give you a good understanding of how the useRef hook helps you manage state in your components.

Okay, 1, 2, 3, let's go!

## 5.1 *Updating state without causing a re-render*

In this section, we use a simple Counter component to introduce refs as a way of persisting state across renders. With the useState hook, calling a state value's updater function usually triggers a re-render. With the useRef hook, we can update our value without a corresponding change to the UI. We start by looking at how the Counter component behaves when a user clicks away on its buttons, incrementing the counters (but not necessarily the UI), and the code required to make it behave that way. Then, having seen useRef in action, we focus on the new hook's API.

### 5.1.1 *Comparing useState and useRef when updating state values*

Figure 5.1 shows four screenshots of the Counter component UI with two buttons, one labeled *count* and one labeled *ref.current*. Each button also has a counter appended to its button text. The buttons behave in different ways.

Clicking the Count button increments its counter, as you can see in the figure, which shows the original component and the result when it's clicked three times. The button counter goes up from 1 to 2 to 3 to 4. Each increase is accompanied by a re-render, so the Counter component shows the latest value.

**Figure 5.1   Clicking the Count button increases the count by 1 each time. Because the event handler increments the count by calling its updater function, React re-renders the component after each change.**

Figure 5.2 shows the result when you then click the Ref.current button three times. Its counter doesn't seem to change. The component shows 1, then 1, then 1. In fact, the value *does* increase, from 1 to 2 to 3 to 4. It's just that changing the ref.current value doesn't cause React to re-render, so the Counter component continues to show an old value.

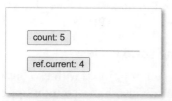

**Figure 5.2   Clicking the Ref.current button three times seems to have no effect. In fact, the event handler does increment** `ref.current` **to 2, then 3, then 4, but React does not re-render the component.**

Clicking the Count button one more time increments its counter from 4 to 5. React re-renders the component to show the latest value, shown in figure 5.3. Doing so also updates the value shown by the Ref.current button, and it jumps to 4, its current value.

**Figure 5.3   Clicking the Count button one more time increases the count to 5. React re-renders the component, which now shows the latest values of** `count` **and** `ref.current`.

In previous chapters, you've seen how to implement a button like the Count button by using the `useState` hook. How do we implement the Ref.current button, where state is persisted across renders but updating the ref doesn't cause a re-render? The following listing shows the code for the button example, including a call to the `useRef` hook for the first time.

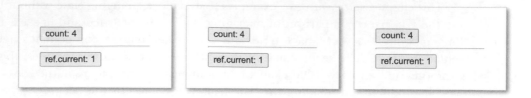

*Live:* **https://gh6xz.csb.app/,** *Code:* **https://codesandbox.io/s/counterstatevsref-gh6xz**

**Listing 5.1   Comparing** `useState` **and** `useRef` **when updating state**

```
import React, { useRef, useState } from "react";

function Counter() {
  const [count, setCount] = useState(1);          Initialize the count
  const ref = useRef(1);                          value with useState.

                                                  Define a handler that calls
  const incCount = () => setCount(c => c + 1);    setCount to increment count.

  const incRef = () => ref.current++;             Define a handler that updates the
                                                  "current" property of the ref.
  return (
    <div className="App">
      <button onClick={incCount}>count: {count}</button>   Call the handler for
                                                           the count value.
```

*Initialize the ref value with useRef.*

```
      <hr />
      <button onClick={incRef}>ref.current: {ref.current}</button>
    </div>
  );
}
```

**Call the handler for the ref value.**

So, why do the buttons behave differently? Well, one uses the `useState` hook, and one uses the `useRef` hook.

The Count button gets React to manage its counter state value by calling `useState`. The button's event handler changes the counter with the state value's updater function, `setCount`. Calling the updater function changes the state and triggers a re-render. React persists the state across renders, each time passing it back to the component, where it is assigned to the `count` variable.

The Ref.current button gets React to manage its counter state value by calling `useRef`. The hook returns an object, a *ref*, which we use to store the state value. Changing the value stored on the ref doesn't trigger a re-render. React persists the state across renders, each time passing the same ref object back to the component, where it is assigned to the `ref` variable.

Both buttons in listing 5.1 include a state value in their button text, `{count}` and `{ref.current}`, and call a handler function when the user clicks them. But what's with the `.current` business? Let's take a closer look at how to work with `useRef`.

### 5.1.2 Calling useRef

In listing 5.1, we obtain a ref from React by calling `useRef`, passing it an initial value of 1. We assign the ref to a variable, `ref`:

```
const ref = useRef(1);
```

The `useRef` function returns an object with a `current` property, as shown in figure 5.4. Every time React runs the component code, each call to `useRef` will return the same ref object for that call.

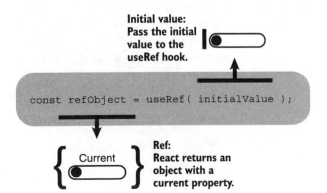

**Initial value:** Pass the initial value to the useRef hook.

```
const refObject = useRef( initialValue );
```

**Ref:** React returns an object with a current property.

**Figure 5.4**  `useRef` returns an object with a current property.

The first time React invokes the component code, it assigns the initial value you pass the useRef function to the ref object's current property:

```
const ref1 = useRef("Towel");
const ref2 = useRef(42);

ref1.current;  // "Towel"
ref2.current;  // 42
```

On subsequent renders, React assigns the same ref objects to the respective variables, based on the order of the useRef calls. You can persist state values by assigning them to the current properties of the refs:

```
ref1.current = "Babel Fish";
ref2.current = "1,000,000,000,000";
```

Assigning new values to the current properties of the ref objects doesn't trigger a re-render. But as React always returns the same ref objects, the new values are available when the component runs again.

Okay, the button example was a bit simple and a bit weird—who wants broken buttons? The time has come for a bit more complexity.

## 5.2    Storing timer IDs with a ref

In the previous section, you saw how to use the useRef hook to maintain state across renders for our function components. To update the ref returned from useRef, we set its current property to the value we want to store. Changing the current property in this way doesn't cause a re-render of the component. In this section, we look at a slightly more complicated example, using the useRef hook to enlist React's help managing the IDs of timers. We return to the bookings app as our context.

Say your boss wants you to create a Presentation Mode for the BookablesList component. Until you click the Stop button, the component should automatically select each bookable in turn on a timer, showing its details, as you can see in figure 5.5. Your boss thinks this would be great for that foyer screen the company bought last year.

Left alone in Presentation Mode, the component cycles through all of the bookables in a group, wrapping back to the first when it leaves the last. We'll use a timer to schedule when the component should move on to the next bookable. If the user clicks the Stop button, Presentation Mode ends, and we cancel any running timer. The following listing shows the ref we use to store the timer ID, the new effect that sets up the timer, and the UI for the Stop button.

**Figure 5.5** In Presentation Mode, the application will automatically advance to each bookable in turn, showing its details, until you click the Stop button (top right).

---

*Branch:* **0501-timer-ref**, *File:* **/src/components/Bookables/BookablesList.js**

### Listing 5.2  Using a ref to hold a timer ID for Presentation Mode

```
import {useReducer, useEffect, useRef, Fragment} from "react";      ⟵  Import the
import {sessions, days} from "../../static.json";                       useRef hook.
import {FaArrowRight} from "react-icons/fa";
import Spinner from "../UI/Spinner";
import reducer from "./reducer";
import getData from "../../utils/api";

const initialState = { /* unchanged */ };

export default function BookablesList () {

  // unchanged variable setup                          Assign a ref to the
                                                       timerRef variable.
  const timerRef = useRef(null);       ⟵

  useEffect(() => { /* load data */ }, []);
                                                       Run an effect when the
  useEffect(() => {                    ⟵              component first mounts.

    timerRef.current = setInterval(() => {       ⟵   Start an interval timer and
      dispatch({ type: "NEXT_BOOKABLE" });            assign its ID to the ref's
    }, 3000);                                          current property.

    return stopPresentation;         ⟵   Return a function
                                          to clear the timer.
  }, []);
```

```
function stopPresentation () {
  clearInterval(timerRef.current);        │  Use the timer ID
}                                          │  to clear the timer.

function changeGroup (e) { /* unchanged */ }
function changeBookable (selectedIndex) { /* unchanged */ }
function nextBookable () { /* unchanged */ }
function toggleDetails () { /* unchanged */ }

// unchanged UI for error and loading

return (
  <Fragment>
    <div>
    { /* list of bookables */ }
    </div>

    {bookable && (
      <div className="bookable-details">
        <div className="item">
          <div className="item-header">
            <h2>
              {bookable.title}
            </h2>
            <span className="controls">
              <label>
                <input
                  type="checkbox"
                  checked={hasDetails}
                  onChange={toggleDetails}
                />
                Show Details
              </label>                    │  Include a Stop
              <button              ◀──────┘  button.
                className="btn"
                onClick={stopPresentation}  ◀──┐  Call the stopPresentation
              >                                 │  function from the button.
                Stop
              </button>
            </span>
          </div>

        { /* further details */ }
        </div>
      </div>
    )}
  </Fragment>
);
}
```

When we set up the timer in the new effect, the browser's setInterval method
returns an ID. We can use the ID to clear the timer if necessary (if the user clicks the
Stop button or navigates to another page in the app). The stopPresentation function needs to access the ID so it can clear the timer. We need to store the ID, but

there's no need to re-render the component when we start or stop the timer, so we don't want to use the useState hook. We use the useRef hook instead, so we need to import it:

```
import {useReducer, useEffect, useRef, Fragment} from "react";
```

We call useRef, passing it null as the initial value because there's no timer yet. Every time the component runs, useRef returns us the same ref object, which we assign to the timerRef variable:

```
const timerRef = useRef(null);
```

We use the ref to store our timer ID by assigning the ID to the ref's current property:

```
timerRef.current = setInterval(/* wibbly-wobbly, timey-wimey stuff */, 3000);
```

The stopPresentation function uses the ID stored in timerRef.current to clear the timer and end Presentation Mode. The function runs when a user clicks the Stop button and, thanks to the second effect returning it as a cleanup function, when the user navigates to another page in the app and the component unmounts:

```
function stopPresentation () {
  window.clearInterval(timerRef.current);
}
```

This section presented another example of using a ref to store state so that updating the state doesn't cause the component to re-render. There's no need to re-run the component code when setting and clearing the timer ID, so using a ref to store its value makes sense. The next section looks at a very common use case for refs, keeping references to DOM elements.

## 5.3 Keeping references to DOM elements

If you're an old hand at working with refs, you may have been surprised at the use we put them to in section 5.2, updating state without re-rendering. If that's the case, you're back in your element in this section, where we call on the useRef hook to help us store references to buttons and form fields. Such references to DOM elements let us interact with the elements directly, bypassing the usual React state-to-UI flow. In particular, we look at two common use cases:

- Setting focus on an element in response to an event
- Reading the value of an uncontrolled text box

We see how to get React to automatically assign DOM element references to our refs' current properties, so we can manipulate or read from those elements directly. Both examples use components from the bookings app. In section 5.3.2, we add a text box to the WeekPicker component. But first, we focus on the BookablesList component, making it easier for users to move from one bookable to the next using the keyboard.

### 5.3.1  *Setting focus on an element in response to an event*

Your boss is back with a new suggestion for the bookings app. Forget Presentation Mode! Wouldn't it be great if, when a user chooses a bookable, the focus automatically shifts to the Next button? Then the user could just press the spacebar to move from bookable to bookable! Figure 5.6 shows the situation.

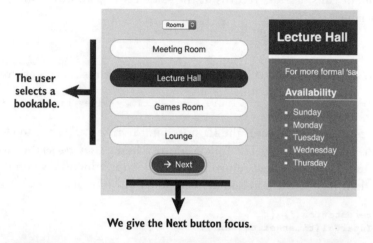

**Figure 5.6   When a user selects a bookable, the focus is automatically set on the Next button.**

We could add an extra piece of state, maybe nextHasFocus, and re-render whenever it changes to give the Next button focus. But the browser has a focus method, so if we just had a reference to the button element, we could call focus and the job would be done:

```
const nextButtonEl = document.getElementById("nextButton");

nextButtonEl.focus();
```

But, having chosen to use React, we prefer to stay within its state-to-UI flow as much as possible. The timing of directly reaching out to the DOM with getElementById could get tricky as React updates the DOM in response to state changes. Also, it's common for the same component to be used multiple times in an app, so using multiple instances of what should be unique id attributes to identify component elements ends up causing problems rather than solving them. Fortunately, React provides a way of automatically assigning DOM element references to refs created with the useRef hook.

Listing 5.3 shows the BookablesList component code with three additions to enable our desired Next button focus behavior. We do the following:

1 Create a new ref, nextButtonRef, to hold a reference to the Next button element.

2 Use the special ref attribute in the JSX to ask React to automatically assign a reference to the button element to nextButtonRef.current.

3 Use our reference, nextButtonRef.current, to set the focus on the Next button.

---

*Branch*: **0502-set-focus**, *File*: **/src/components/Bookables/BookablesList.js**

**Listing 5.3   Using a ref to set focus**

```
import {useReducer, useEffect, useRef, Fragment} from "react";
import {sessions, days} from "../../static.json";
import {FaArrowRight} from "react-icons/fa";
import Spinner from "../UI/Spinner";
import reducer from "./reducer";
import getData from "../../utils/api";

const initialState = { /* unchanged */ };

export default function BookablesList () {          Call useRef and assign the ref to
  // unchanged variable setup                        the nextButtonRef variable.
  const nextButtonRef = useRef();          ◁———

  useEffect(() => { /* load data */ }, []);

  // remove timer effect and stopPresentation function

  function changeGroup (e) { */ unchanged */ }

  function changeBookable (selectedIndex) {
    dispatch({
      type: "SET_BOOKABLE",
      payload: selectedIndex          Use the ref to focus
    });                                the Next button.
    nextButtonRef.current.focus();          ◁———
  }

  function nextBookable () { /* unchanged */ }
  function toggleDetails () { /* unchanged */}

  if (error) {
    return <p>{error.message}</p>
  }

  if (isLoading) {
    return <p><Spinner/> Loading bookables...</p>
  }

  return (
    <Fragment>
      <div>
        <select value={group} onChange={changeGroup}>
          {groups.map(g => <option value={g} key={g}>{g}</option>) }
        </select>
```

```
      <ul className="bookables items-list-nav">
        { /* unchanged */ }
      </ul>
      <p>
        <button
          className="btn"
          onClick={nextBookable}
          ref={nextButtonRef}
          autoFocus
        >
          <FaArrowRight/>
          <span>Next</span>
        </button>
      </p>
    </div>

    {bookable && (
      <div className="bookable-details">
        { /* Stop button removed */ }
      </div>
    )}
  </Fragment>
);
}
```

> ⟵ Assign nextButtonRef to the ref attribute in JSX.

In listing 5.3, we call the `useRef` hook and assign the ref it returns to the `nextButton-Ref` variable:

```
const nextButtonRef = useRef();
```

We don't assign an initial value; we're going to get React to automatically assign a value to the `nextButtonRef.current` property for us. We need to focus the Next button, so, rather than reaching out into the DOM ourselves, we assign our ref to the special `ref` attribute of the button in the JSX for the user interface:

```
<button
  className="btn"
  onClick={nextBookable}
  ref={nextButtonRef}
  autoFocus
>
  <FaArrowRight/>
  <span>Next</span>
</button>
```

Once React has created the button element for the DOM, it assigns a reference to the element to the `nextButtonRef.current` property. We use that reference in the `change-Bookable` function to focus the button by calling the element's `focus` method:

```
function changeBookable (selectedIndex) {
  dispatch({
```

```
    type: "SET_BOOKABLE",
    payload: selectedIndex
  });
  nextButtonRef.current.focus();
}
```

The component calls the `changeBookable` function whenever a user directly selects a bookable in the list of bookables. So, directly selecting a bookable will shift focus to the Next button. That's exactly what the boss wanted! Good job.

This example shows how you can create a ref by using the `useRef` hook and then ask React to assign a reference for a DOM element to that ref. I'll admit it's a little contrived, but it does show the steps involved. Do be careful when programmatically setting the focus of elements on the page; be sure it doesn't confound users' expectations, making your app harder to use. It's a valid technique but may require careful user testing.

### 5.3.2   *Managing a text box via a ref*

Chapter 3 introduced the `WeekPicker` component as a way to navigate from week to week in the bookings app. The user could click the Prev and Next buttons to switch weeks or click the Today button to display the week containing the current day's date. Chapter 3's version of `WeekPicker` is in figure 5.7.

**Figure 5.7   The `WeekPicker` component from chapter 3 with buttons for switching weeks and jumping to the week containing today's date**

But if someone working at the company wants to book a meeting room for an event in a couple of months, they have to click the Next button again and again until they reach the date they want. Entering a specific date and jumping straight to that week would be better. Figure 5.8 shows an improved `WeekPicker` UI with a text box and a Go button.

**Figure 5.8   The `WeekPicker` component with a text box and a Go button, for direct date entry**

The reducer for the `WeekPicker` component already has a `SET_DATE` action; let's put it to use. In the following listing, we add to `WeekPicker` with a text box and Go button for the UI, a ref for the text box, and a `goToDate` handler function for the Go button.

Branch: **0503-text-box**, *File:* **/src/components/Bookings/WeekPicker.js**

Listing 5.4   The `WeekPicker` with a text box and Go button

```
import {useReducer, useRef} from "react";
import reducer from "./weekReducer";
import {getWeek} from "../../utils/date-wrangler";
import {
  FaChevronLeft,
  FaCalendarDay,
  FaChevronRight,
  FaCalendarCheck
} from "react-icons/fa";

export default function WeekPicker ({date}) {
  const [week, dispatch] = useReducer(reducer, date, getWeek);
  const textboxRef = useRef();          ◁─── Create a ref to hold the
                                             reference to the text box.
  function goToDate () {                ◁─ Define a
    dispatch({                            handler
      type: "SET_DATE",                   for the Go    Dispatch the SET_DATE action.
      payload: textboxRef.current.value   button.
    });                                    ◁─── Use the ref to get the text
  }                                          value in the text box.

  return (
    <div>
      <p className="date-picker">
        // Prev button
        // Today button

        <span>
          <input
            type="text"
            ref={textboxRef}              ◁── Add a text box with a
            placeholder="e.g. 2020-09-02"    ref attribute to the UI.
            defaultValue="2020-06-24"
          />
                                          Add the Go
          <button                         button to the UI.
            className="go btn"            ◁──
            onClick={goToDate}            ◁── Assign the handler
          >                                  to set the date.
            <FaCalendarCheck/>
            <span>Go</span>
          </button>
        </span>

        // Next button
      </p>
      <p>
```

```
      {week.start.toDateString()} - {week.end.toDateString()}
    </p>
  </div>
);
}
```

After it renders the component and updates the DOM, React assigns a reference to the input element, our text box, to the `textboxRef` variable's `current` property. The `goToDate` function uses that reference to grab the text from the text box when the user clicks the Go button:

```
function goToDate () {
  dispatch({
    type: "SET_DATE",
    payload: textboxRef.current.value
  });
}
```

So, `textboxRef.current` holds a reference to the input element, the text box, and then `textboxRef.current.value` is the text in the text box.

#### UNCONTROLLED COMPONENTS

The text in the `WeekPicker` text box is part of our component's state. In this example, our component is not managing the text box state. Our component is not interested while the user types characters into the text box, although the browser does show the new characters as the user types. Only when the user clicks the Go button do we read the text state from the DOM, via our ref, and dispatch it to the reducer. Components that let the DOM manage their state in this way are called *uncontrolled components*.

While the `WeekPicker` example demonstrates how to use a ref with a form field, the approach doesn't really fit with the philosophy of managing state with `useState` and `useReducer` and then displaying that state in the UI. React recommends using *controlled components* that make the most of React's help managing the state.

#### CONTROLLED COMPONENTS

To convert the `WeekPicker` component to be fully controlled, we could take back the text box state from the DOM, using a call to the `useState` hook instead:

```
const [dateText, setDateText] = useState("2020-06-24");
```

We could then set the `dateText` state as the `value` property for the text box and use the accompanying updater function, `setDateText`, to change the state whenever the user types in the text box:

```
return (
  <div>
    <input
      type="text"                                        Use the dateText state as        Update the dateText
      value={dateText}              ◁──────               the value for the text box.      state whenever the
      onChange={(e) => setDateText(e.target.value)}      ◁──┘  user types in the
    />                                                                text box.
```

```
      <button onClick={goToDate}>Go</button>
  </div>
);
```

Finally, in the `goToDate` function, we would no longer need the reference to the text box and could simply dispatch the `dateText` value to the reducer:

```
function goToDate () {
  dispatch({
    type: "SET_DATE",
    payload: dateText
  });
}
```

With controlled components, the data flow is from the component to the DOM, in line with the standard React approach.

## Summary

- Call the `useRef` hook when you want React to manage a state value but don't want changes to the value to trigger a re-render. For example, use it for storing IDs for `setTimeout` and `setInterval` or for references to DOM elements. You can pass it an initial value if required. It returns an object with a `current` property set to the initial value:

  ```
  const ref = useRef(initialValue);
  ref.current; // initialValue
  ```

- A call to `useRef` will return the same ref object each time the component runs. Persist values in the ref across renders by assigning them to the ref's `current` property:

  ```
  ref.current = valueToStore;
  ```

- React can automatically assign DOM element references to your ref's `current` property. Assign your ref variable to an element's `ref` attribute in JSX:

  ```
  const myRef = useRef();        ⟵── Create a ref.

  ...

  return (
    <button ref={myRef}>Click Me!</button>     ⟵── Specify the ref in the
  );                                                JSX ref attribute.

  ...
                          The current property will now
                          reference the button element.
  myRef.current;    ⟵──
  ```

- Use the ref to interact with the DOM element. For example, set focus on the element:

```
myRef.current.focus();
```

- Components that read their state from the DOM are called *uncontrolled components*. You can use refs to access and update the state.
- React recommends you use *controlled components*. Use the useState hook or the useReducer hook to manage the state and get React to update the DOM with the latest state values. Your component will be the one source of truth rather than splitting state between the component and the DOM.

# *Managing application state* 6

**This chapter covers**

- Passing shared state to those components that need it
- Coping when state isn't passed down—the props are missing
- Lifting state up the component tree to make it more widely available
- Passing dispatch and updater functions to child components
- Maintaining function identity with the `useCallback` hook

Up to this point, we've seen how components can manage their own state with the `useState`, `useReducer`, and `useRef` hooks and load state data with the `useEffect` hook. It's common, however, for components to work together, using shared state values to generate their UI. Each component may have a whole hierarchy of descendant components nested within it, chirping and chirruping to be fed data, so state values may need to reach deep down into the descendant depths.

In this chapter, we investigate concepts and methods for deciding how to manage the availability of state values for child components that need to consume them, by lifting state to common parents. In chapter 8, we'll see how and when

React's Context API can be used to make values available directly to components that need them. Here, we stick to using props to pass state down to children.

We start, in section 6.1, with a new `Colors` component that shares a selected color with three child components. We see how to update the shared state, managed by the parent, from a child. The rest of the chapter uses the bookings app example to explore two approaches to sharing state: passing a state object and a dispatch function for a reducer to the children and passing a single state value and its updater function to the children. Both approaches are common patterns and help to highlight some common questions regarding state, props, effects, and dependencies. We finish with a look at `useCallback`, a hook that lets us enlist React's help to maintain the identity of functions we pass as props, particularly when child components treat those functions as dependencies.

For our first trick, let's refresh our knowledge of props: pick a color, any color. . . .

## 6.1 *Passing shared state to child components*

When different components use the same data to build their UI, the most explicit way to share that data is to pass it as a prop from parent to children. This section introduces passing props (in particular, passing the state value and updater function returned by `useState`) by looking at a new example, a `Colors` component, shown in figure 6.1. The component includes three UI sections:

- A list of colors with the selected color highlighted
- Text showing the selected color
- A bar with a background set to the selected color

Clicking a color in the list (one of the circles) highlights that selection and updates the text and the color bar. You can see the component in action on CodeSandbox (https://hgt0x.csb.app/).

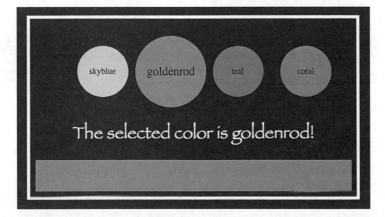

**Figure 6.1** The `Colors` component. When a user selects a color, the menu, text, and color bar all update. When goldenrod is selected, its menu circle is larger, the text says ". . . goldenrod!" and the bar's color is goldenrod.

### 6.1.1  *Passing state from a parent by setting props on the children*

Listing 6.1 shows the code for the `Colors` component. It imports three child components: `ColorPicker`, `ColorChoiceText`, and `ColorSample`. Each child needs the selected color, so the `Colors` component holds that state and passes it to them as a prop, an attribute in the JSX. It also passes the available colors and the `setColor` updater function to the `ColorPicker` component.

---

*Live:* **https://hgt0x.csb.app/,** *Code:* **https://codesandbox.io/s/colorpicker-hgt0x**

**Listing 6.1   The** `Colors` **component**

```
import React, {useState} from "react";

import ColorPicker from "./ColorPicker";              Import the child
import ColorChoiceText from "./ColorChoiceText";      components.
import ColorSample from "./ColorSample";

export default function Colors () {
  const availableColors = ["skyblue", "goldenrod", "teal", "coral"];    Define state
                                                                        values.
  const [color, setColor] = useState(availableColors[0]);

  return (
    <div className="colors">
      <ColorPicker
        colors={availableColors}
        color={color}                  Pass the appropriate
        setColor={setColor}            state values to the
      />                               child components as
      <ColorChoiceText color={color} />    props.
      <ColorSample color={color} />
    </div>
  );
}
```

The `Colors` component passes down two types of props: state values to be used in the children's UI, `colors` and `color`; and a function to update the shared state, `setColor`. Let's look at state values first.

### 6.1.2  *Receiving state from a parent as a prop*

Both the `ColorChoiceText` component and the `ColorSample` component display the currently selected color. `ColorChoiceText` includes it in its message, and `ColorSample` uses it to set the background color. They receive the color value from the `Colors` component, as shown in figure 6.2.

Colors is the closest shared parent of the child components that share the state, so we manage the state within `Colors`. Figure 6.3 shows the `ColorChoiceText` component displaying a message that includes the selected color. The component simply uses the color value as part of its UI; it doesn't need to update the value.

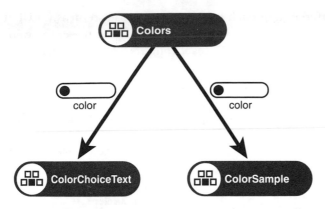

**Figure 6.2  The** `Colors` **component passes the current color state value to the child components.**

The selected color is goldenrod!

**Figure 6.3  The** `ColorChoiceText` **component includes the selected color in its message.**

The `ColorChoiceText` component's code is in listing 6.2. When React calls the component, it passes it as the component's first argument, an object containing all of the props set by the parent. The code here destructures the props, assigning the `color` prop to a local variable of the same name.

*Live:* **https://hgt0x.csb.app/,** *Code:* **https://codesandbox.io/s/colorpicker-hgt0x**

**Listing 6.2  The** `ColorChoiceText` **component**

```
import React from "react";

export default function ColorChoiceText({color}) {
  return color ? (
    <p>The selected color is {color}!</p>
  ) : (
    <p>No color has been selected!</p>
  )
}
```

**Receive the color state from the parent as a prop.**

**Check that there is a color.**

**Use the prop in the UI.**

**Return alternate UI if the parent doesn't set a color.**

What if the parent doesn't set a `color` prop? The `ColorChoiceText` component is happy for there to be no `color` prop; it returns alternate UI saying no color was selected.

The `ColorSample` component, shown in figure 6.4, displays a bar with its background set to the selected color.

**Figure 6.4  The** `ColorSample` **component displays a bar of the selected color.**

ColorSample takes a different approach to a missing prop. It returns no UI at all! In the following listing, you can see the component checking for the color value. If it's missing, the component returns null and React renders nothing at that point in the element tree.

*Live:* **https://hgt0x.csb.app/,** *Code:* **https://codesandbox.io/s/colorpicker-hgt0x**

**Listing 6.3     The ColorSample component**

```
import React from "react";

export default function ColorSample({color}) {          ◁──  Receive the state from
  return color ? (                                            the parent as a prop.
    <div                                      ◁── Check that there
      className="colorSample"                      is a color.
      style={{ background: color }}
    />
  ) : null;          ◁─┤ Don't render any UI if
}                        there's no color.
```

You could set a default value for color as part of the prop's destructuring. Maybe if the parent doesn't specify a color, then it should be white?

```
function ColorSample({color = "white"}) {       ◁── Specify a default
  return (                                            value for the prop.
    <div
      className="colorSample"
      style={{ background: color }}
    />
  );
}
```

A default value will work for some components, but for our color-based components that need to share state, we'd have to make sure all of the defaults were the same. So, we either have alternate UI or no UI. If the component just won't work without a prop, and a default doesn't make sense, you can throw an error explaining that the prop is missing.

Although we won't explore them in this book, you can also use PropTypes to specify expected props and their types. React will use the PropTypes to warn of problems during development (https://reactjs.org/docs/typechecking-with-proptypes.html). Alternatively, use TypeScript rather than JavaScript and type-check your whole application (www.typescriptlang.org).

### 6.1.3   *Receiving an updater function from a parent as a prop*

The ColorPicker component uses two state values to generate its UI: a list of available colors and the selected color. It displays the available color values as list items, and the app uses CSS to style them as a row of colored circles, as you can see in figure 6.5. The selected item, *goldenrod* in the figure, is styled larger than the others.

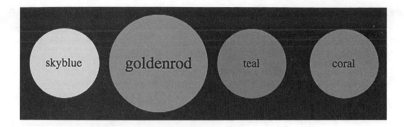

**Figure 6.5  The** `ColorPicker` **component displays a list of colors and highlights the selected color.**

The `Colors` component passes the `ColorPicker` component the two state values it uses. `Colors` also needs to provide a way to update the selected color for all three children. It delegates that responsibility to the `ColorPicker` component by passing it the `setColor` updater function, as illustrated in figure 6.6.

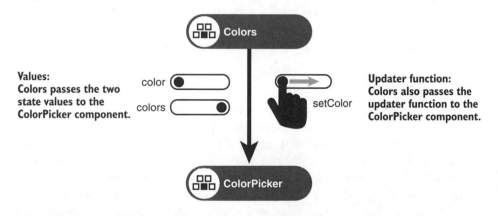

**Values:**
**Colors passes the two state values to the ColorPicker component.**

**Updater function:**
**Colors also passes the updater function to the ColorPicker component.**

**Figure 6.6  The** `Colors` **component passes two state values to** `ColorPicker`**. It also passes the** `setColor` **updater function, so the color state value can be set from the child.**

The following listing shows the `ColorPicker` component destructuring its props argument, assigning the three props to local variables: `colors`, `color`, and `setColor`.

Live: **https://hgt0x.csb.app/,** Code: **https://codesandbox.io/s/colorpicker-hgt0x**

**Listing 6.4  The** `ColorPicker` **component**

```
import React from "react";

export default function ColorPicker({colors = [], color, setColor}) {
  return (
    <ul>                    Receive the state and updater function from the parent as props.
```

```
    {colors.map(c => (
      <li
        key={c}
        className={color === c ? "selected" : null}
        style={{ background: c }}
        onClick={() => setColor(c)}
      >
        {c}
      </li>
    ))}
  </ul>
  );
}
```

Use the updater function
to set the parent's state.

The destructuring syntax includes a default value for `colors`:

```
{colors = [], color, setColor}
```

The `ColorPicker` component iterates over the `colors` array to create a list item for
each available color. Using an empty array as a default value causes the component to
return an empty unordered list if the parent component doesn't set the `colors` prop.

   More interesting (for a book about React Hooks) are the `color` and `setColor`
props. These props have come from a call to `useState` in the parent:

```
const [color, setColor] = useState(availableColors[0]);
```

The `ColorPicker` doesn't care where they've come from; it just expects a `color` prop
to hold the current color and a `setColor` prop to be a function it can call to set the
color somewhere. `ColorPicker` uses the `setColor` updater function in the `onClick`
handler for each list item. By calling the `setColor` function, the child component,
`ColorPicker`, is able to set the state for the parent component, `Colors`. The parent
then re-renders, updating all of its children with the newly selected color.

   We created the `Colors` component from scratch, knowing we needed shared state
to pass down to child components. Sometimes we work with existing components and,
as a project develops, realize they hold state that other siblings may also need. The
next sections look at a couple of ways of lifting state up from children to parents to
make it more widely available.

## 6.2    *Breaking components into smaller pieces*

React gives us the `useState` and `useReducer` hooks as two ways of managing state in
our apps. Each hook provides a means to update the state, triggering a re-render. As
our app develops, we balance the convenience of being able to access local state
directly from a single component's effects, handler functions, and UI against the
inconvenience of that component's state becoming bloated and tangled, with state
changes from one part of the UI triggering re-renders of the whole component.

New components in the app may want a piece of the existing state pie, so we now need to share state that, previously, one component encapsulated. Do we lift state values and updater functions up to parents? Or maybe lift reducers and dispatch functions? How does moving state around change the structure of the existing components?

In this section, we continue building out the bookings app example as a context for these questions. In particular, we explore the following:

- Seeing components as part of a bigger app
- Organizing multiple components within a page's UI
- Creating a `BookableDetails` component

The concepts encountered are nothing new for existing React developers. Our aim here is to consider if and how they change when using React Hooks.

### 6.2.1 *Seeing components as part of a bigger app*

In chapter 5, we left the `BookablesList` component doing double duty: displaying a list of bookables for the selected group and displaying details for the selected bookable. Figure 6.7 shows the component with the list and details visible.

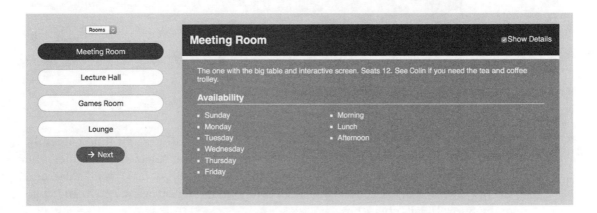

**Figure 6.7    The previous `BookablesList` component, from chapter 5, showed the list of bookables and the details of the selected bookable.**

The component managed all of the state: the bookables, the selected group, and the selected bookable, and flags for displaying details, loading state, and errors. As a single function component with no child components, all of the state was in local scope and available to use when generating the returned UI. But toggling the Show Details check box would cause a re-render of the whole component, and we had to think carefully about persisting timer IDs across renders when using Presentation Mode.

We also need a list of bookables on the Bookings page. Various components will be vying for screen real estate, and we want the flexibility to be able to display the list of bookables separately from the bookable details, as shown in figure 6.8, where the list of bookables is on the left. In fact, as in the figure, we might not want to display the bookable details at all, saving that information for the dedicated Bookables page.

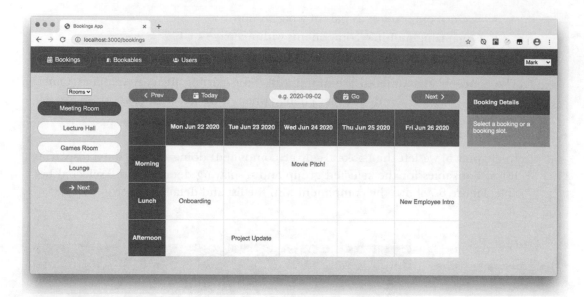

Figure 6.8   The list of bookables (on the left) is also used on the Bookings page.

To be able to use the list and details sections of the `BookableList` UI independently, we'll create a separate component for the details of the selected bookable. The `BookablesList` component will continue to display the groups, list of bookables, and Next button, but the new `BookableDetails` component will display the details and manage the Show Details check box.

The `BookablesPage` component currently imports and renders the `BookablesList` component. We need to do a bit of rearranging to use the new version of the list along with the `BookableDetails` component.

### 6.2.2   *Organizing multiple components within a page's UI*

Both the `BookablesList` and the `BookableDetails` components need access to the selected bookable. We create a `BookablesView` component to wrap the list and details and to manage the shared state. Table 6.1 lists our proliferating bookables components and outlines how they work together.

Table 6.1 Bookables components and how they work together

| Component | Purpose |
|-----------|---------|
| BookablesPage | Shows the BookablesView component (and, later, forms for adding and editing bookables) |
| BookablesView | Groups the BookablesList and BookableDetails components and manages their shared state |
| BookablesList | Shows a list of bookables by group and lets the user select a bookable, either by clicking a bookable or using the Next button |
| BookableDetails | Shows the details of the selected bookable with a check box to toggle the display of the bookable's availability |

In sections 6.3 and 6.4, we look at two approaches to lifting the state up to the BookablesView component:

- Lifting the existing reducer from BookablesList to the BookablesView component
- Lifting the selected bookable from BookablesList to the BookablesView component

First, as shown in the following listing, we update the page component to import and show BookablesView rather than BookablesList.

*Branch*: 0601-lift-reducer, *File*: src/components/Bookables/BookablesPage.js

Listing 6.5 The BookablesPage component

```
import BookablesView from "./BookablesView";          ◁──┐ Import the new
                                                           component.
export default function BookablesPage () {
  return (
    <main className="bookables-page">
      <BookablesView/>                    ◁──┐ Use the new
    </main>                                     component.
  );
}
```

On separate repo branches, we'll create a different version of the BookablesView component for each of the two state-sharing approaches we take. The Bookable-Details component will be the same either way, so let's build that first.

### 6.2.3 Creating a BookableDetails component

The new BookableDetails component performs exactly the same task as the second half of the old BookablesList component UI; it displays the details of the selected bookable and a check box for toggling part of that info. Figure 6.9 shows the Bookable-Details component with the check box and bookable title, notes, and availability.

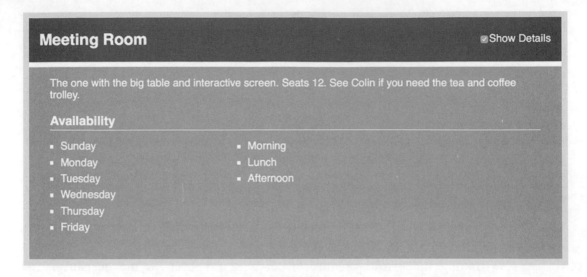

**Figure 6.9**  The `BookableDetails` component with check box, title, notes, and availability

As illustrated in figure 6.10, the `BookablesView` component passes in the selected bookable so that `BookableDetails` has the information it needs to display.

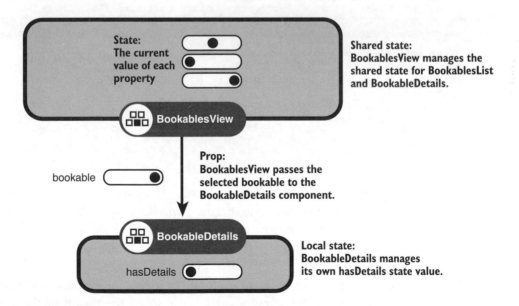

**Figure 6.10**  `BookablesView` manages the shared state and passes the selected bookable to `BookableDetails`.

The code for the new component is in the following listing. The component receives the selected bookable as a prop but manages its own `hasDetails` state value.

Branch: **0601-lift-reducer**, *File:* **src/components/Bookables/BookableDetails.js**

Listing 6.6    The `BookableDetails` component

```
import {useState} from "react";
import {days, sessions} from "../../static.json";

export default function BookableDetails ({bookable}) {          Receive the current
  const [hasDetails, setHasDetails] = useState(true);          bookable via props.

                                                               Use local state to hold
                                                               the hasDetails flag.
  function toggleDetails () {
    setHasDetails(has => !has);                Use the updater function to
  }                                            toggle the hasDetails flag.

  return bookable ? (
    <div className="bookable-details item">
      <div className="item-header">
        <h2>{bookable.title}</h2>
        <span className="controls">
          <label>
            <input
              type="checkbox"                   Toggle the hasDetails flag
              onChange={toggleDetails}          when the check box is clicked.
              checked={hasDetails}
            />                                   Use the hasDetails flag
            Show Details                        to set the check box.
          </label>
        </span>
      </div>
                                               Use the hasDetails flag
      <p>{bookable.notes}</p>                  to show or hide the
                                               availability section.
      {hasDetails && (
        <div className="item-details">
          <h3>Availability</h3>
          <div className="bookable-availability">
            <ul>
              {bookable.days
                .sort()
                .map(d => <li key={d}>{days[d]}</li>)
              }
            </ul>
            <ul>
              {bookable.sessions
                .map(s => <li key={s}>{sessions[s]}</li>)
              }
            </ul>
          </div>
        </div>
      )}
    </div>
  ) : null;
}
```

No other components in BookablesView care about the hasDetails state value, so it makes good sense to encapsulate it completely within BookableDetails. If a component is the sole user of a certain state, putting that state within the component seems like an obvious approach.

BookableDetails is a simple component that just displays the selected bookable. As long as it receives that state value, it's happy. Exactly how the BookablesView component manages that state is more of an open question; should it call useState or useReducer or both? The next two sections explore two approaches. Section 6.4 makes quite a few changes to do away with the reducer. But first, section 6.3 takes an easier path and uses the existing reducer in BookablesList, lifting it up into the BookablesView component.

## 6.3 Sharing the state and dispatch function from useReducer

We already have a reducer that manages all of the state changes for the Bookables-List component. The state the reducer manages includes the bookables data, the selected group, and the index of the selected bookable, along with properties for loading and error states. If we move the reducer up into the BookablesView component, we can use the state the reducer returns to derive the selected bookable and pass it to the child components, as illustrated in figure 6.11.

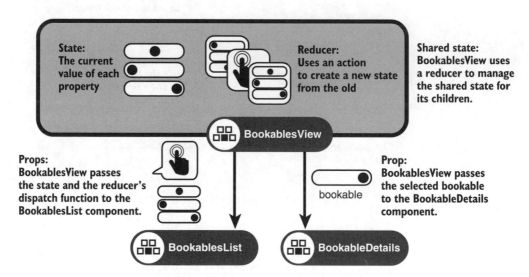

**Figure 6.11**  BookablesView **manages the state with a reducer and passes the selected bookable or the whole state to its children.**

While BookableDetails needs only the selected bookable, BookablesList needs the rest of the state the reducer returns and a way to continue dispatching actions as users select bookables and switch groups. Figure 6.11 also shows `BookablesView` passing the reducer's state and dispatch function to `BookablesList`.

Lifting the state up from `BookablesList` into the `BookablesView` component is relatively straightforward. We complete it in three steps:

- Managing state in the `BookablesView` component
- Removing an action from the reducer
- Receiving state and dispatch in the `BookablesList` component

Let's start by updating the `BookablesView` component to take control of the state.

### 6.3.1 Managing state in the BookablesView component

The `BookablesView` component needs to import its two children. It can then pass them the state they need and the means to update that state if required. In the following listing, you can see the imports for the new components, the state that `Bookables-View` is managing, the call to the `useReducer` hook, and the UI as JSX, with state values and the dispatch function set as props.

> **Branch**: 0601-lift-reducer, *File*: src/components/Bookables/BookablesView.js

> **Listing 6.7   Moving the bookables state into the `BookablesView` component**

```
import {useReducer, Fragment} from "react";

import BookablesList from "./BookablesList";         Import all the components
import BookableDetails from "./BookableDetails";     that make up the UI.

import reducer from "./reducer";          Import the reducer that
                                          BookablesList was using.
const initialState = {
  group: "Rooms",             Set up the initial state
  bookableIndex: 0,           without hasDetails.
  bookables: [],
  isLoading: true,
  error: false
};
                                                        Manage the state
                                                        and reducer within
export default function BookablesView () {              BookablesView.
  const [state, dispatch] = useReducer(reducer, initialState);

  const bookablesInGroup = state.bookables.filter(
    b => b.group === state.group        Derive the
  );                                    selected bookable
  const bookable = bookablesInGroup[state.bookableIndex];     from state.

  return (                                          Pass state and
    <Fragment>                                      dispatch to
      <BookablesList state={state} dispatch={dispatch}/>      BookablesList.
      <BookableDetails bookable={bookable}/>        Pass the selected bookable
    </Fragment>                                     to BookableDetails.
  );
}
```

The `BookablesView` component imports the child components it needs and sets up the initial state that used to live in the `BookablesList` component. We've removed the `hasDetails` property from the state; the new `BookableDetails` component manages its own state for whether to show details or not.

### 6.3.2    *Removing an action from the reducer*

With the `BookableDetails` component happily toggling its own details, the reducer no longer needs to handle an action for toggling a shared `hasDetails` state value, so the following case can be removed from reducer.js:

```
case "TOGGLE_HAS_DETAILS":
  return {
    ...state,
    hasDetails: !state.hasDetails
  };
```

Apart from that, the reducer can stay as it is. Nice!

### 6.3.3    *Receiving state and dispatch in the BookablesList component*

The `BookablesList` component needs a few tweaks. Instead of relying on its own local reducer and actions, it's now dependent on the `BookablesView` component (or any other parent component that renders it). The code for `BookablesList` is relatively long, so we consider it section by section. The structure of the code looks like this:

```
export default function BookablesList ({state, dispatch}) {
  // 1. Variables
  // 2. Effect
  // 3. Handler functions
  // 4. UI
}
```

The following four subsections discuss any changes that are necessary. If you stitch the pieces together, you'll have the complete component.

#### VARIABLES

Apart from the two new props, `state` and `dispatch`, there are no additions to the variables in the `BookablesList` component. But with the reducer lifted up to the `BookablesView` component and the need to display the bookable details removed, there are some deletions. The following listing shows what's left.

> **Branch**: 0601-lift-reducer, *File*: src/components/Bookables/BookablesList.js
>
> **Listing 6.8**  `BookablesList`: 1. Variables

```
import {useEffect, useRef} from "react";
import {FaArrowRight} from "react-icons/fa";
import Spinner from "../UI/Spinner";
import getData from "../../utils/api";
```

```
export default function BookablesList ({state, dispatch}) {    ◁──┐  Assign the state and
  const {group, bookableIndex, bookables} = state;                  dispatch props to
  const {isLoading, error} = state;                                 local variables.

  const bookablesInGroup = bookables.filter(b => b.group === group);
  const groups = [...new Set(bookables.map(b => b.group))];

  const nextButtonRef = useRef();

  // 2. Effect
  // 3. Handler functions
  // 4. UI
}
```

The reducer and its initial state are gone, as is the hasDetails flag. Finally, we no longer need to display the bookable details, so we removed the bookable variable.

**EFFECT**

The effect is pretty much unchanged apart from one small detail. In the following listing, you can see that we have added the dispatch function to the effect's dependency array.

> Branch: 0601-lift-reducer, *File*: src/components/Bookables/BookablesList.js
>
> Listing 6.9   `BookablesList`: 2. Effect

```
export default function BookablesList ({state, dispatch}) {    ◁──┐  Assign the dispatch
  // 1. Variables                                                   prop to a local
                                                                    variable.
  useEffect(() => {
    dispatch({type: "FETCH_BOOKABLES_REQUEST"});

    getData("http://localhost:3001/bookables")
      .then(bookables => dispatch({
        type: "FETCH_BOOKABLES_SUCCESS",
        payload: bookables
      }))
      .catch(error => dispatch({
        type: "FETCH_BOOKABLES_ERROR",
        payload: error
      }));
  }, [dispatch]);              ◁──┐  Include dispatch in
                                    the dependency
  // 3. Handler functions           array for the effect.
  // 4. UI
}
```

In the previous version, when we called useReducer from within the BookablesList component and assigned the dispatch function to the dispatch variable, React knew that the identity of the dispatch function would never change, so it didn't need to be declared as a dependency for the effect. Now that a parent component passes dispatch in as a prop, BookablesList doesn't know where it comes from so can't be sure it won't change. Leaving `dispatch` out of the dependency array prompts a warning in the browser console like the one in figure 6.12.

```
⚠ ▸ src/components/Bookables/BookablesList.js              webpackHotDevClient.js:138
    Line 27:6:  React Hook useEffect has a missing dependency: 'dispatch'. Either
  include it or remove the dependency array. If 'dispatch' changes too often, find
  the parent component that defines it and wrap that definition in useCallback
  react-hooks/exhaustive-deps
```

**Figure 6.12   React warns us when dispatch is missing from the dependency array.**

Including `dispatch` in the dependency array is good practice here; *we* know it won't change (at least for now), so the effect won't run unnecessarily. Notice that the warning in figure 6.12 says "If 'dispatch' changes too often, find the parent component that defines it and wrap that definition in useCallback." We look at using the `useCallback` hook to maintain the identity of functions that are dependencies in section 6.5.

#### HANDLER FUNCTIONS

Now that the details for the selected bookable are shown by a different component, we can remove the `toggleDetails` handler function. Everything else stays the same. Easy!

#### UI

Goodbye, `bookableDetails` div! We completely cut out the second section of the UI, for displaying the bookable details. The following listing shows the updated, super-slim `BookablesList` UI.

> **Branch: 0601-lift-reducer, *File*: src/components/Bookables/BookablesList.js**
>
> **Listing 6.10**  `BookablesList: 4. UI`

```
export default function BookablesList ({state, dispatch}) {
  // 1. Variables
  // 2. Effect
  // 3. Handler functions

  if (error) {
    return <p>{error.message}</p>
  }

  if (isLoading) {
    return <p><Spinner/> Loading bookables...</p>
  }

  return (
    <div>
      <select value={group} onChange={changeGroup}>
        {groups.map(g => <option value={g} key={g}>{g}</option>)}
      </select>
```

```
      <ul className="bookables items-list-nav">
        {bookablesInGroup.map((b, i) => (
          <li
            key={b.id}
            className={i === bookableIndex ? "selected" : null}
          >
            <button
              className="btn"
              onClick={() => changeBookable(i)}
            >
              {b.title}
            </button>
          </li>
        ))}
      </ul>
      <p>
        <button
          className="btn"
          onClick={nextBookable}
          ref={nextButtonRef}
          autoFocus
        >
          <FaArrowRight/>
          <span>Next</span>
        </button>
      </p>
    </div>
  );
}
```

All that's left in the UI is the list of bookables with its associated group picker and Next button. So, we also remove the `Fragment` component that was grouping the two big chunks of UI.

With the bookable details off on their own adventures and the reducer lifted up to the parent, the changes to the `BookablesList` component mostly took the form of deletions. One key addition was the inclusion of `dispatch` in the dependency array for the data-loading effect. Housing the state in the `BookablesView` component (or maybe even higher up the component tree) seems easy. Stick all the data there, and pass a dispatch function to any descendant components that need to make changes to the state. It's a valid approach, and one sometimes used by users of popular state-store libraries like Redux. But before throwing all the state up to the top of the app, even if most components don't care about most of the state that ends up there, let's investigate an alternative.

## 6.4 *Sharing the state value and updater function from useState*

In this section, we try a different approach. We lift only the state that needs to be shared: the selected bookable. Figure 6.13 shows the `BookablesView` component passing the selected bookable to its two child components. The `BookableDetails` and

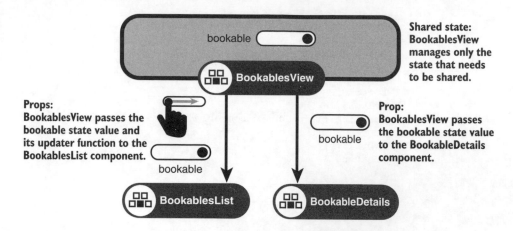

**Figure 6.13** `BookablesView` **manages only the shared state. It passes the bookable to the** `BookableDetails` **component. It passes the bookable and its updater function to** `BookablesList`.

`BookablesList` components still get exactly what they need, and rather than giving `BookablesView` a whole load of state it doesn't need to share, `BookablesList` will manage the rest of the state and functionality that it needs: the loading indicators and errors.

Lifting the selected bookable up from `BookablesList` into the `BookablesView` component requires much less work in `BookablesView` but a number of changes in `BookablesList`. We complete the changes in two steps:

- Managing the selected bookable in the `BookablesView` component
- Receiving the bookable and updater function in `BookablesList`

The `BookablesList` component still needs a way to let `BookablesView` know that a user has selected a new bookable. `BookablesView` passes `BookablesList` the updater function for the selected bookable. Let's take a closer look at the latest code for the `BookablesView` component.

### 6.4.1 *Managing the selected bookable in the BookablesView component*

As you can see in listing 6.11, the `BookablesView` component in this version is very simple; it doesn't have to deal with the reducer, initial state, or deriving the selected bookable from state. It includes a single call to the `useState` hook to manage the selected bookable state value. It then passes the selected bookable to both children and the updater function to `BookablesList`. When a user selects a bookable, the `BookablesList` component can use the updater function to let `BookablesView` know that the state has changed.

---

**Branch**: 0602-lift-bookable, *File*: /src/components/Bookables/BookablesView.js

**Listing 6.11 Putting the selected bookable in the `BookablesView` component**

```
import {useState, Fragment} from "react";

import BookablesList from "./BookablesList";
import BookableDetails from "./BookableDetails";

export default function BookablesView () {                    ←  Manage the selected
  const [bookable, setBookable] = useState();                    bookable as a state value.

  return (                                                    Pass the bookable and its
    <Fragment>                                                   updater function down.
      <BookablesList bookable={bookable} setBookable={setBookable}/>  ←┘
      <BookableDetails bookable={bookable}/>          ←┐
    </Fragment>                                        Pass the
  );                                                   bookable down.
}
```

`BookablesView` no longer needs to do the filtering of the bookables for the current group or grab the current bookable from that filtered list. Let's see how `Bookables-List` changes to adapt to the new approach.

### 6.4.2 *Receiving the bookable and updater function in BookablesList*

By letting the `BookablesView` component manage the selected bookable, we change how the `BookablesList` component works. In the reducer version, `BookablesView` stored the `bookableIndex` and `group` as part of state. Now, with `BookablesList` receiving the bookable directly, those state values are no longer needed. The selected bookable looks something like this:

```
{
  "id": 1,
  "group": "Rooms",
  "title": "Meeting Room",
  "notes": "The one with the big table and interactive screen.",
  "days": [1, 2, 3],
  "sessions": [1, 2, 3, 4, 5, 6]
}
```

It includes an `id` and a `group` property. Whatever group the selected bookable is in is the current group; we don't need a separate `group` state value. Also, it's easy to find the index of the selected bookable within the array of bookables in its group; we don't need a `bookableIndex` state value. With the `group`, `bookableIndex`, and `hasDetails` state values no longer needed, resulting in a smaller, simpler state, let's switch back to using calls to `useState` rather than a reducer.

There are changes to all sections of the `BookablesList` component, so we consider the code section by section. The structure of the code looks like this:

```
export default function BookablesList ({bookable, setBookable}) {
  // 1. Variables
  // 2. Effect
  // 3. Handler functions
  // 4. UI
}
```

Each of the next four subsections discusses one of the code sections. If you stitch the pieces together, you'll have the complete component.

### VARIABLES

The `BookablesList` component now receives the selected bookable as a prop. The selected bookable includes an `id` and a `group` property. We use the `group` property to filter the list and the `id` to highlight the selected bookable.

The following listing shows the updated `BookablesList` component receiving `bookable` and `setBookable` as props and setting up three pieces of local state by calling `useState` three times.

> **Branch**: 0602-lift-bookable, *File*: /src/components/Bookables/BookablesList.js
>
> **Listing 6.12** `BookablesList`: **1. Variables**

```
import {useState, useEffect, useRef} from "react";        Import useState rather
import {FaArrowRight} from "react-icons/fa";              than useReducer.
import Spinner from "../UI/Spinner";
import getData from "../../utils/api";              Receive the selected bookable
                                                    and updater function as props.
export default function BookablesList ({bookable, setBookable}) {
  const [bookables, setBookables] = useState([]);
  const [error, setError] = useState(false);          Manage state
  const [isLoading, setIsLoading] = useState(true);   with calls to the
                                                       useState hook.
  const group = bookable?.group;              Get the current group from
                                              the selected bookable.
  const bookablesInGroup = bookables.filter(b => b.group === group);
  const groups = [...new Set(bookables.map(b => b.group))];

  const nextButtonRef = useRef();

  // 2. Effect
  // 3. Handler functions
  // 4. UI
}
```

Listing 6.12 grabs the current group from the selected bookable by using the *optional chaining operator*, `?.`, a recent addition to JavaScript:

```
const group = bookable?.group;
```

If no bookable is selected, the expression `bookable?.group` returns `undefined`. It saves us from checking whether the bookable exists before accessing the `group` property:

```
const group = bookable && bookable.group;
```

Until a bookable is selected, the group will be undefined and bookablesInGroup will be an empty array. We need to select a bookable as soon as the bookables data is loaded into the component. Let's look at the loading process.

**EFFECT**

The following listing shows the updated effect code. It now uses updater functions rather than dispatching actions.

> **Branch**: 0602-lift-bookable, *File*: /src/components/Bookables/BookablesList.js
>
> **Listing 6.13** BookablesList: **2. Effect**

```
export default function BookablesList ({bookable, setBookable}) {
  // 1. Variables

  useEffect(() => {
    getData("http://localhost:3001/bookables")

      .then(bookables => {          Use the setBookable prop
        setBookable(bookables[0]);  to select the first bookable.
        setBookables(bookables);    Use the local updater function
        setIsLoading(false);        to set the bookables state.
      })

      .catch(error => {
        setError(error);            If there's an error,
        setIsLoading(false)         set the error state.
      });

  }, [setBookable]);       Include the external function
                           in the dependency list.

  // 3. Handler functions
  // 4. UI
}
```

The first effect still uses the getData utility function, created in chapter 4, to load the bookables. But instead of dispatching actions to a reducer, the effect uses all four of the listing's updater functions: setBookable (passed in as a prop) and setBookables, setIsLoading, and setError (from local calls to useState).

When the data loads, it assigns the data to the bookables state value and calls set-Bookable with the first bookable in the array:

```
setBookable(bookables[0]);
setBookables(bookables);
setIsLoading(false);
```

React is able to sensibly respond to multiple state update calls, like the three just listed. It can batch updates to efficiently schedule any re-renders and DOM changes needed.

As we saw with the dispatch prop in the reducer version in section 6.3, React doesn't trust functions passed in as props to be the same on each render. In this version,

BookingsView passes in the setBookable function as a prop, so we include it in the dependency array for the first effect. Indeed, we sometimes might define our own updater functions rather than directly using those that useState returns. We look at how to make such functions work nicely as dependencies in section 6.5, where we introduce the useCallback hook.

If an error was thrown in the course of loading the data, the catch method sets it as the error state value:

```
.catch(error => {
  setError(error);
  setIsLoading(false);
);
```

### HANDLER FUNCTIONS

In the previous version of the BookablesList component, the handler functions dispatched actions to the reducer. In this new version, the handler functions' key task is to set the bookable. In the following listing, notice how each handler function includes a call to setBookable.

> **Branch**: 0602-lift-bookable, *File*: /src/components/Bookables/BookablesList.js
>
> Listing 6.14   BookablesList: 3. Handler functions

```
export default function BookablesList ({bookable, setBookable}) {
  // 1. Variables
  // 2. Effect

  function changeGroup (e) {
    const bookablesInSelectedGroup = bookables.filter(      ⟵  Filter for the
      b => b.group === event.target.value                        selected group.
    );
    setBookable(bookablesInSelectedGroup[0]);      ⟵  Set the bookable to the
  }                                                      first in the new group.

  function changeBookable (selectedBookable) {
    setBookable(selectedBookable);
    nextButtonRef.current.focus();
  }

  function nextBookable () {
    const i = bookablesInGroup.indexOf(bookable);
    const nextIndex = (i + 1) % bookablesInGroup.length;
    const nextBookable = bookablesInGroup[nextIndex];
    setBookable(nextBookable);
  }

  // 4. UI
}
```

The current group is derived from the selected bookable; we no longer have a group state value. So when a user chooses a group from the drop-down, the changeGroup function doesn't directly set the new group. Instead, it selects the first bookable in the chosen group:

```
setBookable(bookablesInSelectedGroup[0]);
```

The `setBookable` updater function is from the `BookablesView` component and triggers a re-render of `BookablesView`. `BookablesView`, in turn, re-renders the `Bookables-List` component, passing it the newly selected bookable as a prop. The `BookablesList` component uses the bookable's `group` and `id` properties to select the correct group in the drop-down, show just the bookables in the group, and highlight the selected bookable in the list.

The `changeBookable` function has no surprises: it sets the selected bookable and moves focus to the Next button. In addition to setting the bookable to the next in the current group, `nextBookable` wraps back to the first if necessary.

### UI

We no longer have the `bookableIndex` value in state. The following listing shows how we use the bookable `id` instead.

> *Branch*: **0602-lift-bookable**, *File*: **/src/components/Bookables/BookablesList.js**
>
> **Listing 6.15** `BookablesList`: 4. UI

```
export default function BookablesList ({bookable, setBookable}) {
  // 1. Variables
  // 2. Effect
  // 3. Handler functions

  if (error) {
    return <p>{error.message}</p>
  }

  if (isLoading) {
    return <p><Spinner/> Loading bookables...</p>
  }

  return (
    <div>
      <select value={group} onChange={changeGroup}>
        {groups.map(g => <option value={g} key={g}>{g}</option>)}
      </select>

      <ul className="bookables items-list-nav">
        {bookablesInGroup.map(b => (
          <li
            key={b.id}
            className={b.id === bookable.id ? "selected" : null}       ⟵── Use the ID to check whether a bookable should be highlighted.
          >
            <button
              className="btn"
              onClick={() => changeBookable(b)}        ⟵── Pass the bookable to the changeBookable handler function.
            >
```

```
                    {b.title}
                  </button>
                </li>
              ))}
            </ul>
            <p>
              <button
                className="btn"
                onClick={nextBookable}
                ref={nextButtonRef}
                autoFocus
              >
                Next
              </button>
            </p>
          </div>
      );
}
```

Some key changes to the UI occur in the list of bookables. The code iterates through the bookables in the same group as the selected bookable. One by one, the bookables in the group are assigned to the b variable. The bookable variable represents the selected bookable. If b.id and bookable.id are the same, the current bookable in the list should be highlighted, so we set its class to selected:

```
className={b.id === bookable.id ? "selected" : null}
```

When a user clicks a bookable to select it, the onClick handler passes the whole bookable object, b, to the changeBookable function, rather than just the bookable's index:

```
onClick={() => changeBookable(b)}
```

And that's the BookablesList component without a reducer again. A few changes were made, but with its more focused role of just listing bookables, it's also simpler overall.

Which approach do you find easier to understand? Dispatching actions to a reducer in the parent or managing most of the state in the component that uses it? In the first approach, we moved the reducer up to the BookablesView component without making many changes. Could we have simplified the state held in the reducer in the same way we did for the variables in the second approach? Whichever implementation you prefer, this chapter gave you a chance to practice calling the useState, useReducer, and useEffect hooks and consider some of the nuances of passing dispatch and updater functions to child components.

### CHALLENGE 6.1

Split the UsersList component into UsersList and UserDetails components. Use the UsersPage component to manage the selected user, passing it to UsersList and UserDetails. Find a solution on the 0603-user-details branch.

## 6.5 Passing functions to useCallback to avoid redefining them

Now that our applications are growing, and we have components working together to provide functionality, it's natural to be passing state values down to children as props. As we've seen in this chapter, those values can include functions. If the functions are updater or dispatch functions from useState or useReducer, React guarantees that their identity will be stable. But for functions we define ourselves, the very nature of components as functions that React calls means our functions will be defined on every render. In this section, we explore the problems such redefining can cause and look at a new hook, useCallback, that can help solve such problems.

### 6.5.1 Depending on functions we pass in as props

In the previous section, the state for the selected bookable is managed by the Bookables-View component. It passes both the bookable and its updater function, setBookable, to BookablesList. BookablesList calls setBookable whenever a user choses a bookable and also within the effect wrapping the data-fetching code, shown here without the catch block:

```
useEffect(() => {
  getData("http://localhost:3001/bookables")
    .then(bookables => {
      setBookable(bookables[0]);      ◁——  Once the data arrives, set the
      setBookables(bookables);              current bookable to the first.
      setIsLoading(false);
    });                               ┐  Include the setBookable
}, [setBookable]);              ◁——   ┘  function as a dependency.
```

We include the setBookable updater function as a dependency. The effect reruns whenever the values in its dependency list change. But up to now, setBookable has been an updater function returned by useState and, as such, is guaranteed not to change value; the data-fetching effect runs only once.

The parent component, BookablesView, assigns the updater function to the set-Bookable variable and sets it directly as one of BookablesList's props. But it's not uncommon to do some kind of validation or processing of values before updating state. Say BookablesView wants to check that the bookable exists and, if it does, add a timestamp property before updating state. The following listing shows such a custom setter.

> Listing 6.16 Validating and enhancing a value in BookablesView before setting state

```
import {useState, Fragment} from "react";

import BookablesList from "./BookablesList";
import BookableDetails from "./BookableDetails";

export default function BookablesView () {
  const [bookable, setBookable] = useState();
```

```
function updateBookable (selected) {
  if (selected) {                              ⊲——⌐  Check that the bookable exists.
    selected.lastShown = Date.now();           ⊲——⌐  Add a timestamp property.
    setBookable(selected);                     ⊲——⌐
  }                                            Set the state.
}

return (
  <Fragment>
    <BookablesList bookable={bookable} setBookable={updateBookable}/>   ⊲——⌐
    <BookableDetails bookable={bookable}/>
  </Fragment>                                  Pass our handler function
);                                             as the updater prop.
}
```

BookablesView now assigns the custom updateBookable function as the setBookable prop for BookablesList. The BookablesList component cares not a jot, and happily calls the new updater function whenever it wants to select a bookable. So, what's the problem?

If you update the code to use the new updater function and load the Bookables page, the Network tab of the Developer Tools highlights some disturbing activity: the bookables are being fetched again and again, as shown in figure 6.14.

| | | | | | |
|---|---|---|---|---|---|
| ☐ users | 200 | fetch | UserPick... | 374 B | 2.... |
| ☐ bookables | 200 | fetch | api.js:3 | 1.1 kB | 2.... |
| ☐ bookables | 200 | fetch | api.js:3 | 374 B | 2.... |
| ☐ bookables | 200 | fetch | api.js:3 | 374 B | 2.... |
| ☐ bookables | 200 | fetch | api.js:3 | 374 B | 2.... |
| ☐ bookables | 200 | fetch | api.js:3 | 374 B | 2.... |
| ☐ bookables | 200 | fetch | api.js:3 | 374 B | 2.... |
| ☐ bookables | 200 | fetch | api.js:3 | 374 B | 2.... |
| ☐ bookables | (pending) | fetch | api.js:3 | 0 B | Pe... |

Figure 6.14  **The Network tab of the Developer Tools shows bookables being fetched repeatedly.**

The parent component, BookablesView, manages the state for the selected bookable. Whenever BookablesList loads the bookables data and sets the bookable, Bookables-View re-renders; React runs its code again, defining the updateBookable function again and passing the new version of the function to BookablesList. The useEffect call in BookablesList sees that the setBookable prop is a new function and runs the effect again, refetching the bookables data and setting the bookable again, restarting the loop. We need a way to maintain the identity of our updater function, so that it doesn't change from render to render.

### 6.5.2 *Maintaining function identity with the useCallback hook*

When we want to use the same function from render to render but don't want it to be redefined each time, we can pass the function to the useCallback hook. React will return the same function from the hook on every render, redefining it only if one of the function's dependencies changes. Use the hook like this:

```
const stableFunction = useCallback(funtionToCache, dependencyList);
```

The function that useCallback returns is stable while the values in the dependency list don't change. When the dependencies change, React redefines, caches, and returns the function using the new dependency values. The following listing shows how to use the new hook to solve our endless fetch problem.

Listing 6.17  Maintaining a stable function identity with `useCallback`

```
import {useState, useCallback, Fragment} from "react";      ◁── Import the
                                                                 useCallback hook.
import BookablesList from "./BookablesList";
import BookableDetails from "./BookableDetails";

export default function BookablesView () {
  const [bookable, setBookable] = useState();
                                                          Pass the updater
  const updateBookable = useCallback(selected => {    ◁── function to useCallback.
    if (selected) {
      selected.lastShown = Date.now();
      setBookable(selected);
    }
  }, []);          ◁──  Specify the                        Assign the stable
                        dependencies.                      function as a prop.
  return (
    <Fragment>
      <BookablesList bookable={bookable} setBookable={updateBookable}/>   ◁──┘
      <BookableDetails bookable={bookable}/>
    </Fragment>
  );
}
```

Wrapping our updater function in useCallback means React will return the same function on every render, unless the dependencies change values. But we've used an empty dependency list, so the values will never change and React will always return the exact same function. The useEffect call in BookablesList will now see that its setBookable dependency is stable, and it'll stop endlessly refetching the bookables data.

The useCallback hook can be useful, in exactly the same way, when working with components that re-render only when their props change. Such components can be created with React's memo function, described in the React docs: https://reactjs.org/docs/react-api.html#reactmemo.

useCallback lets us memoize functions. To prevent the redefinition or recalculation of values more generally, React also provides the useMemo hook, and we'll look at that in the next chapter.

## Summary

- If components share the same state value, lift the value up to the closest shared ancestor component in the component tree and pass the state down via props:

```
const [bookable, setBookable] = useState();
return (
  <Fragment>
    <BookablesList bookable={bookable}/>
    <BookableDetails bookable={bookable}/>
  </Fragment>
);
```

- Pass the updater function returned by useState to child components if they need to update the shared state:

```
const [bookable, setBookable] = useState();
return <BookablesList bookable={bookable} setBookable={setBookable} />
```

- Destructure the props parameter, assigning properties to local variables:

```
export default function ColorPicker({colors = [], color, setColor}) {
  return (
    // UI that uses colors, color and setColor
  );
}
```

- Consider using default values for props. If the prop isn't set, the default value will be used:

```
export default function ColorPicker({colors = [], color, setColor}) {
  return (
    // iterate over colors array
  );
}
```

- Check for undefined or null prop values. Return alternative UI if appropriate:

```
export default function ChoiceText({color}) {
  return color ? (
    <p>The selected color is {color}!</p>
  ) : (
    <p>No color has been selected!</p>
  );
}
```

- Return null when it is appropriate to render nothing.

- To let a child component update the state managed by a parent, pass the child an updater function or a dispatch function. If the function is used in an effect, include the function in the effect's dependency list.
- Maintain the identity of functions across renders by wrapping them in calls to the useCallback hook. React will redefine the function only when the dependencies change:

```
const stableFunction = useCallback(functionToCache, dependencyList);
```

# Managing performance with useMemo

7

**This chapter covers**

- Using the `useMemo` hook to avoid rerunning expensive computations
- Controlling `useMemo` with a dependency array
- Considering the user experience as your app re-renders
- Handling race conditions when fetching data
- Using JavaScript's optional chaining syntax with square brackets

React is great at making it easy to display data in efficient, appealing, and responsive ways. But simply throwing raw data onto the screen is rare. Whether our apps are statistical, financial, scientific, entertaining, or whimsical, we almost always manipulate our data before bringing it to the surface.

Sometimes that manipulation can be complicated or time-consuming. If the time and resources spent are necessary to bring the data to life, the outcome may make up for the cost. But if the user experience is degraded by our computations, we need to consider ways of streamlining our code. Maybe a quest for more-efficient algorithms will pay dividends, or maybe our algorithms are already efficient and there is no way to make them faster. Either way, we shouldn't perform the computations at all if we know their output will be unchanged. In such a case, React provides the use-Memo hook to help us avoid unnecessary and wasteful work.

We start this chapter by being willfully wasteful, running the risk of crashing the browser with some gratuitously resource-intensive anagram generation. We call on useMemo to protect the user from some seriously sluggish UI updates. We then bring the bookings to life in our example app, this time calling useMemo to avoid regenerating grids of booking slots for no reason. When fetching the bookings for the selected week and bookable, we examine a method for coping with multiple requests and responses from within a useEffect call.

The title of section 7.1 is a little messed up; let's find out what it's trying to teach us about React Hooks.

## 7.1 Breaking the cook's heart by calling, "O, shortcake!"

Say you're trying to develop an anagram app that will find amusing anagrams of words, names, and phrases. It's early in the development process and, so far, you have an app that finds all of the combinations of letters in some source text. In figure 7.1, your fledgling app is displaying the 12 distinct anagrams of the source text ball. The app is live on CodeSandbox (https://codesandbox.io/s/anagrams-djwuy).

You can toggle between All anagrams and Distinct anagrams. For example, because "ball" has a repeated letter "l," you could swap their positions and still have

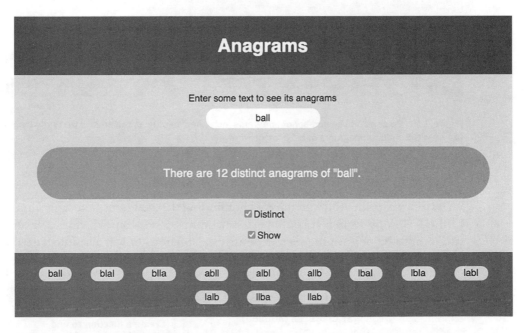

**Figure 7.1 The Anagrams app counts and displays anagrams of text entered by the user. The user can count all anagrams or only distinct anagrams, and can toggle the display of the anagrams.**

the word "ball." The two identical words are counted separately in the All category but not in the Distinct category. You can also hide the generated anagrams, letting the app find new anagrams behind the scenes as you enter the source text, without having to render the new anagrams as you type.

Be careful! The number of anagrams shoots up as the number of letters in the source text increases. There are $n!$ (n factorial) combinations of $n$ letters. For four letters, that's $4 \times 3 \times 2 \times 1 = 24$ combinations. For ten letters, there are 10!, or 3,628,800, combinations, as shown in figure 7.2. The app is limited to ten characters—remove the cap at your own risk!

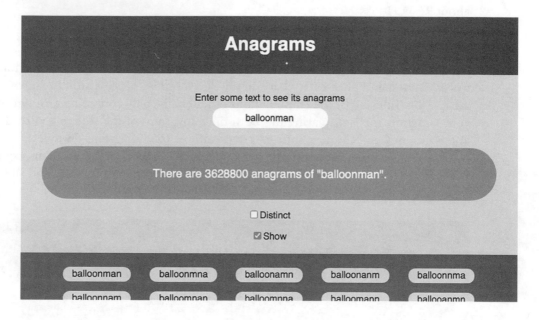

Figure 7.2   Be careful! The number of anagrams increases quickly as the source text gets longer. There are over 3.5 million anagrams of a 10-letter word.

### 7.1.1   Generating anagrams with an expensive algorithm

A coworker provides you with the code for finding the anagrams. The algorithm is shown in the following listing. It could certainly be improved. But whatever the algorithm, you want to be performing such expensive calculations only if absolutely necessary.

*Live:* **https://djwuy.csb.app/,** *Code:* **https://codesandbox.io/s/anagrams-djwuy**

Listing 7.1   Finding anagrams

```
export function getAnagrams(source) {
  if (source.length < 2) {
    return [...source];
  }
}
```
⟵ Create a function to find all combinations of letters in some source text.

```
  const anagrams = [];
  const letters = [...source];

  letters.forEach((letter, i) => {
    const without = [...letters];
    without.splice(i, 1);
    getAnagrams(without).forEach(anagram => {
      anagrams.push(letter + anagram);
    });
  });

  return anagrams;
}

export function getDistinct(anagrams) {
  return [...new Set(anagrams)];
}
```

Call the function recursively on source text with one letter removed.

Create a function to remove duplicates from an array.

The algorithm takes each letter in a word and appends all the anagrams of the remaining letters. So, for "ball" it would find the following:

"b" + anagrams of "all"
"a" + anagrams of "bll"
"l" + anagrams of "bal"
"l" + anagrams of "bal"

The main app calls getAnagrams and getDistinct to get the info it needs to display. The following listing is an earlier implementation. Can you spot any problems?

### Listing 7.2 The anagrams app before the fix

```
import React, { useState } from "react";
import "./styles.css";
import { getAnagrams, getDistinct } from "./anagrams";

export default function App() {
  const [sourceText, setSourceText] = useState("ball");
  const [useDistinct, setUseDistinct] = useState(false);
  const [showAnagrams, setShowAnagrams] = useState(false);

  const anagrams = getAnagrams(sourceText);
  const distinct = getDistinct(anagrams);

  return (
    <div className="App">
      <h1>Anagrams</h1>
      <label htmlFor="txtPhrase">Enter some text...</label>
      <input
        type="text"
        value={sourceText}
        onChange={e => setSourceText(e.target.value.slice(0, 10))}
      />
```

Import the anagram finder functions.

Manage the source text state.

Include flags for toggling distinct anagrams and anagram display.

Use the anagram functions to generate the data.

Cap the number of letters.

```
    <div className="count">
      {useDistinct ? (
        <p>
          There are {distinct.length} distinct anagrams.
        </p>
      ) : (
        <p>
          There are {anagrams.length} anagrams of "{sourceText}".
        </p>
      )}
    </div>

    <p>
      <label>
        <input
          type="checkbox"
          checked={useDistinct}
          onClick={() => setUseDistinct(s => !s)}
        />
        Distinct
      </label>
    </p>
    <p>
      <label>
        <input
          type="checkbox"
          checked={showAnagrams}
          onChange={() => setShowAnagrams(s => !s)}
        />
        Show
      </label>
    </p>

    {showAnagrams && (
      <p className="anagrams">
        {distinct.map(a => (
          <span key={a}>{a}</span>
        ))}
      </p>
    )}
  </div>
  );
}
```

Display the
number of
anagrams.

Display the list
of anagrams.

The key problem is that the code calls the expensive anagram functions on *every* render. But the anagrams change only if the source text changes. You really shouldn't generate the anagrams again if the user clicks either of the check boxes, toggling between All and Distinct anagrams, or showing and hiding the list. Here are the current calls to the anagram functions:

```
export default function App() {
  // variables
```

```
  const anagrams = getAnagrams(sourceText);        | The expensive functions
  const distinct = getDistinct(anagrams);          | run on every render.

  return ( /* UI */ )
}
```

We need a way of asking React to run the expensive functions only if their output is likely to be different. For getAnagrams, that's if the sourceText value changes. For getDistinct, that's if the anagrams array changes.

## 7.1.2 Avoiding redundant function calls

The following listing shows the code for the live example. It wraps the expensive functions in calls to the useMemo hook, providing an array of dependencies for each call.

*Live:* https://djwuy.csb.app/, *Code:* https://codesandbox.io/s/anagrams-djwuy

**Listing 7.3   The anagrams app with** useMemo

```
import React, {useState, useMemo} from "react";        ◁──┐ Import the
import "./styles.css";                                      useMemo hook.
import {getAnagrams, getDistinct} from "./anagrams";

export default function App() {
  const [sourceText, setSourceText] = useState("ball");
  const [useDistinct, setUseDistinct] = useState(false);
  const [showAnagrams, setShowAnagrams] = useState(false);

  const anagrams = useMemo(                   Pass the expensive
    () => getAnagrams(sourceText),       ◁──  function to useMemo.
    [sourceText]                    ◁──┐ Specify a list of
  );                                     dependencies.

  const distinct = useMemo(         ◁──        Assign the value getDistinct
    () => getDistinct(anagrams),    ◁──        returns to a variable.
    [anagrams]              ◁──┐
  );                              Wrap the call to getDistinct
                                  in another function.
  return ( /* UI */ )        Rerun the getDistinct function only
}                            when the anagrams array changes.
```

**Call useMemo.**

In this version, React should call getAnagrams only when sourceText changes, and should call getDistinct only when anagrams changes. Users can toggle at will without causing a cascade of costly calls as the app tries to keep up while rebuilding the same million anagrams again and again.

You could see the last example, decide there's no more to learn, and bury your head in the sand—*some emu*. Or be too timid to ask for more details—*Mouse? Me?* But, be brave, lean on React, and calm those costly calls—*useMemo*!

## 7.2    *Memoizing expensive function calls with useMemo*

If we have a function, `expensiveFn`, that takes time and resources to calculate its return value, then we want to call the function only when absolutely necessary. By calling the function inside the `useMemo` hook, we ask React to store a value computed by the function for a given set of arguments. If we call the function inside `useMemo` again, using the same arguments as the previous call, it should return the stored value. If we pass different arguments, it will use the function to compute a new value and update its store before returning the new value. The process of storing a result for a given set of arguments is called *memoizing*.

When calling `useMemo`, pass it a *create function* and a list of dependencies, as shown in figure 7.3.

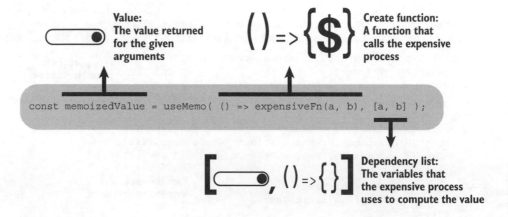

Figure 7.3    Call the `useMemo` hook with a function and a list of dependencies.

The list of dependencies is an array of values and should include all the values the function uses in its computation. On each call, `useMemo` compares the dependency list to the previous list. If each list holds the same values in the same order, `useMemo` may return the stored value. If any value in the list has changed, `useMemo` will call the function and store and return the function's return value. To reiterate, `useMemo` *may* return the stored value. React reserves the right to clear its store if it needs to free up memory. So, it might call the expensive function even if the dependencies are unchanged.

If you omit the dependency list, `useMemo` always runs your function, which kind of defeats the purpose! If you pass an empty array, the values in the list never change, so `useMemo` could always return the stored value. It may, however, decide to clear its store and run your function again anyway. It's almost certainly best to avoid that kind of maybe-or-maybe-not behavior.

That's how `useMemo` works. We see it in action again in the bookings example app in section 7.4, memoizing a function for generating a grid of booking slots. First, we use our state-sharing and React Hooks skills to put the Bookings page components into place and pass them the bits and pieces they need to work nicely together.

## 7.3 Organizing the components on the Bookings page

So far, the Bookables and Users pages have had all the attention in the bookings app; it's about time the Bookings page got some love! We need to put the shared-state concepts from chapter 6 into action and decide which components will manage which state as we let users view bookings for different bookables and different weeks.

Figure 7.4 shows the layout of the Bookings page, with the list of bookables on the left and the bookings info taking up the rest of the page. We have a `BookingsPage` component for the page itself, a `BookablesList` component for the list on the left, and a `Bookings` component for the rest of the page. The bookings info includes a week picker, an area to display a bookings grid, and an area to display the details of a selected booking.

**Figure 7.4  The Bookings page includes two components: one for the list of bookables, and one containing the week picker, bookings grid, and booking details.**

Figure 7.4 has placeholders for the bookings grid and the booking details. We'll bring the bookings grid to life and incorporate the `useMemo` hook in section 7.4. We'll populate the booking details and introduce the `useContext` hook in chapter 8. In this section, we put the pieces into place on the page.

This book uses the bookings app to teach you about React Hooks. To save you time and effort, I'm focusing more on teaching hooks than I am on teaching you how to code the bookings app, which could get very repetitive and wouldn't benefit learning React. So, sometimes, the book sets challenges and points you to the example's GitHub repo to get the latest code for certain components. With the Bookings page, the example app is edging into complexity, so a few more cases of changes in the repo are not fully listed in the book; I'll make it clear when you need to check the repo.

Table 7.1 lists the components in play for the Bookings page, along with their main function and the shared state they manage. In chapter 8, we'll use the `useContext` hook to access the current user from the `BookingDetails` component; although we don't work with the `App` component in this chapter, it's included in the table so you can see the full hierarchy of components.

Table 7.1  Components for the Bookings page

| Component | Role | Managed state | Hook |
|---|---|---|---|
| App | Render header with links to pages. Render user picker. Use routes to render correct page. | Current user | useState + Context API—see chapter 8 |
| BookingsPage | Render `BookablesList` and `Bookings` components. | Selected bookable | useState |
| BookablesList | Render list of bookables and let users select a bookable. | | |
| Bookings | Render `WeekPicker`, `Bookings-Grid`, and `BookingDetails` components. | Selected week and selected booking | useReducer and useState |
| WeekPicker | Let users switch between weeks to view. | | |
| BookingsGrid | Display a grid of booking slots for the selected bookable and week. Populate the grid with any existing bookings. Highlight the selected booking. | | |
| BookingDetails | Display details of the selected booking. | | |

We'll work from the `BookingsPage` down; the listings should give you a good sense of the structure of the page and of the flow of state through the hierarchy of components. The discussion is split into two subsections, using the shared state as the focus:

- Managing the selected bookable with `useState`
- Managing the selected week and booking with `useReducer` and `useState`

All the pieces shown in table 7.1 will need to be in position before the app returns to a working state, but the listings aren't long, so we'll get there soon.

### 7.3.1 *Managing the selected bookable with useState*

Our first piece of shared state is the selected bookable. It's used by the `BookablesList` and `Bookings` components. (Remember, the `Bookings` component is the container for the `WeekPicker`, `BookingsGrid`, and `BookingDetails` components.) Their nearest shared parent is the Bookings page itself.

Listing 7.4 shows the `BookingsPage` component calling `useState` to manage the selected bookable. `BookingsPage` also passes the updater function, `setBookable`, to `BookablesList` so that users can choose a bookable from the list. It no longer directly imports `WeekPicker`.

*Branch*: 0701-bookings-page, *File*: src/components/Bookings/BookingsPage.js

**Listing 7.4  The `BookingsPage` component**

```
import {useState} from "react";
import BookablesList from "../Bookables/BookablesList";
import Bookings from "./Bookings";

export default function BookingsPage () {              ⟵ Manage the selected
  const [bookable, setBookable] = useState(null);        bookable with the
                                                         useState hook.
  return (
    <main className="bookings-page">
      <BookablesList
        bookable={bookable}                           ⟵ Pass the bookable
        setBookable={setBookable}                        down so it can be
      />                                                 highlighted in the list.
      <Bookings                                        ⟵ Pass the updater function so
        bookable={bookable}                              users can select a bookable.
      />
    </main>                                           ⟵ Let the Bookings component
  );                                                     display the bookings for the
}                                                        selected bookable.
```

The page passes the selected bookable to the `Bookings` component (created next) so that it can show the bookable's bookings. To show the correct bookings (and to let users make new bookings), the `Bookings` component also needs to know the selected week. Let's see how it manages that state itself.

### 7.3.2 *Managing the selected week and booking with useReducer and useState*

Users can switch weeks by using the week picker. They can navigate forward a week or back a week and jump straight to the week containing today's date. They can also enter a date into a text box and go to the week for that date. To share the selected date with the bookings grid, we lift the week picker's reducer up into the `Bookings` component, as shown in the following listing.

---

*Branch*: 0701-bookings-page, *File*: src/components/Bookings/Bookings.js

**Listing 7.5   The `Bookings` component**

```
import {useState, useReducer} from "react";
import {getWeek} from "../../utils/date-wrangler";

import WeekPicker from "./WeekPicker";
import BookingsGrid from "./BookingsGrid";
import BookingDetails from "./BookingDetails";

import weekReducer from "./weekReducer";          ◁──── Import the existing
                                                         reducer for the
                                                         week picker.

export default function Bookings ({bookable}) {     ◁──── Destructure the current
                                                          bookable from props.

  const [week, dispatch] = useReducer(        ◁────
    weekReducer, new Date(), getWeek           Manage the shared state
  );                                           for the selected week.

  const [booking, setBooking] = useState(null);   ◁──── Manage the shared state for
                                                         the selected booking.

  return (
    <div className="bookings">
      <div>
        <WeekPicker
          dispatch={dispatch}
        />

        <BookingsGrid
          week={week}
          bookable={bookable}
          booking={booking}
          setBooking={setBooking}
        />
      </div>

      <BookingDetails
        booking={booking}
        bookable={bookable}
      />
    </div>
  );
}
```

The `Bookings` component imports the reducer and passes it in when calling the `useReducer` hook. It also calls the `useState` hook to manage the shared selected booking state for both the `BookingsGrid` and `BookingDetails` components.

### CHALLENGE 7.1

Update the `WeekPicker` component so that it receives `dispatch` as a prop, no longer calling `useReducer` itself. It doesn't need to display the selected date, so remove that from the end of its returned UI, and remove any redundant imports. Check the repo for the latest version (src/components/Bookings/WeekPicker.js).

In section 7.4, we build up the bookings grid to show actual bookings. For the current repo branch, let's just add a couple of placeholder components to check that the page structure is working nicely. The following listing shows our temporary bookings grid.

**Branch**: 0701-bookings-page, *File*: src/components/Bookings/BookingsGrid.js

**Listing 7.6    The** `BookingsGrid` **placeholder**

```
export default function BookingsGrid (props) {
  const {week, bookable, booking, setBooking} = props;

  return (
    <div className="bookings-grid placeholder">
      <h3>Bookings Grid</h3>
      <p>{bookable?.title}</p>
      <p>{week.date.toISOString()}</p>
    </div>
  );
}
```

The following listing shows our temporary details component.

**Branch**: 0701-bookings-page, *File*: src/components/Bookings/BookingDetails.js

**Listing 7.7    The** `BookingDetails` **placeholder**

```
export default function BookingDetails () {
  return (
    <div className="booking-details placeholder">
      <h3>Booking Details</h3>
    </div>
  );
}
```

Everything should now be in place, and the app should be back in working order. The Bookings page should look like figure 7.4 (if you have the latest CSS, or roll your own for the placeholders).

### CHALLENGE 7.2

Make a small change to `BookablesList`, removing the code for moving focus to the Next button. This will just slim down the component for future changes. The updates are on the current branch: /src/components/Bookables/BookablesList.js.

With all the components in place and a sense of where the page manages each piece of shared state, it's time to introduce a new React Hook to the bookings app. The `useMemo` hook will help us run expensive calculations only when necessary. Let's see why we need it and how it helps.

## 7.4    *Efficiently building the bookings grid with useMemo*

With the Bookings page structure and hierarchy in place, we're ready to build up our most complicated component yet, the `BookingsGrid`. In this section, we develop the grid so that it can display booking slots for a bookable in a given week and place any existing bookings in the grid. Figure 7.5 shows the grid with three rows for sessions and five columns for dates. Four existing bookings are in the grid, and the user has selected one of the bookings.

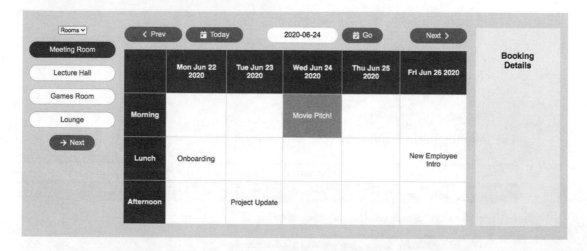

**Figure 7.5**  **The bookings grid showing bookings for the selected bookable and week. A booking in the grid has been selected.**

We develop the component in five stages:

1  Generating a grid of sessions and dates—we want to transform our data to make looking up empty booking slots easier.
2  Generating a lookup for bookings—we want to transform our data to make looking up existing bookings easier.
3  Providing a `getBookings` data-loading function—it will handle building the query strings for our request to the JSON server.
4  Creating the `BookingsGrid` component—this is the meat of the section and is where we enlist the help of `useMemo`.
5  Coping with racing responses when fetching data in `useEffect`.

In stage 5, we see how to manage multiple requests and responses for data within calls to the `useEffect` hook, with later requests superseding earlier ones, and how to manage errors. There's a lot to sink our teeth into, so let's get started by transforming lists of days and sessions into two-dimensional booking grids.

### 7.4.1   Generating a grid of sessions and dates

The bookings grid displays empty booking slots and existing bookings in a table, with sessions as rows and dates as columns. An example grid of booking slots for the Meeting Room bookable is shown in figure 7.6.

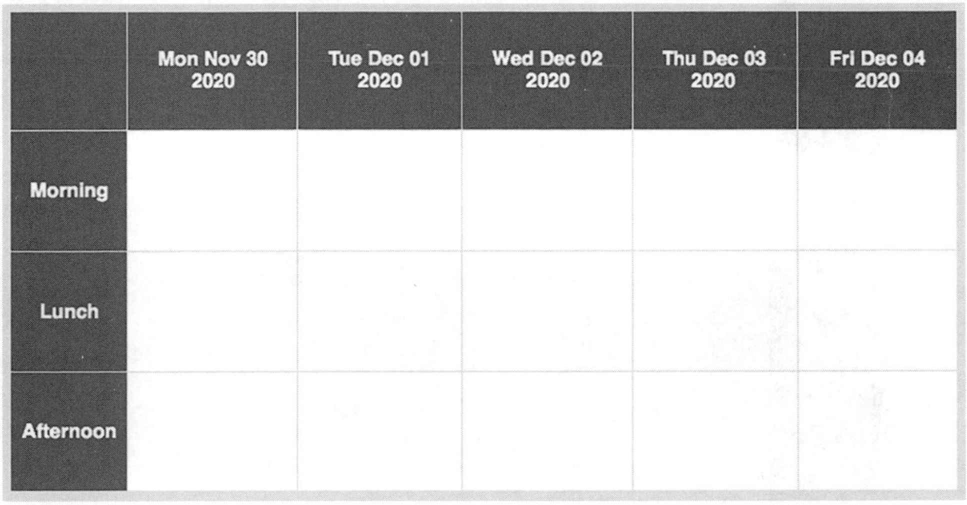

| | Mon Nov 30 2020 | Tue Dec 01 2020 | Wed Dec 02 2020 | Thu Dec 03 2020 | Fri Dec 04 2020 |
|---|---|---|---|---|---|
| Morning | | | | | |
| Lunch | | | | | |
| Afternoon | | | | | |

Figure 7.6   The bookings grid for the Meeting Room bookable. It has rows for each session and columns for each date.

Users book different bookables for different sessions and days of the week. When the user chooses a new bookable, the `BookingsGrid` component needs to generate a new grid, for the latest sessions and dates. Figure 7.7 shows the grid generated when the user switches to the Lounge bookable.

Each cell in the grid corresponds to a booking slot. We want the grid data to be structured so that it's easy to access the data for a specific booking slot. For example, to access the data for the Breakfast session on August 3, 2020, we use this:

```
grid["Breakfast"]["2020-08-03"]
```

For an empty booking slot, the booking data looks like this:

```
{
  "session": "Breakfast",
  "date": "2020-08-03",
  "bookableId": 4,
  "title": ""
}
```

**Figure 7.7   The bookings grid for the Lounge bookable. The Lounge is available for five sessions on every day of the week.**

In the data from the database, each bookable specifies the sessions and days for which it can be booked. Here's the data for the Meeting Room:

```
"id": 1,
"group": "Rooms",
"title": "Meeting Room",
"notes": "The one with the big table and interactive screen.",
"sessions": [1, 2, 3],
"days": [1, 2, 3, 4, 5]
```

The days represent days in the week, where Sunday = 0, Monday = 1, . . . , Saturday = 6. So, the Meeting Room can be booked for sessions 1, 2, and 3, Monday through Friday, as we saw in figure 7.6. To get the specific dates for the bookings, rather than just the day numbers, we also need the start date for the week we want to display. And to get the specific session names, we need to import the array of session names from the config file, static.json.

The grid generator function, getGrid, is in the following listing. The calling code passes getGrid the current bookable and the start date for the selected week.

Branch: **0702-bookings-memo**, *File*: /src/components/Bookings/grid-builder.js

Listing 7.8  The grid generator

**Use the session names and numbers
to create an array of session names.**

**Assign the session names to
the sessionNames variable.**

```
import {sessions as sessionNames} from "../../static.json";
import {addDays, shortISO} from "../../utils/date-wrangler";

export function getGrid (bookable, startDate) {
```
**Accept the current bookable and
week start date as arguments.**

```
  const dates = bookable.days.sort().map(
    d => shortISO(addDays(startDate, d))
  );
```
**Use the day numbers and
start date to create an array
of dates for the week.**

```
  const sessions = bookable.sessions.map(i => sessionNames[i]);

  const grid = {};

  sessions.forEach(session => {
    grid[session] = {};
```
**Assign an object to grid
for each session.**

```
    dates.forEach(date => grid[session][date] = {
      session,
      date,
      bookableId: bookable.id,
      title: ""
    });
  });
```
**Assign a booking
object for each date
to each session.**

```
  return {
    grid,
    dates,
    sessions
  };
}
```
**In addition to the grid,
return the dates and
sessions arrays for
convenience.**

The getGrid function starts by mapping the day and session indexes to dates and session names. It uses a truncated ISO 8601 format for dates:

```
const dates = bookable.days.sort().map(
  d => shortISO(addDays(startDate, d))
);
```

The shortISO function has been added to the utils/date-wrangler.js file that also contains the addDays function. shortISO returns the date part of the ISO-string for a given date:

```
export function shortISO (date) {
  return date.toISOString().split("T")[0];
}
```

For example, for a JavaScript date object representing August 3, 2020, shortISO returns the string "2020-08-03".

The code in the listing also imports the session names from static.json and assigns them to the `sessionNames` variable. The session data looks like this:

```
"sessions": [
  "Breakfast",
  "Morning",
  "Lunch",
  "Afternoon",
  "Evening"
]
```

Each session index from the bookable is mapped to its session name:

```
const sessions = bookable.sessions.map(i => sessionNames[i]);
```

So, if the selected bookable is the Meeting Room, then `bookable.sessions` is the array [1, 2, 3] and `sessions` becomes ["Morning", "Lunch", "Afternoon"].

Having acquired the dates and session names, `getGrid` then uses nested `forEach` loops to build up the grid of booking sessions. You could use the `reduce` array method here, but I find the `forEach` syntax easier to follow in this case. (Don't worry, `reduce` fans; the next listing employs its services.)

### 7.4.2   *Generating a lookup for bookings*

We also want an easy way to look up existing bookings. Figure 7.8 shows a bookings grid with existing bookings in four cells.

| | Mon Jun 22 2020 | Tue Jun 23 2020 | Wed Jun 24 2020 | Thu Jun 25 2020 | Fri Jun 26 2020 |
|---|---|---|---|---|---|
| **Morning** | | | Movie Pitch! | | |
| **Lunch** | Onboarding | | | | New Employee Intro |
| **Afternoon** | | Project Update | | | |

Figure 7.8   **The bookings grid with existing bookings in four cells**

We want to use the session name and date to access the data for an existing booking, like this:

```
bookings["Morning"]["2020-06-24"]
```

The lookup expression should return the data for the Movie Pitch! booking, with this structure:

```
{
  "id": 1,
  "session": "Morning",
  "date": "2020-06-24",
  "title": "Movie Pitch!",
  "bookableId": 1,
  "bookerId": 2
}
```

But the server returns the bookings data as an array. We need to transform the array of bookings into the handy lookup object. Listing 7.9 adds a new function, `transform-Bookings`, to the grid-builder.js file from listing 7.8.

Branch: **0702-bookings-memo**, *File:* **/src/components/Bookings/grid-builder.js**

Listing 7.9  The `transformBookings` function

```
export function transformBookings (bookingsArray) {        Use reduce to step
                                                           through each booking
  return bookingsArray.reduce((bookings, booking) => {     and build up the
                                                           bookings lookup.
    const {session, date} = booking;                       Destructure the session and
                                                           date for the current booking.
    if (!bookings[session]) {
      bookings[session] = {};          Add a property to the lookup
    }                                  for each new session.

    bookings[session][date] = booking;      Assign the booking to
                                            its session and date.
    return bookings;
  }, {});          Start the bookings lookup
}                  as an empty object.
```

The `transformBookings` function uses the `reduce` method to step through each booking in the array and build up the `bookings` lookup object, assigning the current booking to its allotted lookup slot. The lookup object that `transformBookings` creates has entries for only the existing bookings, not necessarily for every cell in the bookings grid.

We now have functions to generate the grid and transform an array of bookings into a lookup object. But where are the bookings?

### 7.4.3   *Providing a getBookings data-loading function*

The BookingsGrid component needs some bookings to display for the selected bookable and week. We could use our existing getData function from within an effect in the BookingsGrid component, building up the necessary URL there. Instead, let's keep our data-access functions in the api.js file. The following listing shows the part of the updated file with our new getBookings function.

---

> **Branch**: 0702-bookings-memo, *File*: /src/utils/api.js
>
> **Listing 7.10   The `getBookings` API function**

```
import {shortISO} from "./date-wrangler";        ⟵──── Import a function to format dates.

export function getBookings (bookableId, startDate, endDate) {    ⟵┐ Export the new
                                                                   │ getBookings
  const start = shortISO(startDate);        Format the dates for    │ function.
  const end = shortISO(endDate);            the query string.

  const urlRoot = "http://localhost:3001/bookings";

  const query = `bookableId=${bookableId}` +        Build up the
    `&date_gte=${start}&date_lte=${end}`;           query string.

  return getData(`${urlRoot}?${query}`);        ⟵── Fetch the bookings,
}                                                    returning a promise.
```

The getBookings function accepts three arguments: bookableId, startDate, and endDate. It uses the arguments to build up the query string for the required bookings. For example, to fetch the bookings for the Meeting Room between Sunday, June 21, 2020, and Saturday, June 27, 2020, the query string is as follows:

```
bookableId=1&date_gte=2020-06-21&date_lte=2020-06-27
```

The json-server we have running will parse the query string and return the requested bookings as an array, ready for transformation into a lookup object.

With the helper functions in place, it's time to put them to good use as we construct the BookingsGrid component.

### 7.4.4   *Creating the BookingsGrid component and calling useMemo*

For a given bookable and week, the BookingsGrid component fetches the bookings and displays them, highlighting any selected booking. It uses three React Hooks: useState, useEffect, and useMemo. We break the code for the component across a number of listings, in this subsection and the next, starting with the imports and component skeleton in the following listing.

---

*Branch*: 0702-bookings-memo, *File*: /src/components/Bookings/BookingsGrid.js

Listing 7.11   The `BookingsGrid` component: Skeleton

```
import {useEffect, useMemo, useState, Fragment} from "react";     ◁ ─┐  Import useMemo to
                                                                       memoize the grid.
import {getGrid, transformBookings} from "./grid-builder";     ◁
                                                                   Import the new
import {getBookings} from "../../utils/api";    ◁ ─┐            grid functions.
                                                    Import a new
import Spinner from "../UI/Spinner";                data-loading
                                                    function.
export default function BookingsGrid () {

    // 1. Variables
    // 2. Effects
    // 3. UI helper
    // 4. UI


}
```

The code imports the helper functions created previously and the three hooks. As you'll see over the next few listings, we use the `useState` hook to manage the state for the bookings and any errors, the `useEffect` hook to fetch the bookings data from the server, and the `useMemo` hook to reduce the number of times we generate the grid data.

#### VARIABLES

The `Bookings` component passes the `BookingsGrid` component the selected bookable, the selected week, and the currently selected booking along with its updater function, as highlighted in the following listing.

---

*Branch*: 0702-bookings-memo, *File*: /src/components/Bookings/BookingsGrid.js

Listing 7.12   The `BookingsGrid` component: 1. Variables

```
export default function BookingsGrid (         ┐ Destructure
    {week, bookable, booking, setBooking}    ◁ ┘ the props.
) {
    const [bookings, setBookings] = useState(null);    ◁ ─┐ Handle the bookings
                                                             data locally.
    const [error, setError] = useState(false);    ◁ ─┐ Handle loading errors locally.

    const {grid, sessions, dates} = useMemo(    ◁ ────────┐  Wrap the grid generator
                                                             function with useMemo.

        () => bookable ? getGrid(bookable, week.start) : {},    ◁
                                                                   Call the grid generator
                                                                   only if there's a
        [bookable, week.start]    ◁ ─┐                            bookable.
    );                               Regenerate the grid
                                     when the bookable
    // 2. Effects                    or week changes.
    // 3. UI helper
    // 4. UI
}
```

BookingsGrid handles the bookings and error state itself with two calls to the use-State hook. It then uses the getGrid function from section 7.4.2 to generate the grid, assigning the returned grid, sessions, and dates data to local variables. We've decided to see getGrid as an expensive function, wrapping it with useMemo. Why might it warrant such treatment?

When the user chooses a bookable on the Bookings page, the Bookings component displays a grid of booking slots for the bookable's available sessions and dates. It generates the data for the grid based on the bookable's properties and the selected week. As we'll see in the next listing, the BookingsGrid component uses the fetch-on-render, data-loading strategy, sending a request for data after the initial render. The grid, shown in figure 7.9, displays a loading indicator in the top-left cell and reduces the opacity of the body cells until the data arrives.

| ⠿ | Mon Jun 22 2020 | Tue Jun 23 2020 | Wed Jun 24 2020 | Thu Jun 25 2020 | Fri Jun 26 2020 |
|---|---|---|---|---|---|
| Morning | | | | | |
| Lunch | | | | | |
| Afternoon | | | | | |

**Figure 7.9  The BookingsGrid component displays a loading spinner in its top-left cell and reduces the opacity of the grid cells while a fetch is in progress.**

When the data arrives, the grid re-renders, hiding the loading indicator and showing the bookings for the selected week. Figure 7.10 shows four bookings in the grid.

With the bookings in place, the user is now free to select an existing booking or an empty booking slot. In figure 7.11, the user has selected the Movie Pitch! booking and, yet again, the component has re-rendered, highlighting the cell.

The component renders for each change in status, as listed in table 7.2, although the underlying grid data for the booking slots hasn't changed.

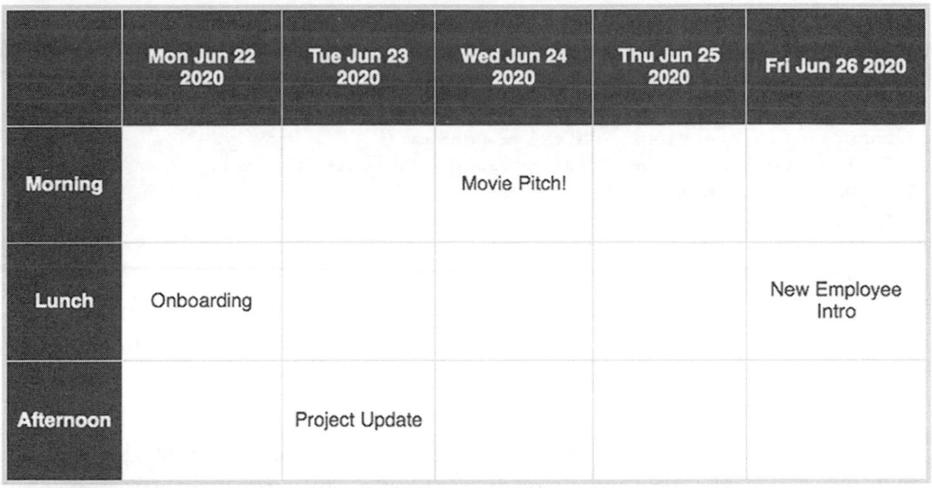

| | Mon Jun 22 2020 | Tue Jun 23 2020 | Wed Jun 24 2020 | Thu Jun 25 2020 | Fri Jun 26 2020 |
|---|---|---|---|---|---|
| **Morning** | | | Movie Pitch! | | |
| **Lunch** | Onboarding | | | | New Employee Intro |
| **Afternoon** | | Project Update | | | |

Figure 7.10   The bookings grid showing four bookings

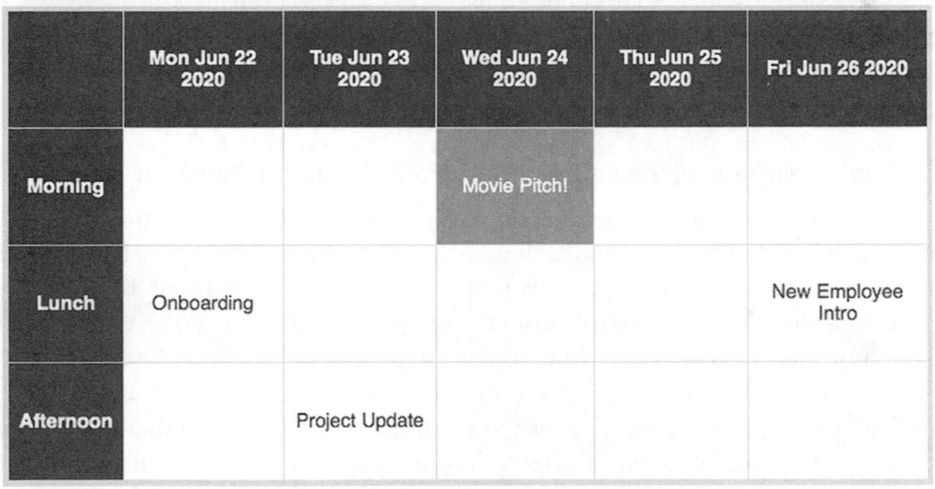

| | Mon Jun 22 2020 | Tue Jun 23 2020 | Wed Jun 24 2020 | Thu Jun 25 2020 | Fri Jun 26 2020 |
|---|---|---|---|---|---|
| **Morning** | | | Movie Pitch! | | |
| **Lunch** | Onboarding | | | | New Employee Intro |
| **Afternoon** | | Project Update | | | |

Figure 7.11   The bookings grid showing a selected booking

Table 7.2   Bookings grid rendering behavior for different events

| Event | Render with |
|---|---|
| Initial render | Blank grid |
| Data fetching | Loading indicator |
| Data loaded | Bookings in cells |
| Booking selected | Highlighted selection |

For the events listed, we don't want to regenerate the underlying grid data on each re-render, so we use the useMemo hook, specifying the bookable and start date for the week as dependencies:

```
const {grid, sessions, dates} = useMemo(
  () => bookable ? getGrid(bookable, week.start) : {},
  [bookable, week.start]
);
```

By wrapping getGrid in useMemo, we ask React to store the generated grid lookup and to call getGrid again only if the bookable or start date changes. For the three re-rendering scenarios in table 7.2 (not for the initial render), React should return the stored grid, avoiding unnecessary computation.

In reality, for the size of grids we're generating, we don't really need useMemo. Modern browsers, JavaScript, and React will hardly notice the work required. There's also some overhead in requiring React to store functions, return values, and dependency values, so we don't want to memoize everything. As we saw with the anagrams example earlier in the chapter, however, sometimes expensive functions can adversely affect performance, so it's good to have the useMemo hook in your toolbelt.

Although the main focus of this chapter is the useMemo hook, a useful technique for data-fetching within a call to useEffect is worth flagging with a subsection heading. Let's see how to avoid getting multiple requests and responses knotted.

### 7.4.5   *Coping with racing responses when fetching data in useEffect*

When interacting with the bookings app, the user might get a little click-happy and switch quickly between bookables and weeks, initiating a flurry of data requests. We want to display the data for only their last selection. Unfortunately, we're not in control of when the data returns from the server, and an older request might resolve after a more recent one, leaving the display out of sync with the user's selection.

We could try to implement a way to cancel in-flight requests. If the data response isn't too large, however, it's easier to simply let the requests run their course and ignore the unwanted data when it arrives. In this subsection, we finish off the BookingsGrid component, fetching the bookings data, and building the UI for display.

#### EFFECTS

The BookingsGrid component loads the bookings for the selected bookable and week. Listing 7.13 shows calls to our helper functions, getBookings and transform-Bookings, wrapped inside a call to useEffect. The effect runs whenever the week or bookable changes.

> *Branch:* 0702-bookings-memo, *File:* /src/components/Bookings/BookingsGrid.js
>
> **Listing 7.13   The BookingsGrid component: 2. Effects**

```
export default function BookingsGrid (
  {week, bookable, booking, setBooking}
```

```
) {
  // 1. Variables

  useEffect(() => {                          Use a variable to track
    if (bookable) {                          whether the bookings
      let doUpdate = true;          ◁───     data is current.

      setBookings(null);                              Call our
      setError(false);                                getBookings
      setBooking(null);                               data-fetching
                                             ◁──┘     function.
      getBookings(bookable.id, week.start, week.end)  ◁─┘
        .then(resp => {                      ◁─────┐ Check if the bookings
          if (doUpdate) {                    ◁───┐ │ data is current.
            setBookings(transformBookings(resp));  │
          }                                      Create a bookings lookup
        })                                       and assign it to state.
        .catch(setError);

      return () => doUpdate = false;   ◁──────┐ Return a cleanup function
    }                                         │ to invalidate the data.
  }, [week, bookable, setBooking]);    ◁──┐
                                          Run the effect when
  // 3. UI helper                         the bookable or
  // 4. UI                                week changes.
}
```

The code uses a doUpdate variable to match each request with its data. The variable is initially set to true:

```
let doUpdate = true;
```

For a particular request, the callback function in the then clause will update the state only if doUpdate is still true:

```
if (doUpdate) {
  setBookings(transformBookings(resp));
}
```

When the user selects a new bookable or switches to a new week, React reruns the component, and the effect runs again to load the newly selected data. The in-flight data from the previous request is no longer needed. Before rerunning an effect, React calls any associated cleanup function for the previous invocation of the effect. Our effect uses the cleanup function to invalidate the in-flight data:

```
return () => doUpdate = false;
```

When the previously requested bookings arrive, the then clause from the associated call to getBookings will see the data is stale and won't update the state.

If the bookings are current, the then clause transforms the linear array of bookings into a lookup structure by passing the response to the transformBookings function. The lookup object is assigned to local state with setBookings.

**UI HELPER FUNCTION**

The contents and behavior of a cell in the bookings grid depend on whether there are any bookings to display and whether the user has selected the cell. Figure 7.12 shows a couple of empty cells and a cell for an existing booking, Movie Pitch!

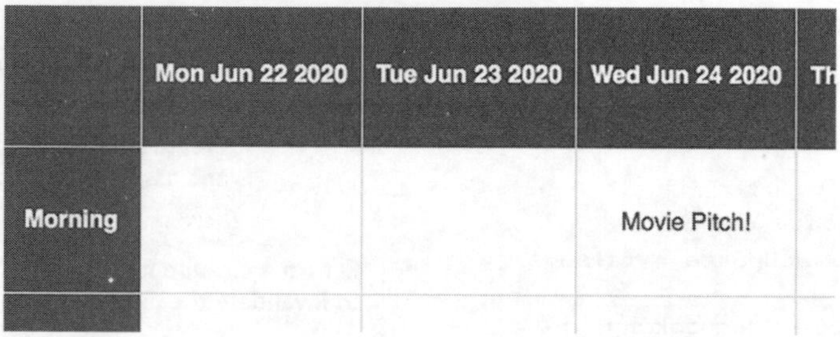

**Figure 7.12    Cells in the grid represent existing bookings where they exist, or just the underlying grid data for session and date.**

When a user selects a cell, that cell should be highlighted, whether the cell shows an existing booking or an empty booking slot. Figure 7.13 shows the grid after the user has selected the Movie Pitch! booking. CSS styles and the cell's class attribute are used to change the cell's appearance.

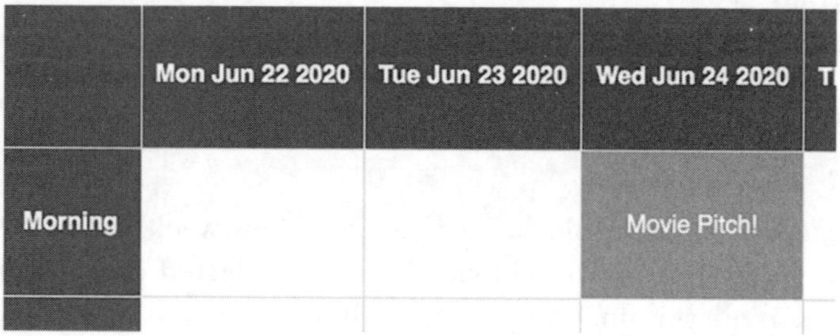

**Figure 7.13    The selected cell is displayed using different CSS styles.**

Listing 7.14 has the code for a cell helper function that returns the UI for a single cell in the bookings grid. It uses the two lookup objects, bookings and grid, to get the data for the cell, set the cell's class, and attach an event handler if there are bookings. The `cell` function is in the scope of `BookingsGrid` and can access the booking, bookings, grid, and `setBookings` variables.

> **Branch: 0702-bookings-memo,** *File:* **/src/components/Bookings/BookingsGrid.js**
>
> **Listing 7.14** The `BookingsGrid` component: 3. UI helper

```
export default function BookingsGrid (
  {week, bookable, booking, setBooking}
) {
  // 1. Variables
  // 2. Effects

  function cell (session, date) {
    const cellData = bookings?.[session]?.[date]      First check the bookings
      || grid[session][date];                          lookup, then the grid lookup.

    const isSelected = booking?.session === session    Use optional chaining because
      && booking?.date === date;                       there might not be a booking.

    return (
      <td
        key={date}
        className={isSelected ? "selected" : null}
        onClick={bookings ? () => setBooking(cellData) : null}  ◁──  Set a handler
      >                                                                only if bookings
        {cellData.title}                                             have been
      </td>                                                          loaded.
    );
  }

  // 4. UI
}
```

The data for a cell comes either from the existing bookings in the `bookings` lookup or from the empty booking slot data in the `grid` lookup. The code uses optional chaining syntax with square-bracket notation to assign the correct value to the `cellData` variable:

```
const cellData = bookings?.[session]?.[date] || grid[session][date];
```

The `bookings` lookup has data for only the existing bookings, but the `grid` lookup has data for every session and date. We need the optional chaining for `bookings` but not for `grid`.

We set the click handler on the cell only if there are bookings. While bookings are loading, when a user switches bookables or weeks, the handler is set to `null` and the user can't interact with the grid.

### UI

The final piece of the `BookingsGrid` puzzle returns the UI. As ever, the UI is driven by the state. We check whether the grid of booking slots has been generated, whether the

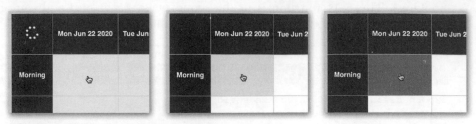

1. **When the grid is not active, the user can't select a cell.**   2. **When the grid is active, the user can select a cell.**   3. **When a cell is selected, it is highlighted.**

**Figure 7.14   The display of a cell depends on whether the grid is active and whether a cell has been selected. While bookings are loading, the UI shows the loading indicator, and the grid is not active.**

bookings have been loaded, and whether there is an error. We then return either alternative UI (loading text) or additional UI (an error message), or we set class names to show, hide, or highlight elements. Figure 7.14 shows the bookings grid for three states:

1 There are no bookings. The grid shows a loading indicator. The grid is inactive, and the user can't interact with the grid.
2 The bookings have loaded. The grid hides the loading indicator. The grid is active, and the user can interact with the grid.
3 The bookings have loaded. The grid hides the loading indicator. The grid is active, and the user has selected a cell.

In figure 7.15, you can see an error displayed right above the date headings for the grid.

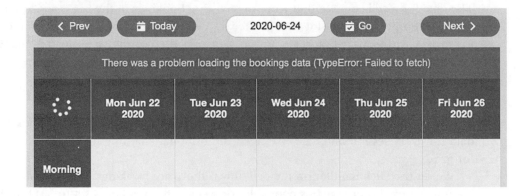

**Figure 7.15   The `BookingsGrid` component displays any errors above the grid.**

The following listing shows the error section, uses class names to control whether the grid is active, and calls our UI helper function, `cell`, to get the UI for each table cell.

Branch: **0702-bookings-memo**, *File:* /src/components/Bookings/BookingsGrid.js

Listing 7.15   The `BookingsGrid` component: 4. UI

```
export default function BookingsGrid (
  {week, bookable, booking, handleBooking}
) {
  // 1. Variables
  // 2. Effects
  // 3. UI helper

  if (!grid) {
    return <p>Loading...</p>
  }

  return (
    <Fragment>
      {error && (
        <p className="bookingsError">
          {`There was a problem loading the bookings data (${error})`}
        </p>
      )}

      <table
        className={bookings ? "bookingsGrid active" : "bookingsGrid"}
      >
        <thead>
        <tr>
          <th>
            <span className="status">
              <Spinner/>
            </span>
          </th>
          {dates.map(d => (
            <th key={d}>
              {(new Date(d)).toDateString()}
            </th>
          ))}
        </tr>
        </thead>

        <tbody>
        {sessions.map(session => (
          <tr key={session}>
            <th>{session}</th>
            {dates.map(date => cell(session, date))}
          </tr>
        ))}
        </tbody>
      </table>
    </Fragment>
  );
}
```

**Show an error section at the top of the grid if there's an error.**

**Include an "active" class when the bookings data has loaded.**

**Include a loading indicator in the top-left cell.**

**Use the UI helper function to generate each table cell.**

If `bookings` is not `null`, a class of `active` is assigned to the table. The CSS for the app hides the loading indicator and sets the cell opacity to 1 when the grid is active.

In the code, we inspect the state ourselves and decide what UI to return from within the component. It's also possible to use React *error boundaries* to specify error UI and React's `Suspense` component to specify fallback UI while data is loading, separately from individual components. We use error boundaries to catch errors and `Suspense` components to catch promises (loading data) in part 2.

Before that, we need to create our `BookingDetails` component to show the details of whichever booking slot or existing booking a user clicks. The new component needs access to the current user of the app, stored all the way up in the root component, `App`. Rather than drilling the user value down through multiple layers of component props, we'll enlist the help of React's Context API and the `useContext` hook.

## Summary

- Try to avoid unnecessarily rerunning expensive computations by wrapping them in the `useMemo` hook.

- Pass `useMemo` the expensive function you want to memoize:

```
const value = useMemo(
  () => expensiveFn(dep1, dep2),
  [dep1, dep2]
);
```

- Pass the `useMemo` hook a list of dependencies for the expensive function:

```
const value = useMemo(
  () => expensiveFn(dep1, dep2),
  [dep1, dep2]
);
```

- If the values in the dependency array don't change from one call to the next, `useMemo` can return its stored result for the expensive function.

- Don't rely on `useMemo` to always use a memoized value. React may discard stored results if it needs to free up memory.

- Use JavaScript's optional chaining syntax with square brackets to access properties of variables that may be `undefined`. Include a period, even when working with square brackets:

```
const cellData = bookings?.[session]?.[date]
```

- When fetching data within a call to `useEffect`, combine a local variable and the cleanup function to match a data request with its response:

```
useEffect(() => {
  let doUpdate = true;
```

```
fetch(url).then(resp => {
  if (doUpdate) {
    // perform update with resp
  }
});

return () => doUpdate = false;
}, [url]);
```

If the component re-renders with a new `url`, the cleanup function for the previous render will set the previous render's `doUpdate` variable to `false`, preventing the previous `then` method callback from performing updates with stale data.

# Managing state with the Context API

8

## This chapter covers

- Providing state via the Context API and its `Provider` component
- Consuming context state with the `useContext` hook
- Avoiding unnecessary re-renders when updating state values
- Creating custom context providers
- Splitting shared state across multiple contexts

We've seen state encapsulated within components, lifted to shared parents, in form fields, persisted across renders, and pulled in from a database, and we've used a whole bunch of hooks to help us set up and work with that state. Our approach has been to keep the state as close to the components that use it as possible. But it's not uncommon for many components, nested on multiple branches, to hunger for the same juicy worms, the same tidbits of application state, like themes, localization info, or authenticated user details. Mmmmmmm, tidbits . . . React's Context API is a way of delivering juicy state tidbits directly to your nest without passing them down through multiple layers of intermediaries who, preferring tacos to tidbits, have no interest in them.

In this chapter, we introduce the Context API, its context objects, `Provider` components, and `useContext` hook. We focus on our bookings app example, where multiple components need the same juicy tidbit: details of the current user. That sets the scene for a rundown of the mechanics of the Context API and we see why, when, where, and how to provide values to whole subtrees of components, and how easy the `useContext` hook makes consuming those values. We finish by wrapping context functionality into our own custom contexts and provider components, and that discussion leads to a deeper understanding of React's rendering behavior, particularly when working with the special `children` prop.

Can you hear that? It's nested components chirping for tasty tidbits. It's feeding time!

## 8.1 Needing state from higher up the component tree

The Bookings page in our example app lets visitors select a bookable and week. The bookings grid on the page then shows the available booking slots and populates the appropriate cells with any existing bookings. Figure 8.1 shows the Bookings page after a visitor has selected the Meeting Room bookable and then the Movie Pitch! booking.

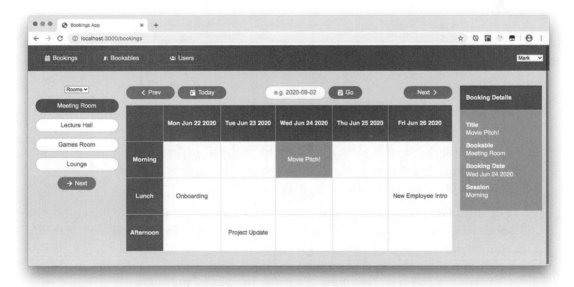

**Figure 8.1** After the user selects a booking, the booking details component (on the right) shows information about the selected booking.

In chapter 7, we worked with a placeholder for `BookingDetails`, the component that displays further information about the selected booking. Figure 8.1 also shows our aim for the `BookingDetails` component in this chapter: it lists a number of the selected booking's properties, such as Title and Booking Date. But when the page first loads, no booking is selected, and the component shows a message encouraging the visitor to select a booking or a booking slot, as you can see in figure 8.2.

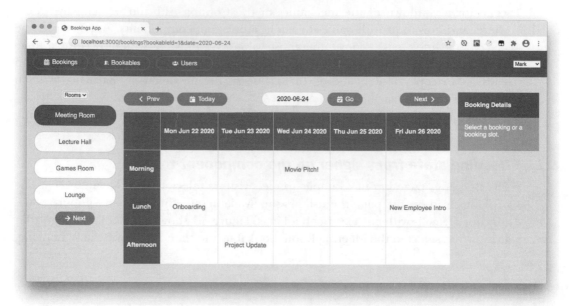

**Figure 8.2    Before the user selects a booking, the booking details component (on the right) shows the message "Select a booking or a booking slot."**

In this chapter, we relieve the `BookingDetails` component of its placeholder duties and promote it to perform these three tasks:

- Displaying a call-to-action message when the page first loads
- Displaying booking information when a visitor selects a booking
- Displaying an edit button for a user's bookings

The third task prompts our investigation of the Context API to make the current user value available to components across the app. Why does the `BookingDetails` component need to know the user? Let's find out.

### 8.1.1    *Displaying a call-to-action message when the page first loads*

When the Bookings page loads, but before a visitor selects a booking, the `Booking-Details` component will display a call-to-action message, shown in figure 8.3.

Listing 8.1 shows how the `BookingDetails` component checks for a booking and either returns UI for the call-to-action message or for an existing booking. The UI for an existing booking is handled by another component, `Booking`; we look at that in section 8.1.2.

Figure 8.3  When the page first loads, the
BookingDetails component shows a
"Select a booking or a booking slot"
message to the user.

---

Branch: **0801-booking-details**, *File:* /src/components/Bookings/BookingDetails.js

**Listing 8.1  The** BookingDetails **component shows a booking or a message**

```
import Booking from "./Booking";          ◁─┐  Import the Booking component.

export default function BookingDetails ({booking, bookable}) {   ◁─┐  Assign booking
  return (                                                          │  and bookable
    <div className="booking-details">                              │  props to local
      <h2>Booking Details</h2>                                     │  variables.

                                           Show the booking info only
                                           if a booking is selected.
      {booking ? (              ◁─────────┘
        <Booking               ◁───  Use the Booking component
          booking={booking}          to display the info.
          bookable={bookable}
        />
      ) : (
        <div className="booking-details-fields">
          <p>Select a booking or a booking slot.</p>   ◁─┐  If no booking is
        </div>                                              selected, show
      )}                                                    a message.
    </div>
  );
}
```

Listing 8.1 uses the JavaScript ternary operator ( a ? b : c ) to return the appropriate
UI, the booking, or the message:

```
{booking ? (
  // return booking UI if there's a booking
) : (
  // return message UI if there's not a booking
)}
```

In later chapters, we add the third UI possibility for a form with its input fields and
submit button. For now, it's an either/or situation: booking or message. Let's see the
code for the booking UI.

### 8.1.2    *Displaying booking information when a visitor selects a booking*

Once the user heeds the call and selects an existing booking, the component displays its information; details for the Movie Pitch! booking are shown in figure 8.4. (If you don't have any booking data, grab db.json from the repo. Get the latest App.css if you need that too.)

**Figure 8.4    The** `BookingDetails`
**component showing information about
the selected booking and bookable**

The information includes a number of fields from the booking and one from the bookable. The following listing shows the `Booking` component receiving the selected booking and bookable as props and returning the booking details as a sequence of labels and paragraphs.

**Branch**: 0801-booking-details, *File*: /src/components/Bookings/Booking.js

**Listing 8.2    The** `Booking` **component**

```
import {Fragment} from "react";

export default function Booking ({booking, bookable}) {      ◁── Assign booking and
                                                                 bookable props to
  const {title, date, session, notes} = booking;      ◁──     local variables.

  return (                                                   Assign booking
    <div className="booking-details-fields">                 properties to
      <label>Title</label>                                   local variables.
      <p>{title}</p>
                                                    Show information
      <label>Bookable</label>                       from the selected
      <p>{bookable.title}</p>              ◁──       bookable.
```

```
        <label>Booking Date</label>
        <p>{(new Date(date)).toDateString()}</p>          ◁─┐  Format the
                                                             │  date property
        <label>Session</label>                               │  nicely.
        <p>{session}</p>

        {notes && (                           ◁─┐  Show the Notes field
          <Fragment>                             │  only if the booking
            <label>Notes</label>                 │  has notes.
            <p>{notes}</p>                       │
          </Fragment>
        )}
      </div>
    )
}
```

The `BookingDetails` component now successfully switches between the call-to-action message when the user is yet to select a booking and the `Booking` component once they make their selection. That's two of the component's three tasks sorted. Good job! But the third task is trickier. What's the problem?

### 8.1.3 Displaying an edit button for a user's bookings: The problem

Our newly minted `BookingDetails` component successfully displays information about the selected bookable. That's great! But plans change, and meetings get cancelled or dates clash. A user should be able to edit their own bookings to update the details or delete them outright. We need to add a button, like the one next to the Booking Details heading on the right of figure 8.5, so the user can switch to editing a booking.

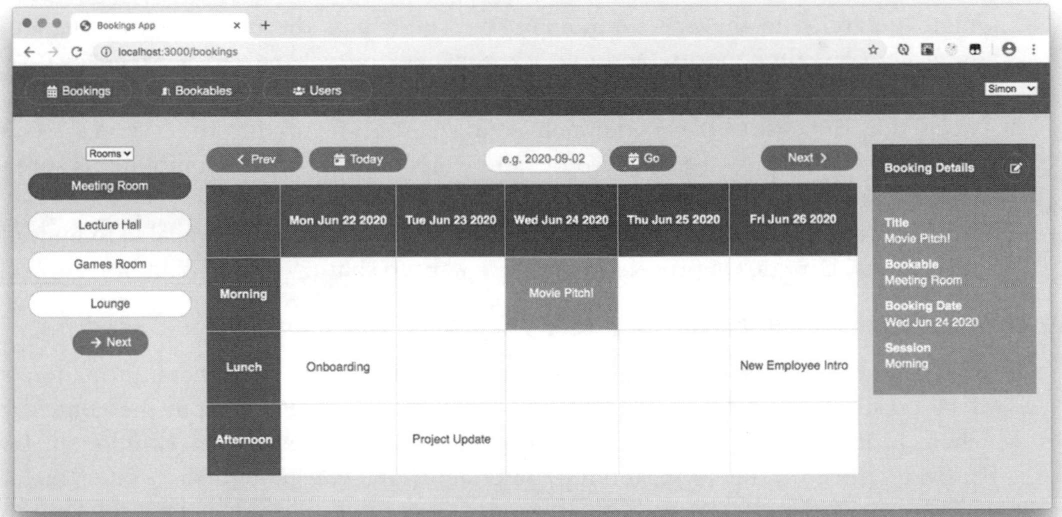

Figure 8.5  When a user selects one of their own bookings, the booking details component (on the right) displays an edit button with an edit icon to the right of the heading.

Figure 8.6 isolates the `BookingDetails` component and shows the edit button (a document-edit icon) on the right of the component's title. The problem is, we want to show the button only if the current user booked the selected booking themselves. For other users, the button should be hidden. The `BookingDetails` component needs to know the `id` of the current user so it can check it against the `bookerId` for the selected booking.

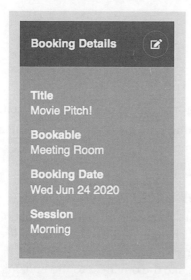

**Figure 8.6   The booking details component with the edit button showing on the right of the heading**

The state for the current user lives all the way up at the top of the application component hierarchy, in the `App` component. We could pass the user down through the intermediate components (`App` to `BookingsPage` to `Bookings` to `BookingDetails`), but the components on the way aren't interested in the user state, and it's also needed by the `UserPicker` component (and will soon be used by the `UsersPage` component too). In this case, a piece of state is needed by several components spread across the app.

The Context API offers an alternative way of making the state available to multiple consumers. How do we provide the state we want to share?

### 8.1.4   *Displaying an edit button for a user's bookings: The solution*

We want to share the current user with all components that need that information, so let's create a `UserContext` object with React's Context API. We put the context to share in its own file, /src/components/Users/UserContext.js. The component that provides the user value, `App`, and the components that consume the user value, including `BookingDetails`, can import the context to set or read its value. The code is in the following listing.

---

*Branch*: **0802-user-context**, *File*: **/src/components/Users/UserContext.js**

**Listing 8.3   Creating and exporting a context object for our user value**

```
import {createContext} from "react";

const UserContext = createContext();

export default UserContext;
```

Yes, that's it! We use the `createContext` method and assign the context object it returns to the `UserContext` variable. That context object, `UserContext`, is the key to sharing the current user value across the app: the `App` component will use it to set the value, and consuming components will use it, along with the `useContext` hook, to read the value.

To use the new context object to provide user state for the bookings app, we update the `App` component in three key ways:

1  Import the context object.
2  Manage state for the current user by calling the `useState` hook.
3  Use the context's `Provider` component to wrap the `Router` component.

The following listing shows the updates in place.

---

*Branch*: **0802-user-context**, *File*: **/src/components/App.js**

**Listing 8.4   Importing the context object and providing its value in `App`**

```
import {useState} from "react";          ⟵  Import the
                                             useState hook.
// unchanged imports

import UserContext from "./Users/UserContext";   ⟵  Import the context
                                                     to be shared.
export default function App () {
  const [user, setUser] = useState();     ⟵  Manage the user state
                                              with the useState hook.
  return (
    <UserContext.Provider value={user}>   ⟵  Wrap the app UI in the
      <Router>                                context provider.
        <div className="App">
          <header>
            <nav>
              // unchanged nav
            </nav>

            <UserPicker user={user} setUser={setUser}/>  ⟵  Pass the user state
          </header>                                          and its updater
                                                             function to
          <Routes>                                           UserPicker.
            // unchanged routes
          </Routes>
        </div>
      </Router>
```

```
    </UserContext.Provider>
  );
}
```

The `App` component imports the `UserContext` object and then wraps the UI in the context's `Provider` component, making the `user` state value available to all components in the tree:

```
<UserContext.Provider value={user}>
  // all app UI
</UserContext.Provider>
```

The provider doesn't have to wrap the whole component tree. As the code stands, with the app passing `user` and `setUser` to the `UserPicker` component as props, we could wrap just the routes in the provider:

```
<Router>
  <div className="App">
    <header>
      // nav and user picker
    </header>

    <UserContext.Provider value={user}>
      <Routes>
        // routes
      </Routes>
    </UserContext.Provider>
  </div>
</Router>
```

But in a later section, we switch the user picker over to using the context rather than props, so it's useful to wrap the whole component tree in the provider. For now, the `UserPicker` component receives the selected user, and its updater function as props. The following listing shows how it works with those props.

---

*Branch*: 0802-user-context, *File*: /src/components/Users/UserPicker.js

**Listing 8.5    Receiving the user and updater function in `UserPicker`**

```
import {useEffect, useState} from "react";
import Spinner from "../UI/Spinner";

export default function UserPicker ({user, setUser}) {      ◁  Assign the user
  const [users, setUsers] = useState(null);                      and setUser props
                                                                 to local variables.
  useEffect(() => {
    fetch("http://localhost:3001/users")
      .then(resp => resp.json())            Once the users have
      .then(data => {                       loaded, set the current
        setUsers(data);                     user to the first.
        setUser(data[0]);     ◁
      });                              Include setUser as
  }, [setUser]);     ◁                 a dependency.
```

```
function handleSelect(e) {
  const selectedID = parseInt(e.target.value, 10);          Use the id
  const selectedUser = users.find(u => u.id === selectedID);  to find the
                                                            selected user
                                                            object.
  setUser(selectedUser);        ◁─┐  Set the
}                                  │  selected user.

if (users === null) {
  return <Spinner/>
}
                                            Specify an event handler
return (                                    for the drop-down.
  <select
    className="user-picker"
    onChange={handleSelect}     ◁──┘    Set the current
    value={user?.id}            ◁──     selection.
  >
    {users.map(u => (                                        Set a value for
      <option key={u.id} value={u.id}>{u.name}</option>  ◁─  each option.
    ))}
  </select>
);
}
```

The UserPicker component loads the user data from the database. Once it has the data, it calls setUser, received as a prop, to set the current user. Because of the updated state, the App component re-renders, setting the updated user as the value on the user context provider. Because App re-renders, all its children re-render too. That includes any descendant components that consume the context, and they'll pick up the new context value. The UserPicker will also show the selected user, setting it as the value of the HTML select element in its UI. (Notice each option element now has a value attribute set to the user's ID.)

To see the whole updated context process in action, we need a component that consumes the user context value. Let's start with the Booking-Details component, as set out in the following listing. Remember, we need the user value to decide whether to show the edit button, shown again in figure 8.7.

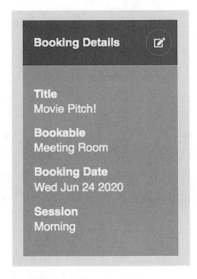

**Figure 8.7** The BookingDetails component shown again with the edit button to the right of the heading

> *Branch:* 0802-user-context, *File:* /src/components/Bookings/BookingDetails.js
>
> **Listing 8.6   The `BookingDetails` component reading the user from context**

```
import {useContext} from "react";          ⟵─ Import the useContext hook.

import {FaEdit} from "react-icons/fa";        ⟵─ Import the icon for
                                                 the edit button.
import Booking from "./Booking";

import UserContext from "../Users/UserContext";   ⟵─ Import our
                                                     shared context.
export default function BookingDetails ({booking, bookable}) {

  const user = useContext(UserContext);                        ⟵─

  const isBooker = booking && user && (booking.bookerId === user.id);

  return (                                 Call useContext with the
    <div className="booking-details">      shared context and assign the
      <h2>                                 value to the user variable.
        Booking Details
        {isBooker && (                ⟵─  Show the edit button only if the
          <span className="controls">     booking belongs to the user.
            <button              ⟵─
              className="btn"
            >                         Render a button, but don't
              <FaEdit/>      ⟵─      attach a handler yet.
            </button>
          </span>            Use the imported edit
        )}                   icon for the button.
      </h2>

      {booking ? (
        // booking
      ) : (
        // message
      )}
    </div>
  );
}
```

*Check if the booking belongs to the user.*

The component imports the `UserContext` context object and passes it to the `useContext` hook, assigning the value the hook returns to the `user` variable. Once `BookingDetails` has a user and a booking, it can check whether the booking was booked by the user:

```
const isBooker = booking && user && (booking.bookerId === user.id);
```

If the current user booked the booking, `isBooker` will be `true`, and the component will show the edit button after the heading:

```
<h2>
  Booking Details
  {isBooker && (
    // edit button UI
  )}
</h2>
```

The button doesn't do anything yet, but it should appear only when the current user (the one selected in the user picker) is the user who booked the selected booking. Test out the showing and hiding logic by selecting a different user and then selecting the different bookings. (When you load the Bookings page, clicking Go in the week picker will take you to the default date—it's set up with some bookings, if you're using db.json from the repo.)

### CHALLENGE 8.1

Update the Users page so that when you switch to the page, it automatically shows the details for the current user. For example, as shown in figure 8.8, if the current user is Clarisse and you switch to the Users page, the details for Clarisse will be shown and Clarisse is selected in the list of users.

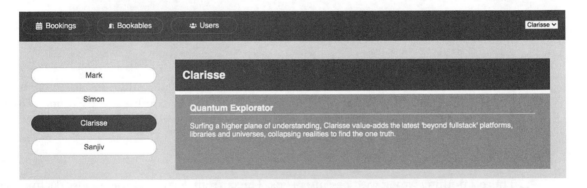

**Figure 8.8   Clarisse is selected as the current user in the user picker (top right). When a visitor switches to the Users page, Clarisse is automatically selected in the user list (left) and her details are shown (right).**

Use the same `UserContext` object we use with the `BookingDetails` component and call `useContext` to get the current user. The completed challenge is on the 0803-users-page branch in the GitHub repo.

React's Context API works well for sharing the selected user in the bookings app. But it raises a few questions: What if we have more than one value to share? Or a more complicated value with many properties? And can we avoid triggering a re-render of the whole component tree when calling `setUser`? Let's dig a little deeper into the nuances of React rendering as we look for answers to those questions.

## 8.2    *Working with custom providers and multiple contexts*

We're successfully feeding tasty tidbits of shared state to components nested deep in our app's tree. We use a context object's `Provider` component to provide a value, and consumer components call `useContext` with the same context object to access the value. Whenever the value changes, the consumers re-render. It would be great if *only* the consumers re-rendered for the values shared via the context. In the bookings app, updating the user state in the `App` component causes the whole tree to re-render. It's not just the tidbit tasters that update; it's the taco munchers (the components that aren't interested in the user) that update too.

In this section, we look at four ways of extending our use of the context. The first, using objects as values, can cause problems. The second and third, using custom providers and multiple contexts, may help us solve those problems. And the last way lets us specify a default value for our context.

### 8.2.1    *Setting an object as the context provider's value*

In listing 8.4, our `App` component enlists the help of the `useState` hook to manage the current user state. It makes the `user` value available to descendant components by setting the `value` prop of a context object's `Provider` component:

```
<UserContext.Provider value={user}>
  // app JSX
</UserContext.Provider/>
```

One of those descendants, `UserPicker`, needs the `user` state value *and* its updater function, `setUser`. Because it needs more than just the `user` value, we use good old props to fulfill its desires:

```
<UserPicker user={user} setUser={setUser}/>
```

There's nothing wrong with passing props. The current version of the app works fine, and the data flow is easy to follow. But, seeing as we already have the `user` state value available in the context of the app, let's update the `UserPicker` component to consume that state. We want this:

```
<UserPicker/>
```

But the `UserPicker` needs the `user` value and the `setUser` function. Can we put them both in the context? Sure!

```
<UserContext.Provider value={{user, setUser}}>
  // app JSX
</UserContext.Provider/>
```

Now that we assign a JavaScript object as the value on the provider, the components consuming the value must destructure the properties they need from the value object. For example, the `BookingDetails` component will grab the user value like this:

```
const {user} = useContext(UserContext);
```

The assignment now has curly braces around the `user` variable name. That wasn't so bad. But what about the `UsersPage` component (updated in challenge 8.1)? It previously assigned the context value to a `loggedInUser` variable. No problem:

```
const {user : loggedInUser} = useContext(UserContext);
```

The colon syntax lets us assign a property to a differently named variable when destructuring an object. In the previous snippet, the `user` property of the context value is assigned to a variable named `loggedInUser`.

The final component to use the context value is the `UserPicker` component. In fact, because it wants the `user` and the `setUser` updater function, it's the reason we switched to an object for the value. That's okay; when destructuring, we can assign all the properties we need to local variables:

```
const {user, setUser} = useContext(UserContext);
```

That's three different components using the context value in three different ways. In section 8.2.2, we take things a bit further and develop our own custom provider for the user context. If you want code for switching the context value to an object, as just discussed, check the solution branch for challenge 8.2.

**CHALLENGE 8.2**
Update App.js so that the `App` component sets an object, with `user` and `setUser` properties, as the `value` prop on the `Provider` component for the user context. Update the `BookingDetails`, `UsersPage`, and `UserPicker` components to use the new object value via destructuring. The code for the completed challenge is on the 0804-object-value branch in the GitHub repo.

### 8.2.2 *Moving the state to a custom provider*

The current user for the booking app is determined by the `UserPicker` component (although in a real app, users would log in). The state value for the current user is managed by the `App` component; that's where the context provider, `UserContext.Provider`, wraps the tree of components. When a visitor to the site chooses a user in the user picker, the `UserPicker` component calls `setUser` to update the `user` state value in the `App` component. React notices the state has changed and re-renders the component that manages that state, `App`. Because `App` re-renders, *all of its children re-render*, as shown in figure 8.9.

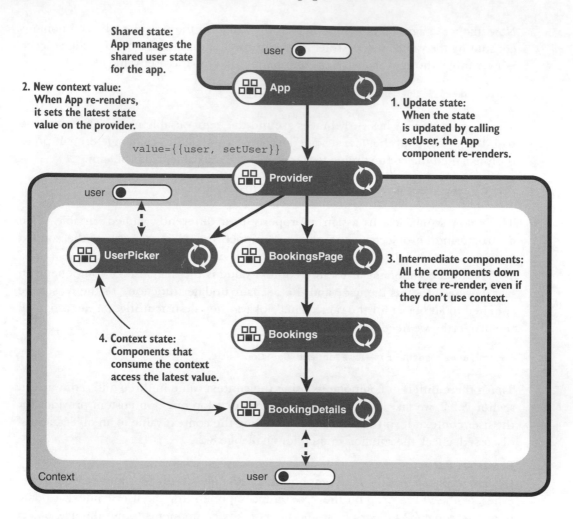

**Figure 8.9   Calling setUser in the `App` component re-renders the whole tree. The gray band around the components after the Provider represents the context: `UserPicker` and `BookingDetails` access the user value from the context.**

Re-rendering is not inherently bad—we fixate on the state, and React calls the components, does its diffing, and tickles the DOM—and if your app is performing well, there's no need to complicate the code. But, if slower, more involved components are in the tree, you might want to avoid re-renders that won't change the UI. We want a way of updating the context provider value without setting off a cascade of updates all the way down the component tree. We want the context consumers (the components that call `useContext`) to re-render in response to a change of value on the provider, not just because the whole tree is re-rendering. Can we avoid updating the state in the `App` component?

Answering that question involves a good understanding of React's rendering behavior. We discuss the concepts and how to apply them in the following four subsections:

- Creating a custom provider
- Using the `children` prop to render wrapped components
- Avoiding unnecessary re-renders
- Using the custom provider

### CREATING A CUSTOM PROVIDER

If App is managing the `user` state only so it can pass it to `UserContext.Provider`, and we already have a separate file for `UserContext`, why not manage the state in the same place as the context? Can we build a `UserProvider` component that we use to wrap the component tree and that manages the user state itself? You bet we can! The following listing shows our very own custom provider component, `UserProvider`.

---

**Branch:** 0805-custom-provider, **File:** /src/components/Users/UserContext.js

**Listing 8.7  Exporting a custom provider along with the user context**

```
import {createContext, useState} from "react";          ┐  Export the context object
                                                         │  so that other components
const UserContext = createContext();                     │  can import it.
export default UserContext;                         ◁────┘

                                                         ┐  Assign the special children
export function UserProvider ({children}) {         ◁────┘  prop to a local variable.
  const [user, setUser] = useState(null);           ◁──┐  Manage the user state
                                                        │  within the component.
  return (
    <UserContext.Provider value={{user, setUser}}>  ◁──┐  Set an object as
      {children}                                       │  the context value.
    </UserContext.Provider>                      ┐
  );                                             │  Render the children
}                                                │  inside the provider.
```

---

`UserContext` is still the default export, so no files that import and use it directly need to change. But the context file now has a named export, `UserProvider`, our custom provider component. The custom provider calls `useState` to manage the user value and to get an updater function. It passes the value and function, wrapped in an object, to the `UserContext.Provider` component as the value to share for the context:

```
<UserContext.Provider value={{user, setUser}}>
  {children}
</UserContext.Provider>
```

When we use our custom provider, we wrap it around part or all of our app in JSX. All of the wrapped components get access to the value set by the provider (if they call useContext with UserContext):

```
<UserProvider>
  // app components
</UserProvider>
```

Let's look at that `children` prop in a bit more detail.

### USING THE CHILDREN PROP TO RENDER WRAPPED COMPONENTS

Whenever a component wraps other components, React assigns the wrapped components to the `children` prop of the wrapper. For example, here's a `Wrapper` component with a `MyComponent` component as a child:

```
<Wrapper>
  <MyComponent/>
</Wrapper>
```

When React calls `Wrapper` to get its UI, it passes `Wrapper` the child component, `MyComponent`, assigning it to the `children` prop. (React has always been doing this; we just haven't used the `children` prop until now.)

```
function Wrapper ({children}) {          ←  React assigns any child
                                            components to the children prop.
  return <div className="wrapped">{children}</div>    ←  Use the child components
                                                          when returning the UI.
}
```

When returning its UI, `Wrapper` uses the components React has assigned to `children`. The UI becomes the following:

```
<div className="wrapped"><MyComponent/></div>
```

For the `Wrapper` example, `children` is a single component. If `Wrapper` wraps multiple, sibling components, then `children` is an array of components. Find out more about working with the `children` prop in the React docs: https://reactjs.org/docs/react-api.html#reactchildren.

Back in our `App` component, React assigns to the `children` prop of `UserProvider`, the components that `UserProvider` wraps. `UserProvider` uses the `children` prop to make sure the `UserContext.Provider` component still renders the components that our custom `UserProvider` component now wraps:

```
export function UserProvider ({children}) {          ←  React assigns the
  const [user, setUser] = useState(null);               wrapped components
                                                         to the children prop.
  return (
    <UserContext.Provider value={{user, setUser}}>
      {children}                                     ←  Render the wrapped
    </UserContext.Provider>                             components within the
  );                                                    provider for a context.
}
```

It wraps the child components in the user context's provider and sets the provider's `value`, making the `user` value and `setUser` function available to the wrapped children. The context and the state are now in the same place. That's nice for organization, understanding, and maintainability. But there's an optimization benefit too.

### AVOIDING UNNECESSARY RE-RENDERS

When a descendant (the user picker, for example) calls `setUser` to update the user state value in the `UserProvider` component, React notices the state has changed and re-renders the component that manages that state, `UserProvider`. But for `User-Provider`, all of its children *don't* re-render, as illustrated in figure 8.10.

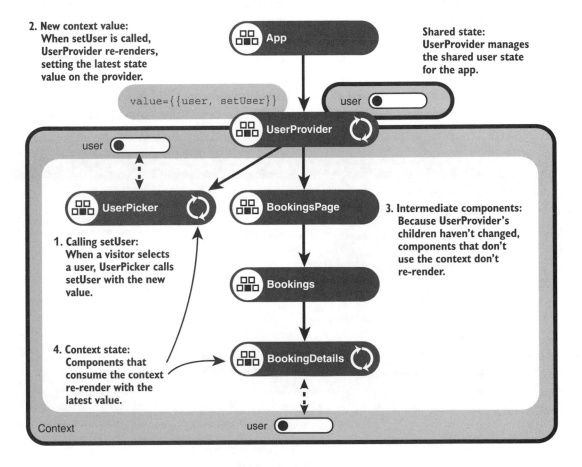

**Figure 8.10**  When `UserProvider` re-renders, only the context consumers, not the whole tree, re-render.

It may be unexpected, but it's standard React rendering behavior; no special memoizing function is being applied here. What makes `UserProvider` behave differently from our `App` component, when `App` was managing the user state? What stops React from rendering the provider's children?

It's because `UserProvider` accesses its children as a prop, and updating the state *within* the component doesn't change its props. The identity of `children` doesn't change when a descendant calls `setUser`. It's exactly the same object as it was before. There's no need to re-render all the children, so React doesn't.

Except for the context consumers! Context consumers *always* re-render when the value of the closest provider for their context changes. Our custom provider provides an updater function to its consumers. When a component calls the updater function, the custom provider re-renders, updating its context value. React knows the provider's children haven't changed, so doesn't re-render them. Any components that consume the context, however, do re-render in response to the change of value on the provider, not because the whole tree of components has re-rendered.

#### USING THE CUSTOM PROVIDER

Now that our custom provider is looking after the user state, we can simplify the App component, removing the import and calling of useState and the need to set a value on the provider. The following listing shows the slimmer code. Notice, also, that we no longer set props on UserPicker; it was switched over to using context in challenge 8.2.

Branch: 0805-custom-provider, *File:* /src/components/App.js

Listing 8.8   Using the custom provider in the App component

```
// remove import for useState
// unchanged imports

import {UserProvider} from "./Users/UserContext";        ◁┘ Import the
                                                              custom provider.
export default function App () {
  return (                          ┐ Wrap the app UI
    <UserProvider>        ◁─────────┘ in the provider.
      <Router>
        <div className="App">
          <header>
            // nav
                                  ┐ Don't pass props
            <UserPicker/>   ◁─────┘ to the user picker.
          </header>

          <Routes>
            // routes
          </Routes>
        </div>
      </Router>                  ┐ Wrap the app UI
    </UserProvider>     ◁────────┘ in the provider.
  );
}
```

Because, in the JSX, UserProvider wraps Router, the Router component is assigned to the UserProvider component's children prop, and UserProvider, our custom provider, wraps it in UserContext.Provider, the actual context provider component. That way, every component in the app gets access to the user context. In chapter 9, we'll see how custom hooks can be used to more easily work with the Context API from the consumers' perspective.

Our custom provider assigns an object, {user, setUser}, as the value for the context provider component. In the next section, we look at downsides to using an object in this way.

### 8.2.3 Working with multiple contexts

Now that we have a mechanism for sharing values across the whole application, you may be tempted to create a single, monstrous store for the app's state and let components anywhere consume the bloated, gassy value it provides. But—as you might have guessed from the previous sentence's hyperbole—that's not always the best idea. If a component needs some state, try to manage it in the component.

Keeping the state with the component that uses it makes it easier to work with and reuse the component. If the app develops and a sibling now needs the same state, lift the state into a shared parent and pass it down via props. If extra levels of nested components are introduced between the state and some of the components that use it, consider *component composition* before reaching for the Context API. The React docs have some information about composition: http://mng.bz/PPjY.

If you find you really do have state that doesn't change often and that is used by many components at different levels across your app, the Context API sounds like a good fit. But even then, a single state object provided by context can be inefficient. Say your context state value looks like this:

```
value = {
  theme: "lava",
  user: 1,
  language: "en",
  animal: "Red Panda"
};

<MyContext.Provider value={value}><App/></MyContext.Provider>
```

Across your component hierarchy, some components use the theme, some the user, others the language, and yet others use the animal. The problem is, if a single property value changes (say the theme changes from lava to cute), *all* of the components that consume the context will re-render, even if they're not interested in the changed value. A nested component with a craving for just the juiciest state tidbits gets tacos, tapioca, and a huge lamb tagine too! Fortunately, there's an easy fix. (Although, if I can keep the tagine, I'll be sorted for a few days. Mmmmmmm tagine . . .)

#### SPLITTING THE CONTEXT VALUES ACROSS MULTIPLE PROVIDERS

You can use as many contexts as you need, and nested components can call the use-Context hook on just the contexts they consume. Here's what the providers look like if each shared value gets its own:

```
<ThemeContext.Provider value="lava">
  <UserContext.Provider value=1>
    <LanguageContext.Provider value="en">
      <AnimalContext.Provider value="Red Panda">
```

```
        <App/>
      </AnimalContext.Provider>
    </LanguageContext.Provider>
  </UserContext.Provider>
</ThemeContext.Provider>
```

Then, nested components consume only the values they need and re-render when their selected values change. Here are two components that access a pair of context values each:

```
function InfoPage (props) {
  const theme = useContext(ThemeContext);
  const language = useContext(LanguageContext);

  return (/* UI */);
}


function Messages (props) {
  const theme = useContext(ThemeContext);
  const user = useContext(UserContext);

  // subscribe to messages for user

  return (/* UI */);
}
```

### USING A CUSTOM PROVIDER FOR MULTIPLE CONTEXTS

You want to put your providers as close to the components that consume their contexts as possible, wrapping subtrees rather than the whole app. Sometimes, however, the context really is used across the whole app, and the providers can go at or close to the root. The code at the root often doesn't change much, so don't worry about nesting multiple providers; you don't have to see the nesting as "wrapper hell" or a "pyramid of doom." If you prefer, and the providers are likely to stay together, you can always create a custom provider that groups multiple providers in one place, like this:

```
function AppProvider ({children}) {
  // maybe manage some state here

  return (
    <ThemeContext.Provider value="lava">
      <UserContext.Provider value=1>
        <LanguageContext.Provider value="en">
          <AnimalContext.Provider value="Red Panda">
            {children}
          </AnimalContext.Provider>
        </LanguageContext.Provider>
      </UserContext.Provider>
    </ThemeContext.Provider>
  );
}
```

Then the app can use the custom provider(s):

```
<AppProvider>
  <App/>
</AppProvider>
```

As we saw in section 8.2.2, using a custom provider with a `children` prop can help with unnecessary child component re-renders too.

### USING SEPARATE CONTEXTS FOR A STATE VALUE AND ITS UPDATER FUNCTION

When a context provider's value changes, its consumers re-render. A provider might also re-render as a result of its parent re-rendering. If the provider's value is an object that the code creates every time the provider renders, the value changes on each render, even if the property values you assign to the object stay the same.

Take another look at our custom `UserProvider` component in the bookings app:

```
export function UserProvider ({children}) {
  const [user, setUser] = useState(null);

  return (
    <UserContext.Provider value={{user, setUser}}>
      {children}
    </UserContext.Provider>
  );
}
```

> A new object is assigned to the value prop on every render.

We assign an object, `{user, setUser}`, to the `value` prop of the provider. Every time the component renders, it's a fresh object that's assigned, even if the two properties, `user` and `setUser`, are the same. The consumers of the context—`UserPicker`, `Users-Page`, and `BookingDetails`—re-render whenever `UserProvider` re-renders.

Also, by using an object as the value, if a nested component uses only one of the properties on the object, it will still re-render when the other property changes (it's tidbits and tacos again). In our case, that's not a problem; `setUser` never changes, and the only component that uses it, `UserPicker`, also uses the `user` property. But if we were to build a proper login system, we could easily create a logout button that didn't need the current user but that did need to call `setUser`. There's no need to re-render the button every time the user changes.

So, we have two problems:

- A new object is assigned to the provider value every render.
- Changing one property on the value re-renders consumers that may not consume that value.

We can solve both problems by using two contexts rather than one in our custom provider, as shown in the following listing.

Branch: **0806-multiple-contexts**, *File:* **/src/components/Users/UserContext.js**

**Listing 8.9   Using separate providers for a value and its updater function**

```
import {createContext, useState} from "react";

const UserContext = createContext();
export default UserContext;

export const UserSetContext = createContext();      ◁──┐ Create a separate context
                                                         for setting the current user.

export function UserProvider ({children}) {
  const [user, setUser] = useState(null);

  return (                                          ┌── Set the user
    <UserContext.Provider value={user}>        ◁──┘    as a value.
      <UserSetContext.Provider value={setUser}>  ◁──┐ Set the updater
        {children}                                    function as a value on
      </UserSetContext.Provider>                      its own provider.
    </UserContext.Provider>
  );
}
```

user and setUser are not re-created every render, and we now use a separate context and provider for each value, so consumers of one value are not affected by changes to the other.

The latest branch also updates the consumer components; they don't need to destructure values from a value object, and UserPicker imports and uses the new UserSetContext context object.

### 8.2.4   *Specifying a default value for a context*

Working with the Context API involves providers and consumers: the provider sets a value, and the consumer reads the value. But working with two separate parts can require a little trust. What if we call useContext with a context object, but no corresponding provider is set further up the tree? If appropriate, when creating a context object, we can specify a default value for just such an occurrence, like this:

```
const MyContext = createContext(defaultValue);
```

The useContext hook will return the context object's default value if no value is set by a corresponding provider for that context. This could be useful if your app uses a default language or theme; a provider could be used to override the default, but everything would still work if no provider was included.

## Summary

- For rarely changing values used by many components, consider using the Context API.
- Create a context object to manage a particular value that components will access:

```
const MyContext = createContext();
```

- Export the context object to make it available to other components. (Or create the context object in the same scope as the provider and consumer components.)
- Import the context object into the provider and consumer component files.
- Wrap the component tree that needs access to the shared state value with the context object's provider component, setting the value as a prop:

```
<MyContext.Provider value={value}>
  <MyComponent />
</MyContext.Provider>
```

- Access context values with the `useContext` hook, passing it the context object:

```
const localValue = useContext(MyContext);
```

Whenever the context value changes, the consuming component will re-render.
- Optionally, specify a default value for a context when creating it:

```
const MyContext = createContext(defaultValue);
```

The `useContext` hook will return the default value if no provider for the context is set further up the component tree.
- Use multiple contexts for values that aren't usually consumed together. Consumer components that consume one value can re-render independently of those that consume another value.
- Create custom providers to manage state for shared values.
- Use the `children` prop in custom components to avoid re-rendering descendants that don't consume the context.

# Creating your own hooks

React Hooks promise to simplify component code and to promote encapsulation, reusability, and maintainability. They let function components work closely with React to manage state and hook into life-cycle events for mounting, rendering, and unmounting. Function components with hooks collocate related code and remove the need to mix unrelated code within and across the separate life-cycle methods of class-based components.

Figure 9.1 contrasts the location of code in class-based and function-based versions of a `Quiz` component that loads question data and subscribes to a user service. Whereas the class component spreads the functionality across its methods, the `Quiz` function component manages local state with calls to `useState` or `useReducer` and wraps up the loading of question data and the subscription to a user service within separate calls to `useEffect`.

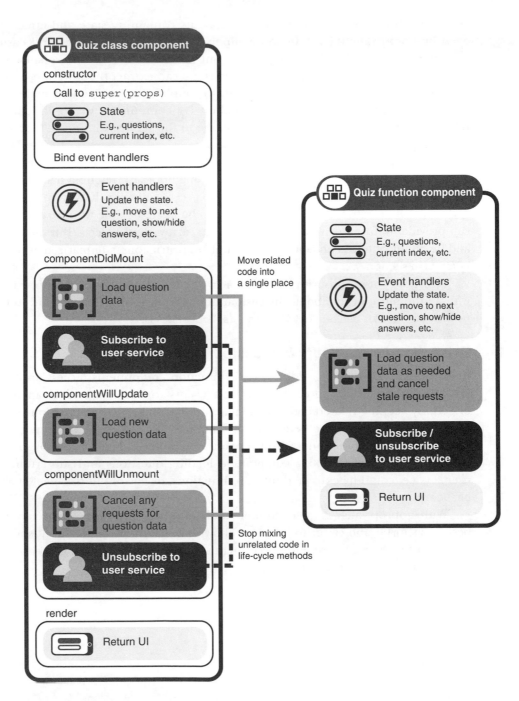

**Figure 9.1** React Hooks let us move related code into a single place and stop mixing unrelated code in life-cycle methods.

We could stop there, with function components containing state and effects managed by hooks. The Quiz function component already looks neater and easier to reason about than the class component. But in the same way that we split longer functions into a number of shorter functions, we can extract the work the hooks do into *custom hooks* outside the component, to simplify the component code and to prepare the functionality for reuse. For the Quiz component, we could load question data with a useFetch hook and subscribe to the service with a useUsers hook, for example.

This chapter includes custom hooks, some based on code we've seen before (examples of useEffect from chapter 4, including hooks for fetching data) and some extending previous code (we create a hook to access context values from chapter 8). The examples illustrate how custom hooks can be made flexible with parameters and can provide useful return values with functions, arrays, and objects. But the neatness and flexibility of hooks do come with a couple of restrictions, summarized as the *Rules of Hooks* in section 9.2.

Before we get serious with the rules or in-depth with the bookings app, let's start with a little more detail about why custom hooks are a good thing and with our first two custom hooks, useRandomTitle and useDocumentTitle.

## 9.1    *Extracting functionality into custom hooks*

React hooks let us manage local state in function components, access application state via context, and hook into life-cycle events to perform and clean up side effects. By keeping related code in one place, rather than spread across various class methods, they let us make better use of functions. We can extract commonly used code into separate functions, simplifying our components. Figure 9.2 shows how the key functionality of the Quiz component, loading questions and subscribing to a user service, could be extracted into two functions, or custom hooks, useFetch and useUsers.

With appropriately named custom hooks, the code for the Quiz component becomes shorter and easier to follow, as shown on the left of figure 9.3. It should be clear that the Quiz component is accessing user information by calling useUsers and fetching data by calling useFetch.

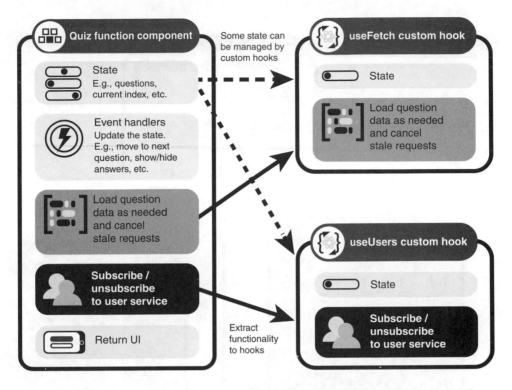

**Figure 9.2  With custom hooks, we can move some state and functionality into separate functions.**

Moving the functionality into custom hooks also lets us reuse that functionality in multiple components, and figure 9.3 shows a second component, Chat, calling the same useUsers hook. Particularly useful hooks can be shared across a team or even published and made available to developers across the world.

Library authors can create hooks to make key functionality available to function components, and we look at a couple of examples—routing with React Router and fetching data with React Query—in chapter 10. In this section, we say hello again to a simple component from chapter 4 that accesses the document's title from within an effect. We consider the following:

- Recognizing functionality that could be shared
- Defining custom hooks outside your components
- Calling custom hooks from custom hooks

In creating our first examples, we encounter the naming convention for custom hooks, setting up the need for a few rules in section 9.2.

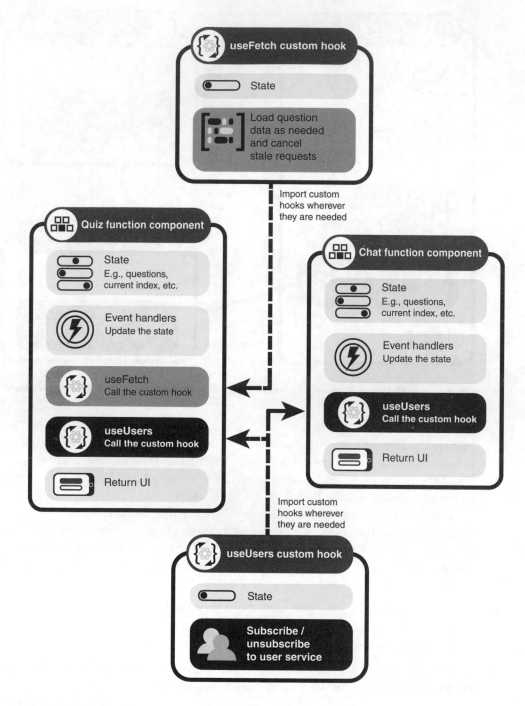

**Figure 9.3    Many components can call our custom hooks.**

### 9.1.1   Recognizing functionality that could be shared

We have a SayHello component that displays greetings in the document's title. On first loading, the component shows a random greeting and a Say Hi button. It updates the greeting whenever the button is clicked, as shown in figure 9.4.

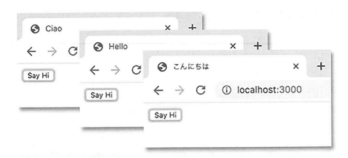

**Figure 9.4   Three views of the browser document with different greetings as titles**

The component performs two main tasks:

- Chooses a greeting from a list
- Sets the document title to the chosen greeting

In the subsections that follow, we extract the title-setting code into our first custom hook, useDocumentTitle, and the random title selection into our second, useRandom-Title. The original code for the SayHello component is shown again in listing 9.1, where you can see the call to the useEffect hook that sets the document's title. (The effect in this listing now has index specified as a dependency; it sets the title only when the index changes.)

> *Live:* **https://jhijd.csb.app,** *Code:* **https://codesandbox.io/s/sayhello-jhijd**

##### Listing 9.1   Updating the browser title

```
import React, {useState, useEffect} from "react";          ⟵ Import the
                                                              useEffect hook.
function SayHello () {
  const greetings = ["Hello", "Ciao", "Hola", "こんにちは"];
  const [index, setIndex] = useState(0);
                                          Pass the useEffect hook
                                          a function, the effect.
  useEffect(() => {                   ⟵
    document.title = greetings[index];          ⟵ Update the browser title
  }, [index]);                                     from inside the effect.

  function updateGreeting () {
    setIndex(Math.floor(Math.random() * greetings.length));
  }

  return <button onClick={updateGreeting}>Say Hi</button>
}
```

Update the title only if the index changes.

Setting a document's title is functionality we might like to use on multiple pages and in multiple projects. As functions, hooks let us extract and share functionality easily. Components can pass arguments to our hooks, and the hooks can return state values and functions to give the components the powers they need to complete their tasks. Let's see how.

### 9.1.2 *Defining custom hooks outside your components*

Setting a document title is a simple example, and you could easily just re-create the effect whenever you want the functionality. But its simplicity lets us focus on the extraction to a custom hook without any cognitive strain related to what the effect does. Listing 9.2 shows the same friendly SayHello component from listing 9.1, this time with the effect moved into a separate function, useDocumentTitle, outside the component definition.

> **Listing 9.2  Extracting an effect into the `useDocumentTitle` hook**

```
import React, {useState, useEffect} from "react";      Define the custom hook as a
                                                        function whose name begins
function useDocumentTitle (title) {                     with "use."
  useEffect(() => {
    document.title = title;                  Call the original useEffect hook
  }, [title]);                               from within the custom hook.
}
                                          Update the document title
                                          only if the title changes.
export default function SayHello () {
  const greetings = ["Hello", "Ciao", "Hola", "こんにちは"];
  const [index, setIndex] = useState(0);

  function updateGreeting () {
    setIndex(Math.floor(Math.random() * greetings.length));
  }
                                          Call the custom hook,
                                          passing it the title to show.
  useDocumentTitle(greetings[index]);

  return <button onClick={updateGreeting}>Say Hi</button>
}
```

In listing 9.2, the custom hook has been defined outside the component but in the same file. You could, and often do, move the custom hook into its own file (or a file with multiple utility hooks) and import it into any components that need it.

We called the custom hook useDocumentTitle. When using hooks, there are a couple of rules to follow to keep your components running smoothly, as discussed in section 9.2, and starting the name of all hooks with "use" helps enforce those rules. It's an important enough naming convention to warrant its own sidebar.

> ### Start the names of custom hooks with "use"
>
> To make it clear that a function is a custom hook and should follow the rules of hooks, start its name with `use`, for example, `useDocumentTitle`, `useFetch`, `useUsers`, or `useLocalStorage`.

It's not only components that we can power up by calling custom hooks. Our custom hooks are free to make the most of extra powers too! It's just functions calling functions at the end of the day.

### 9.1.3 *Calling custom hooks from custom hooks*

In doing their jobs, your freshly sculpted hooks might perform useful tasks that could be extracted into their own custom hooks, with one hook calling one or more other hooks. And your hooks can return values to the calling component, either for inclusion in the UI or to update a hook-controlled state. For example, for the `SayHello` component in listing 9.2, we could also extract the "choose a random greeting" functionality. Listing 9.3 shows the final, compact form of our title-setting component, `SayHello`, with the key title-setting functionality extracted into a `useRandomTitle` hook imported from another file (shown in listing 9.4).

---

Live: **https://ynmc2.csb.app/**, *Code:* **https://codesandbox.io/s/userandomtitle-ynmc2**

**Listing 9.3 A compact, title-setting `SayHello` component**

```
import React from "react";
import useRandomTitle from "./useRandomTitle";      ← Import our custom hook.

const greetings = ["Hello", "Ciao", "Hola", "こんにちは"];

export default function SayHello () {
  const nextTitle = useRandomTitle(greetings);      ← Pass the custom hook the greetings to use and assign the function it returns to a variable.

  return <button onClick={nextTitle}>Say Hi</button>  ← Use the function returned by the hook to update the document title whenever the button is clicked.
}
```

In listing 9.3, we pass the `useRandomTitle` hook the list of greetings from which to choose the document title. The hook returns a function we invoke to generate the next title. We have abstracted how the title is generated into the hook but, by using sensible hook and variable names, the component code is easy to follow. Figure 9.5 shows the component calling one hook, which calls another.

Listing 9.4 shows the code for the `useRandomTitle` hook. It includes two hook calls of its own, one to the built-in `useState` hook and one to our `useDocumentTitle` custom hook, now moved to its own file (shown in listing 9.5).

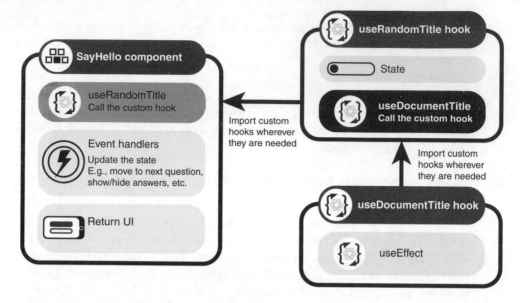

**Figure 9.5    The simplified** `SayHello` **component calls the** `useRandomTitle` **hook, which calls the** `useDocumentTitle` **hook.**

*Live:* **https://ynmc2.csb.app/,** *Code:* **https://codesandbox.io/s/userandomtitle-ynmc2**

**Listing 9.4    The** `useRandomTitle` **custom hook calls** `useDocumentTitle`

```
import {useState} from "react";                                          Import our
import useDocumentTitle from "./useDocumentTitle";                       custom hook.

const getRandomIndex = length => Math.floor(Math.random() * length);     ← Define this
                                                                           function
                                                                           outside
export default function useRandomTitle (titles = ["Hello"]) {            ← the hook.

                                                                        Provide a default
  const [index, setIndex] = useState(                                   list of greetings.
    () => getRandomIndex(titles.length)
  );                                      ← Provide a function to choose a random
                                            greeting index for the initial state.

  useDocumentTitle(titles[index]);

  return () => setIndex(getRandomIndex(titles.length));   ←
}
                                          Return a function so code using
Call our imported custom hook             this hook can update the title.
to update the document title.
```

The `useRandomTitle` custom hook uses the `useState` hook to manage the index of the title to be shown. Code that uses the hook doesn't need to know how the hook manages the current title; it just needs to be able to ask for a new title to be shown. The hook returns a function so code that uses the hook can ask for the next title. The useRandomTitle custom hook also calls our useDocumentTitle custom hook from earlier, and the following listing shows that custom hook exported from its own file.

> *Live:* https://ynmc2.csb.app/, *Code:* https://codesandbox.io/s/userandomtitle-ynmc2

**Listing 9.5   The useDocumentTitle hook exported from its own file**

```
import {useEffect} from "react";

export default function useDocumentTitle (title) {    ◁──┐ Specify a parameter
  useEffect(() => {                                        for the title.
    document.title = title;      ┌── Update the document title only
  }, [title]);                   │   when the title value changes.
}                                ◁──┘
```

Set the document's title to the value passed in. ──▷

Listings 9.3, 9.4, and 9.5, together, show how custom hooks can call custom hooks and return only what's needed by components that use them. But before we get carried away by our extraction/abstraction enthusiasm, we need to understand a little about how React manages these hook calls and how to make sure they work as intended. Yes, there are rules!

## 9.2   Following the Rules of Hooks

We've seen many advantages of hooks so far in this book and in this chapter. The way they help to organize and clarify code and their promise of efficient code abstraction and reuse are both very appealing. But in order for hooks to deliver on their promises, the React team has made some interesting implementation decisions. While React doesn't generally impose too many idioms on your JavaScript, with hooks the team has laid down some rules:

- Start the names of custom hooks with "use."
- Call hooks only at the top level.
- Call hooks only from React functions.

When you call hooks like useState and useEffect, you're enlisting React's help to manage state and side effects, batch updates, calculate UI differences, and schedule DOM changes. For React to successfully and reliably track your components' state, the hook calls from those components need to be consistent in order and number. The three rules of hooks are there to ensure that the call order of your hooks doesn't change from one render to the next.

> **The Rules of Hooks**
> - Start hook names with "use."
> - Call hooks only at the top level.
> - Call hooks only from React functions.

Let's look at the last two rules in a little more detail.

### 9.2.1   *Call hooks only at the top level*

It's important that components call hooks consistently each time they run. You shouldn't call hooks only on some occasions but not on others, and you shouldn't call them a different number of times each time a component runs. To help ensure that your hook calls are consistent, follow these conventions:

- *Don't* put hooks inside conditionals.
- *Don't* put hooks inside loops.
- *Don't* put hooks inside nested functions.

Each of those three scenarios can lead to you skipping hook calls or changing the number of times you call the hooks for a component.

   If you have an effect that should run only under certain conditions, and the conditions aren't covered by the dependency array, put the conditions inside the effect function. *Don't do this*:

```
if (condition) {
  useEffect(() => {
    // perform effect
  }, [dep1, dep2]);
}
```
**Don't put the hook call inside the condition.**

Hiding an effect in a condition may skip the effect depending on the condition. But our effects must *always* run. Instead, *do this*:

```
useEffect(() => {
  if (condition) {
    // perform task.
  }
}, [dep1, dep2]);
```
**Do put the condition inside the hook call.**

This code always calls the hook but checks the condition before performing the effect's task.

### 9.2.2   *Call hooks only from React functions*

Hooks allow function components to have state and to manage when they use or cause side effects. Components that use hooks should be easy to understand, maintain, and share. Their state should be predictable and reliable. Expected changes of state should be visible within the component, although you might extract exact implementations of those state changes into custom hooks. To help your components work sensibly:

- *Do* call hooks from React function components.
- *Do* call hooks from custom hooks (with names starting with "use").

Don't call hooks from other, regular JavaScript functions. Keep your hook calls within function components and custom hooks.

### 9.2.3 Using an ESLint plugin for the rules of hooks

Undoubtedly, these "rules" may raise a few eyebrows. But I think the pros of hooks outweigh the cons of the three rules. To help you spot when you may have overlooked the rules in your code, there's an ESLint plugin called `eslint-plugin-react-hooks`. If you've used `create-react-app` to generate your project skeleton, the plugin is already in place.

## 9.3 Extracting further examples of custom hooks

In chapter 4, we saw a few other examples of side effects: getting the window size, using local storage, and fetching data. Although we wrapped the side effects inside calls to `useEffect`, they were still within the embrace of the components using them. But the functionality is worth sharing, so let's extract and export it.

In this section, we create a couple more custom hooks:

- `useWindowSize`—Returns the height and width of the document window
- `useLocalStorage`—Gets and sets a value using the browser's local storage API

In section 9.4, we access context via a custom hook, and in section 9.5 we set up a custom hook to make it easy to fetch data.

As functions, hooks can return whatever values are needed to expose their functionality. We've already seen no return value from `useDocumentTitle` and a function return value from `useRandomTitle`. The two examples that follow return two further types of values: `useWindowSize` returns an object with properties, and `useLocalStorage` returns an array. As you read through the examples, consider how the different return types work for the custom hooks and the components that use the hooks. First up is a hook that returns the window length and width as properties of a single object.

### 9.3.1 Accessing window dimensions with a useWindowSize hook

Say you want to measure the width and height of a browser window and show the dimensions onscreen, updating them automatically if the user resizes the window. Figure 9.6 shows the same window reporting its dimensions at two different sizes.

As we saw in chapter 4, this requires adding and removing event listeners to the window's resize event. With a custom hook, we can simplify the component that uses the dimensions. The following listing shows how simple the `WindowSizer` component becomes.

*Live:* https://zswj6.csb.app/, *Code:* https://codesandbox.io/s/usewindowsize-zswj6

**Listing 9.6  A compact component showing the window width and height**

```
import React from "react";
import useWindowSize from "./useWindowSize";          ← Import the custom hook.

export default function WindowSizer () {
  const {width, height} = useWindowSize();            ← Call the hook and assign the
                                                        returned dimensions to variables.
  return <p>Width: {width}, Height: {height}</p>      ← Use the dimensions in the UI.
}
```

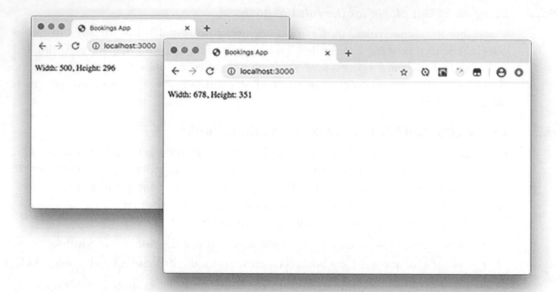

**Figure 9.6  Displaying the width and height of a window as it's resized**

The `WindowSizer` component gets ahold of the window dimensions in a single line of code. It doesn't care how the values are arrived at and doesn't have to set up and tear down any event listeners itself:

```
const {width, height} = useWindowSize();
```

Any projects and components that need the dimensions can import and use the custom hook. The hook's abstracted magic is shown in listing 9.7. It performs the same actions as the dimension-reporting component from chapter 4, but now the call to `useEffect` and the event-related code is separated from any individual component.

> *Live*: **https://zswj6.csb.app/**, *Code*: **https://codesandbox.io/s/usewindowsize-zswj6**

**Listing 9.7   The `useWindowSize` custom hook**

```
import {useState, useEffect} from "react";        ◁── Define a function that returns
                                                       the dimensions of the window.
function getSize () {
  return {
    width: window.innerWidth,         Read the dimensions from
    height: window.innerHeight        the window object.
  };
}

export default function useWindowSize () {
  const [size, setSize] = useState(getSize());
```

```
useEffect(() => {
  function handleResize () {
    setSize(getSize());
  }

  window.addEventListener('resize', handleResize);

  return () => window.removeEventListener('resize', handleResize);
}, []);

  return size;
}
```

**Update the state, triggering a re-render.**

**Register an event listener for the resize event.**

**Return a cleanup function to remove the listener.**

**Pass an empty array as the dependency argument.**

**Return the object containing the dimensions.**

The call to useEffect includes an empty dependency array (it runs only when the calling component first mounts), and it returns a cleanup function (it removes the event listener when the calling component unmounts). The useWindowSize custom hook returns an object with width and height properties. The next custom hook, useLocal-Storage, takes a different approach, returning an array with two elements, just like the useState hook.

### 9.3.2 Getting and setting values with a useLocalStorage hook

Our fourth custom hook comes from the third useEffect example in chapter 4. We have a user picker that lets us select a user from a drop-down menu. We store the selected user in the browser's local storage, so the page remembers the selected user from visit to visit, as shown in figure 9.7.

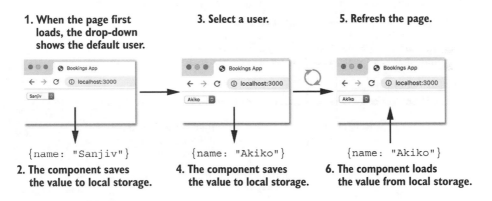

Figure 9.7    Once you select a user, refreshing the page automatically reselects the same user.

We want our custom hook to manage setting and retrieving the selected user from local storage. As shown in the following listing, the useLocalStorage hook returns the user and an updater function to the UserPicker component as two elements in an array.

Listing 9.8    A user picker component that uses local storage

```
import React from "react";
import useLocalStorage from "./useLocalStorage";       ◁ — Import the
                                                            custom hook.
export default function UserPicker () {
  const [user, setUser] = useLocalStorage("user", "Sanjiv");   ◁ — Call the hook
                                                                    with a key and
                                                                    initial value.
  return (
    <select value={user} onChange={e => setUser(e.target.value)}>   ◁
      <option>Jason</option>
      <option>Akiko</option>                            Use the state and
      <option>Clarisse</option>                         updater function
      <option>Sanjiv</option>                           returned by the hook.
    </select>
  );
}
```

The `UserPicker` component uses array destructuring to assign the saved user and the updater function to local variables, `user` and `setUser`. Again, the component doesn't care how the custom hook does its thing; it cares only about the saved user (so it can select the appropriate option in the drop-down list) and the updater function (so any change to the selection can be saved). The following listing shows the code we extract into the custom hook.

Listing 9.9    The `useLocalStorage` custom hook

```
import {useEffect, useState} from "react";
                                                            Accept a key
                                                            and an initial
export default function useLocalStorage (key, initialValue) {   ◁   value.
  const [value, setValue] = useState(initialValue);        ◁ — Manage the
                                                                 state locally.
  useEffect(() => {
    const storedValue = window.localStorage.getItem(key);   ◁   Get any local
                                                                storage value
    if (storedValue) {              Update the local state    for the key.
      setValue(storedValue);        if there's a value from
    }                               local storage.
  }, [key]);       ◁
                        Rerun this effect if
                        the key changes.
  useEffect(() => {                                   Save the latest value
    window.localStorage.setItem(key, value);          to local storage.
  }, [key, value]);        ◁
                                Rerun this effect for
                                a new key or value.
  return [value, setValue];   ◁
}                                 Return an array.
```

The code calls the `useState` hook to manage the selected user state locally. It also uses two calls to the `useEffect` hook, to retrieve any saved value from local storage and to save changed values. Check back in chapter 4 if you want a step-by-step account of how the two effects work together to use local storage to save and retrieve the selected user. In this chapter, we move on to a context we first encountered in chapter 8.

## 9.4 *Consuming a context value with a custom hook*

In chapter 8, we saw how to use React's Context API to share values across an application or subtree of the application by wrapping components in a context provider and setting the provider's `value` prop. Any components that consume the context value need to import the provider's corresponding context object and pass it to the `useContext` hook. In the bookings app, multiple components need access to the current user, and we created a custom provider to make that value available across the app.

The consuming components don't need to know where the values come from or what mechanism is used to make them available; we can abstract the details behind a custom hook. For the bookings app, let's create a `useUser` hook that provides the current user and an updater function for any components that need to set the user. We'll use it like this:

```
const [user, setUser] = useUser();
```

Or, for components that need only the value, we do this:

```
const [user] = useUser();
```

The following listing expands on the custom user provider from chapter 8. The file exports the existing provider and our new custom hook.

> Branch: 0901-context-hook, *File*: /src/components/Users/UserContext.js
>
> Listing 9.10  The `useUser` custom hook

```
import {createContext, useContext, useState} from "react";

const UserContext = createContext();          Don't export
const UserSetContext = createContext();       the contexts.

export function UserProvider ({children}) {
  const [user, setUser] = useState(null);

  return (
    <UserContext.Provider value={user}>
      <UserSetContext.Provider value={setUser}>
        {children}
      </UserSetContext.Provider>
    </UserContext.Provider>
  );
}
                                        Export the
                                        custom hook.
export function useUser () {            ◁─┘
```

```
const user = useContext(UserContext);          │ Consume the contexts
const setUser = useContext(UserSetContext);     │ from inside the hook.

if (!setUser) {
  throw new Error("The UserProvider is missing.");      ◁─── Throw an error if the
}                                                             provider is missing.

return [user, setUser];        ◁─── Return the two context
}                                    values in an array.
```

The custom hook, useUser, consumes the two context values set up in the provider, returning the user value and updater function as the two elements in an array. It performs a check to make sure a provider component has been used further up the component tree and throws an error if it's missing.

With our custom hook ready to go, we can simplify the components that need access to the current user: UserPicker, UsersPage, and BookingDetails. They no longer need to import the contexts they consume; they simply import and call the useUser hook. The following listing shows the UserPicker component.

> **Branch**: 0901-context-hook, *File*: /src/components/Users/UserPicker.js
>
> Listing 9.11   Calling the useUser hook from the UserPicker component

```
import {useEffect, useState} from "react";
import Spinner from "../UI/Spinner";            ◁─── Remove unused
                                                      imports.

import {useUser} from "./UserContext";     ◁─── Import the
                                                custom hook.
export default function UserPicker () {
  const [user, setUser] = useUser();        ◁─── Call the hook and assign the
  const [users, setUsers] = useState(null);      user and updater function
                                                 to local variables.
  useEffect(() => {
    // unchanged
  }, [setUser]);

  function handleSelect (e) { /* unchanged */ }

  if (users === null) {
    return <Spinner/>
  }

  return ( /* unchanged UI */ );
}
```

Because the call to useUser returns an array, we can destructure the return value by using variable names we choose. The UserPicker component uses user and setUser.

The BookingDetails component needs only the user, so its useUser call can look like this:

```
const [user] = useUser();
```

The `UsersPage` component names the current user from the context `loggedInUser`, so its `useUser` call can look like this:

```
const [loggedInUser] = useUser();
```

With more functionality moved into custom hooks, the components themselves become simpler, starting to resemble presentational components that just receive and display state. Before hooks, presentational components would leave any business logic to wrapper components. With hooks, the business logic can be more easily encapsulated, reused, and shared.

#### CHALLENGE 9.1

Update the `UsersPage` and `BookingDetails` components to call the `useUser` hook rather than the `useContext` hook. The current branch, 0901-context-hook, already has the latest code.

## 9.5 *Encapsulating data fetching with a custom hook*

It's common for multiple components in an application to display data, usually fetched from data sources over a network or over the internet. As our applications get bigger and the data consumed by components starts to intersect, we may need to reach for centralized data stores that efficiently manage retrieval, caching, and updating. (We look at the React Query library in chapter 10.) But many applications function perfectly well with components fetching their own data, usually within calls to the `useEffect` hook. Often, all that changes from component to component is the URL from which to grab the data.

In this section, we create a custom hook for fetching data. We supply the hook with the URL, and it returns the data, along with a status value and maybe an error object if something goes wrong. We use the hook like this:

```
const {data, status, error} = useFetch(url);
```

As you can see, the hook returns an object with the three properties we need. The hook works equally well for fetching users or bookables in our example app. Bookings, however, require a bit of extra work to be most useful, so we'll create a specialized hook for fetching those. This section is divided into three parts:

- Creating the `useFetch` hook
- Using the data and status values that the `useFetch` hook returns
- Creating a more specialized data-fetching hook: `useBookings`

The `useFetch` hook could be used in multiple projects, so let's look at it in some detail.

### 9.5.1   *Creating the useFetch hook*

Our custom `useFetch` hook accepts a URL and returns an object with `data`, `status`, and `error` properties, as shown in listing 9.12. It uses the `useState` hook to manage the data (which could be `undefined`, a primitive, an object, or an array), the status (which can be `idle`, `loading`, `success`, or `error`), and the error object (which can be `null` or a JavaScript error object). The hook uses our `getData` API function from within `useEffect`, just as our components did in previous chapters.

---

**Branch: 0902-use-fetch, *File:* /src/utils/useFetch.js**

**Listing 9.12   The `useFetch` hook**

```
import {useEffect, useState} from "react";
import getData from "./api";

export default function useFetch (url) {
  const [data, setData] = useState();
  const [error, setError] = useState(null);
  const [status, setStatus] = useState("idle");          ⟵  Set the initial
                                                             status as "idle."
  useEffect(() => {
    let doUpdate = true;                 Just before sending a
                                         request, set the status
    setStatus("loading");         ⟵     to "loading."
    setData(undefined);
    setError(null);

    getData(url)
      .then(data => {
        if (doUpdate) {                  If the data comes back
          setData(data);                 successfully, set the
          setStatus("success");    ⟵    status to "success."
        }
      })
      .catch(error => {                  If there was a problem
        if (doUpdate) {                  fetching, set the status
          setError(error);          ⟵   to "error."
          setStatus("error");
        }
      });

    return () => doUpdate = false;
  }, [url]);

  return {data, status, error};
}
```

---

Rather than using Booleans like `isLoading` and `isError`, the `useFetch` hook uses a status value, set to a string. (Rather than having strings scattered across the application, it would be better to export the possible status values as variables from their own file and import them wherever they're needed. But for the purposes of the example app, we'll stick with the simpler, if slightly more error-prone, naked string approach.) Components that call useFetch can check the status to decide what UI to return. To see useFetch in action, let's update the BookablesList component, making use of the status value.

### 9.5.2 Using the data, status, and error values the useFetch hook returns

We designed the useFetch hook to return more than just the data; it also gives us a status string and an error object. The status is great for deciding what UI to show, and the updated BookablesList component in listing 9.13 uses it to choose between an error message, a loading spinner, or the list of bookables.

> **Branch:** 0902-use-fetch, *File:* src/components/Bookables/BookablesList.js

> **Listing 9.13  Calling the** useFetch **hook from the** BookablesList **component**

```
import {useEffect} from "react";
import {FaArrowRight} from "react-icons/fa";
import Spinner from "../UI/Spinner";

import useFetch from "../../utils/useFetch";          ◁── Import our new
                                                          useFetch hook.

export default function BookablesList ({bookable, setBookable}) {

  const {data : bookables = [], status, error} = useFetch(      Call useFetch and
    "http://localhost:3001/bookables"                           destructure the
  );                                                            object it returns.

  const group = bookable?.group;
  const bookablesInGroup = bookables.filter(b => b.group === group);
  const groups = [...new Set(bookables.map(b => b.group))];

  useEffect(() => {              ◁──  Select the first bookable
    setBookable(bookables[0]);        when the bookables load.
  }, [bookables, setBookable]);

  function changeGroup (event) { /* unchanged */ }
  function nextBookable () { /* unchanged */ }
                                                     Check the status to see if
                                                     an error has occurred.
  if (status === "error") {        ◁──
    return <p>{error.message}</p>       ◁──  Display the message property
  }                                          of the error object.

  if (status === "loading") {                          Check the status to see if
    return <p><Spinner/> Loading bookables...</p>  ◁── the bookables are loading.
  }

  return ( /* unchanged UI */ );
}
```

Listing 9.13 calls `useFetch` and destructures the object it returns, assigning the properties to local variables:

```
const {data : bookables = [], status, error} = useFetch(
  "http://localhost:3001/bookables"
);
```

It assigns the `data` property to the `bookables` variable and includes a default value of an empty array for when the `data` property is `undefined`:

```
data : bookables = []
```

If you check our implementation of `useFetch` in listing 9.12, you'll see that no initial value was passed to `useState` for the `data` value, and it's explicitly set to `undefined` every time a new data fetch is started. `useFetch` returns the data fetched from the server or `undefined`. When destructuring an object, JavaScript assigns a specified default value whenever the property value is `undefined`. `BookablesList` uses that behavior to assign an empty array to `bookables` whenever `data` is `undefined`.

### CHALLENGE 9.2

Update the `UserPicker` and `UsersList` components to call `useFetch` to get the list of users from the database. Use the `status` value to determine what UI to show. Again, the current branch, 0902-use-fetch, already has the changed files.

### 9.5.3  *Creating a more specialized data-fetching hook: useBookings*

Custom hooks make it easy to encapsulate and share functionality across components, and our `useFetch` hook makes it easy to fetch data from any component. We have the `BookablesList`, `UserPicker`, and `UsersList` components all calling `useFetch` to manage their data-loading only when they first mount. For interactive applications, though, we continue fetching data in response to user choices. For example, the bookings grid displays bookings for a chosen bookable and week, as shown in figure 9.8, and the user can choose new bookables and new weeks at will, so we need to fetch new data to keep everything synchronized.

To display a grid filled with bookings, we generate the grid for the chosen bookable and week and transform the bookings data into a form that's easy to reference when filling the grid. So, there's more to it than just fetching the bookings. We'll split the code into three parts:

- `useBookings`—A custom hook to load and transform the booking data
- `useGrid`—A custom hook to generate the empty grid of booking slots
- `BookingsGrid`—The updated component that calls the two custom hooks

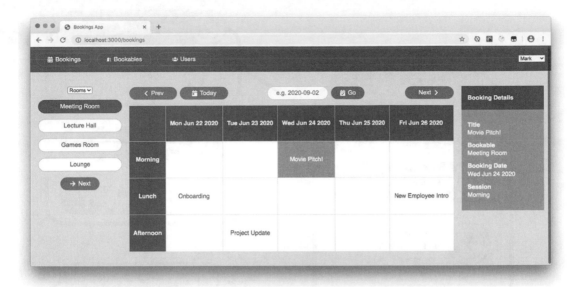

**Figure 9.8  The `BookingsGrid` shows bookings for a chosen bookable (Meeting Room) and week (containing 2020-06-24).**

The relationships of the three parts are shown in figure 9.9, which includes one component, three custom hooks, and two built-in React hooks.

Okay, let's dig in to the code, starting with the two custom hooks, `useBookings` and `useGrid`, in a new bookingsHooks.js file.

### USEBOOKINGS

This is where more specialized custom hooks can come in handy. Listing 9.14 shows the `useBookings` hook. It fetches bookings data for a specified bookable ID, start date, and end date. It also uses our previously created `transformBookings` function to return the data in a format that the bookings grid finds easy to work with.

> **Branch**: 0903-use-bookings, **File**: /src/components/Bookings/bookingsHooks.js

**Listing 9.14  The `useBookings` hook**

```
import {shortISO} from "../../utils/date-wrangler";        ← Import our useFetch
import useFetch from "../../utils/useFetch";                  custom hook.
import {transformBookings} from "./grid-builder";

export function useBookings (bookableId, startDate, endDate) {    ← Use parameters
  const start = shortISO(startDate);                                to specify the
  const end = shortISO(endDate);                                    data to fetch.

  const urlRoot = "http://localhost:3001/bookings";

  const queryString = `bookableId=${bookableId}` +          Build the query string
    `&date_gte=${start}&date_lte=${end}`;                   for the specified data.
```

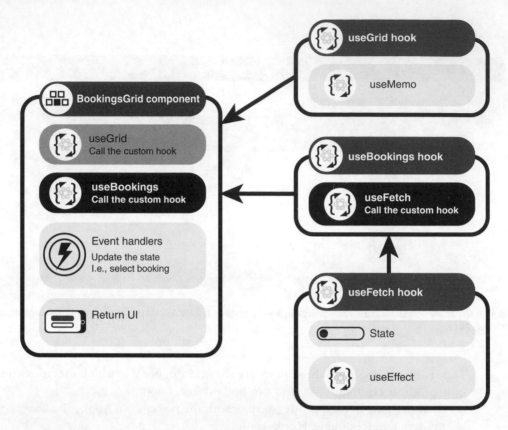

**Figure 9.9** The `BookingsGrid` **component calls the** `useBookings` **and** `useGrid` **custom hooks, and the** `useBookings` **hook calls the** `useFetch` **custom hook. React's** `useMemo` **and** `useEffect` **hooks are also used.**

```
const query = useFetch(`${urlRoot}?${queryString}`);          ← Call the useFetch hook
                                                                with the specific URL.
return {
  bookings: query.data ? transformBookings(query.data) : {},  ←
  ...query
};                                                            Transform loaded data
}                                                             before returning it.
```

The `useBookings` hook uses the `bookableId` and the `startDate` and `endDate` values converted to strings, `start` and `end`, to build the URL for the specific data we want, in a format that our data server, `json-server`, understands:

```
const queryString = `bookableId=${bookableId}&date_gte=${start}&date_lte=${end}`;
```

Listing 9.14 splits the query string across two lines to fit this book's formatting, but it's the same string. Our `useBookings` hook then passes the generated URL to our useFetch hook to grab the data, status, and error values wrapped in an object it assigns to query:

```
const query = useFetch(`${urlRoot}?${queryString}`);
```

Finally, just like the useFetch hook, the useBookings hook returns an object with the data and status and error values. As it's a more specialized data-fetching hook, we rename the data property to bookings. We could call it data to make it consistent with useFetch but, seeing as we're using it only to fetch bookings, calling it bookings seems like a good choice, and the data property will still be there in the return object because the query object (data, status, and error) is spread into the return object too.

### USEGRID

Each bookable can be booked only on certain days of the week and for certain sessions during the day. The BookingsGrid component displays the appropriate grid for the current bookable. But, to run the grid creation logic only when the bookable changes, we wrap the call to getGrid in the useMemo hook. Although this code could happily remain within the BookingsGrid itself, we pull it into its own custom hook, useGrid, shown in the following listing, to continue our component simplification process.

---

> *Branch*: **0903-use-bookings**, *File*: **/src/components/Bookings/bookingsHooks.js**
>
> **Listing 9.15** The `useGrid` hook

```
import {useMemo} from "react";
import {getGrid} from "./grid-builder";

export function useGrid (bookable, startDate) {
  return useMemo(
    () => bookable ? getGrid(bookable, startDate) : {},
    [bookable, startDate]
  );
}
```

The useGrid and useBookings hooks could remain in the same file as BookingsGrid because that's the only place they're used, but we'll have more booking hooks and utility functions later in the book, so a dedicated bookingsHooks.js file will work for us. I've mostly tended toward splitting functions, hooks, and components into their own files for the purposes of the code listings in this book. But don't feel that that's a recommendation; you can follow a course that makes the most sense and is the most useful to you and your team.

With our hooks ready and waiting, let's put the bookings, status, and error, and grid, sessions, and dates values they return to good use in the BookingsGrid.

### BOOKINGSGRID

With our two new custom hooks, useBookings and useGrid, in place, we can update the BookingsGrid component to call them. As the following listing shows, with functionality hidden away in the custom hooks, BookingsGrid itself is almost exclusively concerned with displaying the grid and its bookings.

> **Branch**: 0903-use-bookings, *File*: /src/components/Bookings/BookingsGrid.js
>
> **Listing 9.16  The BookingsGrid component**

```
import {Fragment, useEffect} from "react";
import Spinner from "../UI/Spinner";

import {useBookings, useGrid} from "./bookingsHooks";      ◁─── Import our new
                                                                custom hooks.
export default function BookingsGrid (
  {week, bookable, booking, setBooking}
) {
  const {bookings, status, error} = useBookings(           Call the useBookings
    bookable?.id, week.start, week.end                     hook with the specified
  );                                                       bookable and dates.

  const {grid, sessions, dates} = useGrid(bookable, week.start);   ◁──┐ Call the
                                                                       │ useGrid hook
  useEffect(() => {                                                    │ with the
    setBooking(null);                                                  │ specified
  }, [bookable, week.start, setBooking]);  ◁──┐ Deselect the booking   │ bookable
                                               │ when switching weeks  │ and date.
  function cell (session, date) {             │ or bookables.
    const cellData = bookings[session]?.[date]
      || grid[session][date];

    const isSelected = booking?.session === session
      && booking?.date === date;

    return (
      <td
        key={date}
        className={isSelected ? "selected" : null}
        onClick={
          status === "success"       ◁──┐ Use the status value to
            ? () => setBooking(cellData)  │ check if the bookings
            : null                        │ are available.
        }
      >
        {cellData.title}
      </td>
    );
  }

  if (!grid) {
    return <p>Waiting for bookable and week details...</p>
  }
```

```
   return (
     <Fragment>
       {status === "error" && (          ◁——  Use the status value to
         <p className="bookingsError">          check for an error.
           {`There was a problem loading the bookings data (${error})`}    ◁——
         </p>
       )}                                                           Display the
       <table                                                       error message.
         className={
           status === "success"          ◁——  Use the status
             ? "bookingsGrid active"            value to set the
             : "bookingsGrid"                   class of the grid.
         }
       >
         <thead>{ /* unchanged */ }</thead>
         <tbody>{ /* unchanged */ }</tbody>
       </table>
     </Fragment>
   );
}
```

The component now uses the `status` and `error` values that `useBookings` returns to enable interaction with the grid and show a message if there's a problem.

Moving functionality into custom hooks has made our components simpler and made it easier to share functionality across components and projects. Our custom hook examples became increasingly sophisticated over the course of the chapter, but they're just scratching the surface of what can be achieved. In chapter 10, we introduce third-party hooks for routing and data fetching, and start to see how custom hooks let us access the power of existing third-party libraries with ease.

## Summary

- To simplify components and share functionality that uses React Hooks, create custom hooks outside the components.
- To make it clear that a function is a custom hook and should follow the Rules of Hooks, start its name with "use." Examples include `useDocumentTitle`, `useFetch`, `useUsers`, and `useLocalStorage`.
- It's important that components call hooks consistently each time they run. You shouldn't call hooks only on some occasions but not on others, and you shouldn't call them a different number of times each time a component runs. To help ensure that your hook calls are consistent, follow these conventions:
  - Don't put hooks inside conditionals.
  - Don't put hooks inside loops.
  - Don't put hooks inside nested functions.
- If you need side-effect code to run only under certain conditions, put the condition check inside the effect:

```
useEffect(() => {
  if (condition) {
    // perform task.
  }
}, [dep1, dep2]);
```

- Don't call hooks from regular JavaScript functions; keep your hook calls within function components and custom hooks.

- To help you spot when you may have misused hooks in your code, use the ESLint plugin called `eslint-plugin-react-hooks`. If you've used `create-react-app` to generate your project skeleton, the plugin is already in place.

- Manage state and effects related to a hook's functionality within the hook and return only the value(s) that components need:

```
function useWindowSize () {
  const [size, setSize] = useState(getSize());

  useEffect(() => {/* perform effect */}, []);

  return size;
}
```

- Pass hooks values they need and return nothing, primitives, functions, objects, or arrays—whatever is most useful:

```
useDocumentTitle("No return value");
const nextTitle = useRandomTitle(greetings);
const [user, setUser] = useUser();
const {data, status, error} = useFetch(url);
```

# Using third-party hooks

*10*

**This chapter covers**

- Making the most of third-party hooks
- Accessing state in the URL with React Router's `useParams` and `useSearchParams` hooks
- Switching to a new route with React Router's `useNavigate` hook
- Efficiently fetching and caching data with React Query's `useQuery` hook
- Updating data on the server with React Query's `useMutation` hook

Chapter 9 introduced custom hooks as a way to extract functionality from components, making the functionality reusable and simplifying the components. Custom hooks provide a simple, readable way to access all kinds of functionality from a function component, whether that's simple tasks like changing the document title or managing a state value with local storage, or increasingly complex tasks like fetching data or working with an application state manager. Many existing libraries have been quick to provide hooks to allow function components to make the most of the libraries' features, and this chapter tries some out to improve the bookings example app.

The bookings app has been using React Router to switch between its page components for bookings, bookables, and users. But React Router can handle more complicated scenarios, and in sections 10.1 and 10.2 we introduce three of its hooks. The first, `useParams`, lets us specify the bookable to show on the Bookables page by including its ID in the URL path. The second, `useNavigate`, lets us navigate to a new URL when a user clicks the Next button or selects a different group. The third, `useSearch-Params`, lets us get and set search parameters in a URL's query string to specify a bookable ID and date on the Bookings page.

We've been loading data with our own `useFetch` hook without considering caching or re-fetching, techniques that help us more efficiently retrieve data and update the UI. It's time to up our data game, and the React Query library can do some great things for us with minimal setup. In section 10.3, we have a go at using its `useQuery` hook and pave the way for sending changes to the server via the `useMutation` hook.

Let's introduce our first third-party custom hook and see how we can access state that's specified in a URL.

## 10.1 Accessing state in the URL with React Router

React Router gives us navigational components (`Router`, `Routes`, `Route`, and `Link`, for example) that we use to match UI with URL routes. When a user navigates to a URL, React Router displays the associated React component for that route and, as you'll see, makes any parameters in the URL available to nested components via hooks. Figure 10.1 shows the home page at https://reactrouter.com, where you can find out more.

**Figure 10.1   The web page for React Router: Learn Once, Route Anywhere**

The bookings app includes three pages—for Bookings, Bookables, and Users—and we already use React Router to show the appropriate page depending on the URL: /bookings, /bookables and /users. The association of the URL with the page component is in the App.js file, which includes this code:

```
<Routes>
  <Route path="/bookings" element={<BookingsPage/>}/>
  <Route path="/bookables" element={<BookablesPage/>}/>
  <Route path="/users" element={<UsersPage/>}/>
</Routes>
```

But your boss is back and has decided it would be great if visitors could navigate directly to specific bookables and dates. For example, to show the bookable with an ID of 3, a visitor would use this URL:

```
/bookables/3
```

To see the bookings for the same bookable on June 24, 2020, the visitor would use this:

```
/bookings?bookableId=3&date=2020-06-24
```

These URLs contain state for the application, either as part of the URL path (/bookables/3) or as search parameters in the query string (bookableId=3&date=2020-06-24). In section 10.2, we'll update the Bookings page to work with the query string and the useSearchParams hook. In this section, we start with the Bookables page and focus on the URL path and the useParams and useNavigate hooks. The section is split into four subsections, each working with one component, as shown in table 10.1.

**Table 10.1  The four components we'll change in this section**

| Section | Component | Change |
|---------|-----------|--------|
| 10.1.1 | App | Setting up routes to enable nesting |
| 10.1.2 | BookablesPage | Adding nested routes to the Bookables page |
| 10.1.3 | BookablesView | Accessing URL parameters with the useParams hook |
| 10.1.4 | BookablesList | Navigating with the useNavigate hook |

Let's take our first steps on the path to parameters by updating App.js to accept the new routes we're going to add.

### 10.1.1  *Setting up routes to enable nesting*

To display the details of a bookable and to edit and create bookables, users will navigate to URLs like these:

```
/bookables/3        ◁─── Display the details for the
                         bookable with an ID of 3.
/bookables/3/edit   ◁───
/bookables/new      ◁───         Edit the bookable
                    Create a new  with an ID of 3.
                    bookable.
```

Two of the three components associated with the three routes are in figure 10.2: the details view for the bookable with an ID of 3, and the form for creating a new bookable.

**Show the form for creating a new bookable.**
/bookables/new

/bookables/3
**Show the details for the bookable with an ID of 3.**

**Figure 10.2   Different views are associated with different URLs.** /bookables/3 **shows the details of the bookable with an ID of 3, and** /bookables/new **shows the form for creating a new bookable.**

Now that we have multiple routes that start with /bookables, we need to update App.js to make sure the BookablesPage component is rendered for all of them. The following listing shows the changed path attribute for the /bookables route with its appended /*.

---

*Branch*: 1001-bookables-routes, *File*: /src/components/App.js

**Listing 10.1   Extending the** BookablesPage **route in the** App **component**

```
// imports

export default function App () {
  return (
    <UserProvider>
      <Router>
        <div className="App">
```

```
      <header>
        {/* unchanged */}
      </header>

      <Routes>
        <Route path="/bookings" element={<BookingsPage/>}/>
        <Route path="/bookables/*" element={<BookablesPage/>}/>      ◁──┐
        <Route path="/users" element={<UsersPage/>}/>
      </Routes>
    </div>
  </Router>
</UserProvider>
  );
}
```

**Match any URL that
starts with "bookables."**

Now, any path that starts with /bookables/ will render the BookablesPage component. That small change lets the component set up the three nested routes we need.

### 10.1.2 Adding nested routes to the Bookables page

React Router lets us render different components depending on the *location* or URL.
We use Route components to match a path with a component to render. In listing 10.1,
we specified that any path starting with /bookables should render the BookablesPage
component. Listing 10.2 sets up some nested routes to show more-specific components
on the Bookables page. (We've also added BookableEdit and BookableNew components
to the repo so that the app will compile. We'll discuss them in section 10.3.)

**Branch: 1001-bookables-routes,** *File:* **/src/components/Bookables/BookablesPage.js**

**Listing 10.2   Nested routes in the BookablesPage component**

```
import {Routes, Route} from "react-router-dom";

import BookablesView from "./BookablesView";
import BookableEdit from "./BookableEdit";
import BookableNew from "./BookableNew";

export default function BookablesPage () {
  return (
    <Routes>                          ◁──        Specify a set of
      <Route path="/:id">             ◁──┐       nested routes.
        <BookablesView/>                 │  Use a parameter to catch
      </Route>                           │  the specified bookable ID.
      <Route path="/">                ◁──┐
        <BookablesView/>                 │  Render the BookablesView component
      </Route>                           │  even when no ID is specified.
      <Route path="/:id/edit">        ◁──┐
        <BookableEdit/>                  │  Use a parameter to show an edit
      </Route>                           │  form for the specified bookable ID.
      <Route path="/new">             ◁──┐
        <BookableNew/>                   │  Include a separate route for
      </Route>                           │  the new bookables form.
    </Routes>
  );
}
```

In the listing, we use opening and closing `Route` tags, rather than an `element` prop, just to show that you can specify the UI for a matching route as enclosed JSX rather than as a prop. We add two routes that render the `BookablesView` component and two more routes for creating and editing bookables. The first `Route` in listing 10.2 includes a parameter to catch the ID of the bookable to display:

```
<Route path="/:id">
  <BookablesView/>
</Route>
```

Match URLs of the form /bookables/:id.

Because these routes are nested within the `BookablesPage` component, which is rendered by React Router when the URL matches /bookables/*, this route is rendered for URLs of the form /bookables/:id. For example, when navigating to /bookables/3, React Router will render the `BookablesPage` component and then the `BookablesView` component within it. React Router will also set the id parameter to 3. So, how do we access that parameter from within a rendered component? Here comes our first third-party custom hook!

### 10.1.3  *Accessing URL parameters with the useParams hook*

React Router's `useParams` hook returns an object with properties corresponding to URL parameters set up in a `Route` component's `path` attribute. Say we have a `Route` component like this one:

```
<Route path="/milkshake/:flavor/:size" element={<Milkshake/>}/>
```

Its path attribute includes two parameters, `flavor` and `size`. Say, also, that a shake enthusiast visits this URL:

```
/milkshake/vanilla/medium
```

React Router will render the `Milkshake` component. When the `Milkshake` component calls `useParams`, the hook will return an object with properties corresponding to the two parameters:

```
{
  flavor: "vanilla",
  size: "medium"
}
```

The `Milkshake` component could access the parameters by assigning them to local variables:

```
const {flavor, size} = useParams();
```

Mmmm, now I want a milkshake. It'll have to wait; we have bookables to view. . . .

The Bookables page renders one of three components. Two of them, `Bookables-View` and `BookableEdit`, need to know which bookable they're working with. That bookable's ID is specified in the URL. Listing 10.3 shows the `BookablesView` component. It used to manage just the *selected* bookable with `useState`, but now fetches the data for *all* bookables with our `useFetch` hook from chapter 9 and manages the selected bookable by accessing the `id` parameter from the URL. (These changes will temporarily break the application.)

> *Branch*: 1001-bookables-routes, *File*: /src/components/Bookables/BookablesView.js
>
> **Listing 10.3** `BookablesView` **accessing ID from the URL**

```
import {Link, useParams} from "react-router-dom";        ◁—— Import the
import {FaPlus} from "react-icons/fa";                        useParams hook.

import useFetch from "../../utils/useFetch";        ◁—— Import our useFetch
                                                         custom hook.
import BookablesList from "./BookablesList";
import BookableDetails from "./BookableDetails";
import PageSpinner from "../UI/PageSpinner";
                                                              Retrieve the
export default function BookablesView () {                    bookables
  const {data: bookables = [], status, error} = useFetch(  ◁  with useFetch.
    "http://localhost:3001/bookables"
  );

  const {id} = useParams();        ◁—— Assign the ID parameter
                                        value to a local variable.
  const bookable = bookables.find(
    b => b.id === parseInt(id, 10)     ◁—— Use the ID to get the
  ) || bookables[0];                        specified bookable.

  if (status === "error") {
    return <p>{error.message}</p>
  }

  if (status === "loading") {
    return <PageSpinner/>
  }

  return (
    <main className="bookables-page">
      <div>
        <BookablesList
          bookable={bookable}                  Provide a function
          bookables={bookables}                to generate URLs
          getUrl={id => `/bookables/${id}`}  ◁  for bookables.
        />

        <p className="controls">
          <Link
            to="/bookables/new"       ◁—— Include a link to the
            replace={true}                 form for creating
            className="btn">               new bookables.
            <FaPlus/>
            <span>New</span>
```

```
        </Link>
      </p>
    </div>

    <BookableDetails bookable={bookable}/>
  </main>
 );
}
```

The `BookablesView` component calls React Router's `useParams` custom hook to get an object with all the parameters set in the URL. It uses object destructuring to assign the `id` parameter to a local variable with the same name:

```
const {id} = useParams();
```

The parameters are returned as strings, but each bookable's `id` property is a number, so `parseInt` is used when finding the specified bookable in the collection of all bookables:

```
const bookable = bookables.find(
  b => b.id === parseInt(id, 10)
) || bookables[0];
```

If the bookable can't be found, the first bookable in the collection, `bookables[0]`, is selected instead. Once the bookables have loaded, and assuming there are no errors, `BookablesView` renders the `BookablesList` and `BookableDetails` components. It passes `BookablesList` a function for generating URLs for each bookable. Let's see how that function is used and introduce a second React Router custom hook, `useNavigate`.

### 10.1.4  *Navigating with the useNavigate hook*

React Router's `useNavigate` hook returns a function we can use to set a new URL, prompting the router to render whichever UI has been associated with the new path. (Remember, we're using the beta version of React Router 6, so it's possible the API may change. If that happens, I'll add some extra, updated listings to the GitHub repo.) Say an app is currently showing a `Milkshake` component. (Sorry, I just can't get them out of my head. So . . . creamy . . .) Say, also, that the user is a neuralgia-phobe and prefers bubble tea. To provide a way to navigate from the milkshake page to the bubble tea page, the `Milkshake` component could do this:

```
const navigate = useNavigate();        ◄──┤ Assign a URL-setting function
                                            to the navigate variable.

navigate("/bubbletea");        ◄──┐  Use the function to set a new URL.
```

Assigning the URL-setting function to the local `navigate` variable gives the component a way to set the URL, in event handlers, for example. It could also render some links that point to the new URLs. Let's use both approaches in the bookings app.

In the `BookablesView` component, rather than getting the selected bookable and its updater function with a call to `useState`, we now specify the selection in the URL. Here's the URL for the bookable with an ID of 1:

```
/bookables/1
```

To switch to a new bookable, we set a new URL:

```
/bookables/2
```

To update the state, we either need a link that points to a new URL or a function that navigates to the new URL (fired by the Next button, for example):

```jsx
// JSX
<Link to="/bookables/2">Lecture Hall</Link>
```
← **Use React Router's Link component.**

```js
// js
navigate("/bookables/2");
```
← **Use the function that React Router's useNavigate hook returns.**

Figure 10.3 shows the app after a user has navigated to /bookables/1. The `Bookables-List` component on the left shows the group selector, the list of bookable links in the current group, and the Next button. The `BookablesView` component also renders a New button outside `BookablesList`.

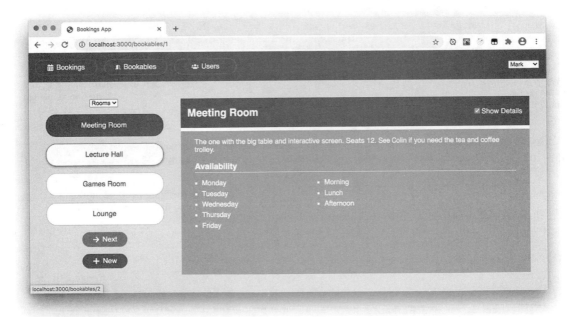

**Figure 10.3**  The `BookablesView` component displays the New button and each bookable as links that lead to a new URL. The Next button and the group selector change the URL by calling a function.

The bookable links and the New button are rendered using `Link` components, and the group drop-down and Next buttons navigate within event handlers. Table 10.2 lists the elements and how they function.

**Table 10.2    Elements and components used in navigation**

| Element/component | Text | Action |
| --- | --- | --- |
| select | e.g., Rooms | Call navigate function |
| Link | Meeting Room | Set link to /bookables/1 |
| Link | Lecture Hall | Set link to /bookables/2 |
| Link | Games Room | Set link to /bookables/3 |
| Link | Lounge | Set link to /bookables/4 |
| button | Next | Call navigate function |
| Link | New | Set link to /bookables/new |

Listing 10.4 shows the `BookablesList` component using both approaches. The `BookablesList` component is used on different pages (the Bookables page and the Bookings page) that use different structures for their URLs. The component needs to know how to generate the URL from a bookable ID, so its parent component has to pass it a function, `getUrl`, for that purpose.

> **Branch**: 1001-bookables-routes, *File*: /src/components/Bookables/BookablesList.js
>
> **Listing 10.4    `BookablesList` using two approaches for navigation**

**Import the useNavigate hook.**

**Accept the current bookable, list of bookables, and getUrl function as props.**

```
import {Link, useNavigate} from "react-router-dom";
import {FaArrowRight} from "react-icons/fa";

export default function BookablesList ({bookable, bookables, getUrl}) {
  const group = bookable?.group;
  const bookablesInGroup = bookables.filter(b => b.group === group);
  const groups = [...new Set(bookables.map(b => b.group))];

  const navigate = useNavigate();

  function changeGroup (event) {
    const bookablesInSelectedGroup = bookables.filter(
      b => b.group === event.target.value
    );
    navigate(getUrl(bookablesInSelectedGroup[0].id));
  }

  function nextBookable () {
    const i = bookablesInGroup.indexOf(bookable);
    const nextIndex = (i + 1) % bookablesInGroup.length;
    const nextBookable = bookablesInGroup[nextIndex];
```

**Call the useNavigate hook, assigning the navigation function to a variable.**

**Navigate to the URL for the first bookable in the new group.**

```
      navigate(getUrl(nextBookable.id));                    ◁─┐  Navigate to the URL for
  }                                                            │  the next bookable in the
                                                               │  current group.
  return (
    <div>
      <select value={group} onChange={changeGroup}>
        {groups.map(g => <option value={g} key={g}>{g}</option>)}
      </select>

      <ul className="bookables items-list-nav">
        {bookablesInGroup.map(b => (
          <li
            key={b.id}
            className={b.id === bookable.id ? "selected" : null}
          >
            <Link                          ◁─┐  Specify links with
              to={getUrl(b.id)}              │  React Router's Link
              className="btn"               │  component.
              replace={true}
            >
              {b.title}
            </Link>
          </li>
        ))}
      </ul>
      <p>
        <button
          className="btn"
          onClick={nextBookable}
          autoFocus
        >
          <FaArrowRight/>
          <span>Next</span>
        </button>
      </p>
    </div>
  );
}
```

**Use the getUrl function to generate the URL for each link.**

(At this point, you should be able to load the Bookables page and the Users page but not the Bookings page.) React Router's useNavigate hook returns a function we use to update the URL, switching to the selected bookable. Listing 10.4 assigns the function to a local variable called navigate, and the changeGroup and nextBookable functions call navigate (rather than the setBookable updater function from previous incarnations of BookablesList). For example, here's the changeGroup function calling navigate with the URL for the first bookable in the newly selected group:

```
function changeGroup (event) {
  const bookablesInSelectedGroup = bookables.filter(
    b => b.group === event.target.value
  );
  navigate(getUrl(bookablesInSelectedGroup[0].id));
}
```

changeGroup uses the `getUrl` function we pass to `BookablesList` as a prop. On the Bookables page, the `getUrl` function looks like this:

```
id => `/bookables/${id}`
```

It just appends the `id` to the end of the URL. The Bookings page will use a different `getUrl` prop that matches that page's use of URLs to specify state. It uses query strings and React Router's `useSearchParams` hook. Let's go there now:

```
navigate("/react-hooks-in-action/10/2");
```
◁─┤ **Go to section 10.2 of this chapter.**

## 10.2 *Getting and setting query string search parameters*

In the preceding section, you saw how to use the `path` attributes for `Route` components to extract state values for our app. This section introduces another approach for storing state in the URL: *search parameters* in the *query string*. Here's a URL with two search parameters:

```
/path/to/page?key1=value1&key2=value2
```

The query string, in bold, is at the end of the URL and starts with a question mark. The search parameters are `key1` and `key2`. The key-value pairs specifying the values for each parameter are separated by the `&` character. We can append further parameters if necessary, and it's easy to include or omit them. Bear in mind these three points when specifying state in the URL:

- Which state values you want as parameters
- How to cope with missing or invalid parameters
- How to update the URL when the state needs to change

Before you see how React Router lets us work with search parameters (getting them in section 10.2.1 and setting them in section 10.2.2), let's briefly consider how the three points just listed relate to our needs for the Bookings page in the example app.

On the Bookings page, to show the grid of bookings for the Meeting Room (the bookable with an ID of 1) for the week containing June 24, 2020 (specified as 2020-06-24), we want to navigate to the following:

```
/bookings?bookableId=1&date=2020-06-24
```

So, our search parameters in the URL are `date` and `bookableId`. Figure 10.4 shows the Bookings page for that URL with the specified bookable highlighted on the left and the specified date present in the bookings grid.

But the URL a user enters might not include the date or the bookable ID, so we need to either throw or report an error when parameters are missing or use sensible default values. We'll use the state value policy set out in table 10.3.

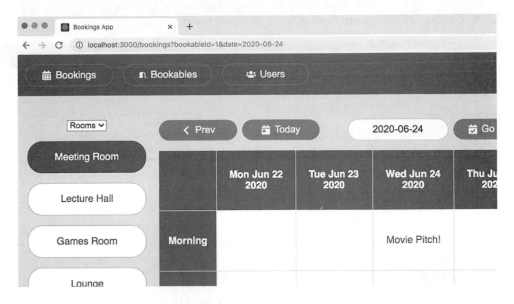

**Figure 10.4** The Bookings page using key-value pairs in the URL to specify bookable and date

**Table 10.3** The state value policy for different URLs

| URL | State |
|---|---|
| /bookings?bookableId=1&date=2020-06-24 | Use the specified date and bookable. |
| /bookings?date=2020-06-24 | Use the specified date and the first bookable. |
| /bookings?bookableId=1 | Use today's date and the specified bookable. |
| /bookings | Use today's date and the first bookable. |

As with any user-entered state, we need to make sure it's valid. The date parameter must be a date, and the bookableId must be an integer. We'll treat invalid values as missing values and follow the policy set out in the table.

Choosing a bookable (by clicking one in the list, switching groups, or clicking the Next button) or moving to a different week (by clicking one of the buttons in the week picker) should update the URL, to set the appropriate date and bookableId state values, and re-render the page.

Working with the query string involves getting and setting the search parameter values. React Router provides the useSearchParams hook for both actions, and we explore the details of first getting and then setting in the next two subsections as we update the Bookings page to use state from the URL.

### 10.2.1  *Getting search parameters from the query string*

To do its job, the `BookingsPage` component needs to know the selected bookable and a date in the week of bookings the user wants to see. Both of those state values will be in the page's URL, like this:

```
/bookings?bookableId=1&date=2020-08-20
```

We want to access each parameter in the query string by the names in bold:

```
searchParams.get("date");
searchParams.get("bookableId");
```

How do we get access to the `searchParams` object? React Router provides the `useSearchParams` hook that returns an array containing an object with the `get` method for accessing the search parameters and a function for setting them:

```
const [searchParams, setSearchParams] = useSearchParams();
```

Because we no longer manage the state with `useState` and are giving users the ability to enter state in the URL, we need to check the validity of that state more carefully. Rather than accessing the parameters directly from a component, let's create a custom hook to get and sanitize them before using that hook in the `BookingsPage` and `Bookings` components.

#### CREATING A USEBOOKINGSPARAMS HOOK

In the following listing, our new hook, `useBookingsParams`, looks for the `date` and `bookableId` parameters in the URL and checks to make sure `date` is a valid date and `bookableId` is an integer. We add the hook to the bookingsHooks.js file.

> **Branch**: 1002-get-querystring, *File*: /src/components/Bookings/bookingsHooks.js
>
> **Listing 10.5   Accessing search parameters with the `useBookingsParams` hook**

```
import {useSearchParams} from "react-router-dom";
import {shortISO, isDate} from "../../utils/date-wrangler";

export function useBookingsParams () {              ◁─── Get a searchParams object.
  const [searchParams] = useSearchParams();

                                                          Use the searchParams object
  const searchDate = searchParams.get("date");      ◁─── to access the date parameter.
  const bookableId = searchParams.get("bookableId"); ◁──┐ Use the searchParams
                                                         │ object to access the
  const date = isDate(searchDate)         Use today's date if  bookableId parameter.
    ? new Date(searchDate)                the date parameter
    : new Date();             ◁───────────is invalid.

  const idInt = parseInt(bookableId, 10);  ◁──┐ Try converting bookableId
  const hasId = !isNaN(idInt);                 │ to an integer.
```

**Check that the date parameter is a valid date.** (margin note pointing to `const date = isDate(searchDate)`)

```
    return {
      date,
      bookableId: hasId ? idInt : undefined          ◁──┐  Set bookableId to undefined
    };                                                   │  if it's not an integer.
}
```

We upgrade the useBookingsParams hook to *set* query string parameters in section 10.2.2. For now, we don't need to set the query string, so the hook code in listing 10.5 destructures only the first element from the array that useSearchParams returns:

```
const [searchParams] = useSearchParams();
```

Once we have the searchParams object, we call its get method to retrieve the value for any parameter in the query string. To get the value for the two keys we're interested in, we use the following:

```
const searchDate = searchParams.get("date");
const bookableId = searchParams.get("bookableId");
```

Having checked the validity of the two values, the new hook returns an object with date and bookableId properties. Components that call the hook can destructure the return value:

```
const {date, bookableId} = useBookingsParams();
```

#### USING THE QUERY PARAMETERS IN THE BOOKINGSPAGE COMPONENT

For example, the BookingsPage component must add only that single line of code to access the two query string search parameters it needs, as shown in the following listing.

Branch: **1002-get-querystring**, *File*: **/src/components/Bookings/BookingsPage.js**

Listing 10.6   BookingsPage **accessing query string search parameters**

```
import useFetch from "../../utils/useFetch";
import {shortISO} from "../../utils/date-wrangler";            Import the
import {useBookingsParams} from "./bookingsHooks";     ◁──    useBookingsParams
                                                              custom hook.
import BookablesList from "../Bookables/BookablesList";
import Bookings from "./Bookings";
import PageSpinner from "../UI/PageSpinner";

export default function BookingsPage () {
  const {data: bookables = [], status, error} = useFetch(
    "http://localhost:3001/bookables"
  );                                                           Call useBookingsParams
                                                               and destructure the
  const {date, bookableId} = useBookingsParams();     ◁──     object it returns.

  const bookable = bookables.find(          Use the bookableId
    b => b.id === bookableId            ◁── parameter to find the
  ) || bookables[0];                        selected bookable.
```

```
function getUrl (id) {
  const root = `/bookings?bookableId=${id}`;
  return date ? `${root}&date=${shortISO(date)}` : root;      ◁——   Check the date
}                                                                     value is defined
                                                                      before using it.
if (status === "error") {
  return <p>{error.message}</p>
}

if (status === "loading") {
  return <PageSpinner/>
}

return (
  <main className="bookings-page">
    <BookablesList
      bookable={bookable}
      bookables={bookables}
      getUrl={getUrl}
    />
    <Bookings
      bookable={bookable}
    />
  </main>
);
}
```

If the bookableId value is undefined (it's missing from the URL or can't be parsed as an integer) or there's no booking with that ID, we fall back to the first bookable in the list of bookables returned by the server:

```
const bookable = bookables.find(
  b => b.id === bookableId)
) || bookables[0];
```

If you find users are confused when they specify an ID that is invalid but are still presented with bookings for a default bookable, you could choose to throw or report an error for invalid values instead.

The BookingsPage component passes a getUrl function to the BookablesList component (which we updated to accept such a prop in section 10.1), so the list can generate URLs in the correct format for the current page:

```
function getUrl (id) {
  const root = `/bookings?bookableId=${id}`;
  return date ? `${root}&date=${shortISO(date)}` : root;
}
```

getUrl uses the date value derived from the URL search parameter, so it makes sure date is not falsy before including it in the generated URL.

The Bookings component also uses the specified date; it generates an object that represents the week containing the date. It then uses the week object in three ways:

1 It fetches the bookings for the specified week.
2 It sets the selected booking to null if the user switches to another week.
3 It passes the week object to the BookingsGrid component.

The following listing shows the Bookings component calling the new useBookingsParams hook to get the date from the URL and highlights the week-related code in bold.

> *Branch*: 1002-get-querystring, *File*: /src/components/Bookings/Bookings.js

**Listing 10.7  Bookings accessing query string search parameters**

```
import {useEffect, useState} from "react";

import {getWeek, shortISO} from "../../utils/date-wrangler";
import {useBookingsParams, useBookings} from "./bookingsHooks";   ⟵  Import the
                                                                      useBookings-
import WeekPicker from "./WeekPicker";                                 Params
import BookingsGrid from "./BookingsGrid";                            custom hook.
import BookingDetails from "./BookingDetails";
                                                     Call useBookingsParams
export default function Bookings ({bookable}) {       and assign the date to a
  const [booking, setBooking] = useState(null);       local variable.

  const {date} = useBookingsParams();            ⟵   Use the date to generate
  const week = getWeek(date);                    ⟵   a week object.
  const weekStart = shortISO(week.start);        ⟵   Create a date string to
                                                     use as a dependency.
  const {bookings} = useBookings(bookable?.id, week.start, week.end);   ⟵
  const selectedBooking = bookings?.[booking?.session]?.[booking.date];
                                                     Get bookings for the
  useEffect(() => {                                  specified week.
    setBooking(null);
  }, [bookable, weekStart]);       ⟵   Set the currently selected
                                       booking to null if the start
  return (                             date changes.
    <div className="bookings">
      <div>
        <WeekPicker/>           ⟵   Remove props
                                    from WeekPicker.
        <BookingsGrid
          week={week}           ⟵   Pass the week object
          bookable={bookable}       to BookingsGrid.
          booking={booking}
          setBooking={setBooking}
        />
      </div>

      <BookingDetails
        booking={selectedBooking || booking}
```

```
        bookable={bookable}
      />
    </div>
  );
}
```

If a user has selected a booking in the grid and then switches to another bookable or week, the effect in the listing sets the selected booking back to null. It uses a simple date string, weekStart, in the dependency list rather than the Date object assigned to week.start. A new Date object is assigned to week.start on every render and, even though the object might represent the same date, the effect will see it as a new object when it compares its dependency list elements. We don't want the selected booking set to null after every render! Have a go at changing weekStart to week.start in the dependency list to see the problem for yourself.

The Bookings and BookingsPage components can now continue to do their jobs by grabbing state from the URL. If you try switching bookables or manually updating the URL to new dates, you should see the page load the appropriate bookings. But switching dates in the UI is managed by the WeekPicker component. It used to manage its state with a reducer. Let's see how to update it to work with the query string when a user clicks one of its buttons.

### 10.2.2  Setting the query string

The WeekPicker component lets the user move to the previous week, the next week, the week containing a specific date, or the week containing today's date. Figure 10.5 shows the WeekPicker UI with its four buttons and text box.

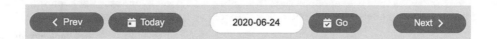

**Figure 10.5    The WeekPicker component has buttons for switching to different weeks.**

The state for the currently selected date is stored in the query string. Say it's 2020 and the user navigates to the Bookings page to show bookings for the week containing July 20. The URL is as follows:

```
/bookings?bookableId=1&date=2020-07-20
```

If today's date is September 1 and the date in the week picker text box is June 24, we want the WeekPicker buttons to set the URL to the values shown in table 10.4.

We could convert the WeekPicker buttons to links that point to the URLs in the table. But we don't know the date for the Go button until the user types it into the text box. As an alternative to links, we'll keep all of the buttons and set the query string by

**Table 10.4   Matching URLs with buttons**

| Button | URL |
|--------|-----|
| Prev | `/bookings?bookableId=1&date=2020-07-13` |
| Next | `/bookings?bookableId=1&date=2020-07-27` |
| Today | `/bookings?bookableId=1&date=2020-09-01` |
| Go | `/bookings?bookableId=1&date=2020-06-24` |

using a function when the buttons are clicked. In section 10.1.4, you saw how React Router's `useNavigate` hook returns a function we use to set the whole URL. The `useSearchParams` hook provides a way to set just the query string. It returns an array whose second element is a function we can use for that purpose. For example, here we assign the setter function to a variable called `setSearchParams`:

```
const [searchParams, setSearchParams] = useSearchParams();
```

To update the URL with new search parameters in the query string, we pass `setSearchParams` an object with properties that will make up the parameters. For example, to produce this URL

```
/bookings?bookableId=3&date=2020-06-24
```

we would pass `setSearchParams` this object:

```
{
  bookableId: 3,
  date: "2020-06-24"
}
```

At the beginning of section 10.2.1, we created the `useBookingsParams` hook to *get* the date and `bookableId` parameters (with some simple validation mixed in for good measure). Now that we want to *set* the `date` parameter, we need to update the hook. The following listing adds a `setBookingsDate` function to the hook, making the new function available as a property on the object the hook returns.

> **Branch:** 1003-set-querystring, *File:* /src/components/Bookings/bookingsHooks.js
>
> **Listing 10.8   Providing a way to set search parameters with `useBookingsParams`**

```
export function useBookingsParams () {
  const [searchParams, setSearchParams] = useSearchParams();
  const searchDate = searchParams.get("date");
  const bookableId = searchParams.get("bookableId");

  const date = isDate(searchDate)
    ? new Date(searchDate)
    : new Date();
```

```
  const idInt = parseInt(bookableId, 10);
  const hasId = !isNaN(idInt);

  function setBookingsDate (date) {
    const params = {};

    if (hasId) {params.bookableId = bookableId}
    if (isDate(date)) {params.date = date}

    if (params.date || params.bookableId !== undefined) {
      setSearchParams(params, {replace: true});
    }
  }

  return {
    date,
    bookableId: hasId ? idInt : undefined,
    setBookingsDate
  };
}
```

**Create a function to update the parameters with a new date.**

**Create an empty object to hold the parameters.**

**Include parameters only for valid values.**

**Update the URL with the new parameters.**

**Include the new function in the hook's return value.**

The new setBookingsDate function creates a parameters object and adds properties for the specified date and existing bookableId value, if they're valid. If it sets at least one property, the function passes the parameters object to setSearchParams, updating the URL with a query string that matches the new parameters:

```
setSearchParams(params, {replace: true});
```

Components that consume the search parameters will re-render, using the fresh values as the latest state. The {replace: true} option causes the browser to replace the current URL in its history with the new one. This will prevent each visited date from appearing in the browser's history. The browser's Back button won't step back through each date selected in the WeekPicker. If you think it would be useful for your app's users to be able to navigate back through each selected date, you can omit the option argument.

Listing 10.9 shows the WeekPicker component calling useBookingsParams to get the date parameter and the setter function, setBookingsDate. It uses the setter function (that it renames goToDate) to update the query string when a user clicks one of its buttons.

**Branch: 1003-set-querystring, *File*: /src/components/Bookings/WeekPicker.js**

**Listing 10.9   WeekPicker getting and setting search parameters**

```
import {useRef} from "react";
import {
  FaChevronLeft,
  FaCalendarDay,
  FaChevronRight,
  FaCalendarCheck
} from "react-icons/fa";
```

```
import {addDays, shortISO} from "../../utils/date-wrangler";
import {useBookingsParams} from "./bookingsHooks";
```
Import the
useBookingsParams
custom hook.

```
export default function WeekPicker () {
  const textboxRef = useRef();

  const {date, setBookingsDate : goToDate} = useBookingsParams();
```
Call the
hook to get
the date
and setter
function.

```
  const dates = {
    prev: shortISO(addDays(date, -7)),
    next: shortISO(addDays(date, 7)),
    today: shortISO(new Date())
  };
```
Create a dates lookup
for the previous,
next, and today's
weeks.

```
  return (
    <div>
      <p className="date-picker">
        <button
          className="btn"
          onClick={() => goToDate(dates.prev)}
        >
          <FaChevronLeft/>
          <span>Prev</span>
        </button>
```
Call the setter
function with the
appropriate date.

```
        <button
          className="btn"
          onClick={() => goToDate(dates.today)}
        >
          <FaCalendarDay/>
          <span>Today</span>
        </button>

        <span>
          <input
            type="text"
            ref={textboxRef}
            placeholder="e.g. 2020-09-02"
            id="wpDate"
            defaultValue="2020-06-24"
          />
```

Call the setter
function with
the text box
date.

```
          <button
            onClick={() => goToDate(textboxRef.current.value)}
            className="go btn"
          >
            <FaCalendarCheck/>
            <span>Go</span>
          </button>
        </span>

        <button
          className="btn"
          onClick={() => goToDate(dates.next)}
        >
```

```
            <span>Next</span>
            <FaChevronRight/>
          </button>
        </p>
      </div>
    );
  }
```

Both the Bookables and the Bookings pages now manage some of their state in the URL. The Bookables page uses separate URLs for creating and editing bookables. The Bookings page, however, doesn't use separate URLs for creating and editing bookings. That's because the interconnections among booking, bookable, and date are a little more complicated, and the user may not need to navigate directly to the edit form for an individual booking. If you feel it would be useful for users to navigate directly to the views for particular states in your app, you now have the tools to implement that functionality.

Whatever path you take for specifying bookables, dates, and bookings, you'll need to load in the relevant data. Up to now, we've been using our own, fairly naïve useFetch hook to get ahold of data. It's time to up our data game with a couple more third-party hooks.

## 10.3  *Streamlining data-fetching with React Query*

The data needs of the bookings app are pretty modest. The most data-intensive component is the bookings grid, and even that loads only one grid of bookings at a time. But we can make improvements that will make the app feel more responsive when the network is slow. And, if your app's data needs increase, these kinds of improvements can make a big difference in your users' perceptions of your app's performance—no one wants a slew of loading spinners strewn across their screen after every interaction!

The bookings app is a single-page application—although we call our three main views (Bookings, Bookables, and Users) *pages* within the app. It uses React Router to display different components for different URLs. Some of those components use the same data; the BookablesList fetches all the bookables from the database on both the Bookings page and the Bookables page, and both the user picker and the Users page fetch all the users. If the Bookables page has already loaded the bookables, we shouldn't need to wait for them to load again when switching to the Bookings page. This section introduces React Query and makes use of its useQuery and useMutation hooks. There are four subsections:

- *Introducing React Query*—What is it? Why is it helpful? Where do we get it?
- *Giving components access to a React Query client*—Creating a client instance and setting it as a prop on a provider component that wraps the component tree.
- *Fetching data with* useQuery—Defining queries, specifying query keys, and using status and error properties. Background re-fetching and request deduping.
- *Updating server state with* useMutation—Defining mutations, taking action when mutations are complete, and working with the query cache.

### 10.3.1 Introducing React Query

*React Query* is a library for managing server state from your React apps. It has defaults that produce great results with no configuration. Figure 10.6 shows the home page for the React Query website, https://react-query.tanstack.com/, where you can find docs, examples, and links to further learning resources. (React Query's author, Tanner Linsley, has created open source React packages to help with forms, tables, charts, and more. Check out his GitHub pages at https://github.com/tannerlinsley.)

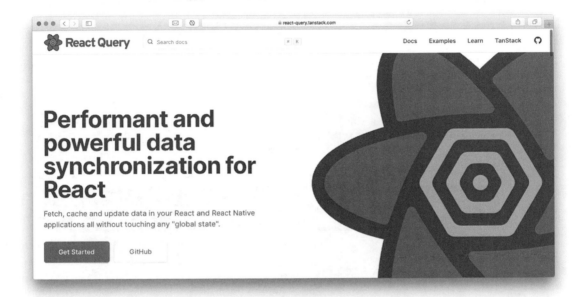

**Figure 10.6**    **The web page for React Query: Performant and powerful data synchronization for React**

React Query's docs list some of the ways it can improve on our own `useFetch` hook. They include the following:

- Caching
- Deduping multiple requests for the same data into a single request
- Updating out-of-date data in the background
- Knowing when data is out of date
- Reflecting updates to data as quickly as possible

Switching from our `useFetch` to React Query's `useQuery` is simple. First, we need to get ahold of the React Query package. You can use the npm package manager to install it, like this:

```
npm install react-query
```

For the bookings app, React Query will provide caching, merging of multiple requests, background fetching to get the latest data, and useful status codes and flags for keeping users informed. If you need them, it has a whole host of configuration options to help you create powerful but streamlined data-driven applications. But why do we need something like React Query for our bookings app?

If you haven't been running `json-server` with a delay, you may not have noticed any issues. Switching from page to page and bookable to bookable is swift and snappy—what a great application! But try adding in that delay; restart `json-server` like this:

```
json-server db.json --port 3001 --delay 3000
```

With the delay, when we click the link for the Bookables page, we get the loading indicator shown in figure 10.7.

**Figure 10.7   When navigating to the Bookables page, we get a loading indicator as the bookables data loads.**

After three seconds, the bookables have loaded, and the expected display appears with the `BookablesList` and `BookableDetails` components. If the network is slow, there's no problem having a loading indicator; we just need to be patient. But, if from the Bookables page we navigate to the Bookings page, we get the loading indicator again as the Bookings page reloads the bookables. In fact, every page reloads existing data.

Here's a list of some of the ways the three main types of data are reloaded following user interactions:

- *Bookables*—Both the Bookings page and the Bookables page fetch the full list of bookables.
- *Bookings*—The Bookings and BookingsGrid components load the same list of bookings. On the Bookings page, switching from one bookable to another and then back again reloads the bookings for the first bookable, and switching from one week to the next and back again reloads the bookings for the first week.
- *Users*—Even after the UserPicker component has loaded the list of users, switching to the Users page will load them again.

To prevent this data-fetching duplication, should we move all the data-fetching code into a central store and access that single source from the components that need it? With React Query, we don't need to do any of the work involved in creating such a store. It lets us keep the data-fetching code in the components that need the data, but behind the scenes it manages a data cache, passing already-fetched data to components when they ask for them. Let's see how to give our components access to that cache.

### 10.3.2 Giving components access to a React Query client

For components to access a shared React Query cache, we make the cache available by wrapping our app JSX in a provider component. React Query uses a *client* object to hold the cache and configuration and to provide further functionality. The following listing shows how to create a client and pass it to the provider component that wraps the app's component tree.

---

**Branch: 1004-use-query,** *File:* /src/components/App.js

**Listing 10.10   Wrapping the app in a** QueryClientProvider **component**

```
import {QueryClient, QueryClientProvider} from "react-query";          ◁──

                                          Import the client constructor and
// other imports                          provider component from React Query.

const queryClient = new QueryClient();      ◁──┐ Create a client
                                                │ instance.
export default function App () {
  return (
    <QueryClientProvider client={queryClient}>       ◁──┐
      <UserProvider>
        <Router>                                          Wrap the app in
          {/* unchanged JSX */}                           the provider,
        </Router>                                         setting the client
      </UserProvider>                                     as a prop.
    </QueryClientProvider>                           ◁──┘
  );
}
```

Wrapping the component tree in the provider makes the client object available to React Query's hooks when we call the hooks from descendant components. Let's start by fetching data with the useQuery hook.

### 10.3.3 *Fetching data with useQuery*

Our own useFetch custom hook is a simple solution to data fetching that works well when network speeds are fast but shows its limitations when latency is introduced. To create apps that consistently feel responsive and avoid unnecessary loading states, we want a way for components to fetch data from the server that doesn't make us wait for previously fetched data. React Query will manage caching for us and provides the useQuery hook for fetching data.

React Query's useQuery hook is similar to our own useFetch hook in that it returns an object with properties for the data, status, and error object. But where we passed useFetch a URL, we pass useQuery a *key* and an asynchronous function that returns the data:

```
const {data, status, error} = useQuery(key, () => fetch(url));
```

useQuery uses the key to identify the data in its cache; it can return the data corresponding to existing keys straightaway and then fetch the latest data from the server in the background. The key can be a string or a more complicated array or object that can be serialized.

#### USING A STRING AS THE QUERY KEY

The simplest key we can pass to useQuery is a primitive value like a string. For example, in the bookings app, we can fetch the list of bookables like this:

```
const {data: bookables = [], status, error} = useQuery(      Specify a key
  "bookables",                                                for the query.
  () => getData("http://localhost:3001/bookables")      Provide an asynchronous
);                                                        data-fetching function.
```

We use the string "bookables" as the key. Whenever any component subsequently calls useQuery with "bookables" as the key, React Query will return the previously fetched bookables data from its cache and then fetch the latest data in the background. That behavior makes the UI seem super-responsive. You'll be able to see the behavior in action after we update both BookablesView and BookingsPage to call use-Query rather than useFetch to retrieve the list of bookables from the server. The following listing updates the BookablesView component first.

> Branch: **1004-use-query**, *File*: **/src/components/Bookables/BookablesView.js**
>
> Listing 10.11   **BookablesView** with **useQuery**

```
import {Link, useParams} from "react-router-dom";
import {FaPlus} from "react-icons/fa";
```

```
import {useQuery} from "react-query";                    ◁──────┐   Import the
import getData from "../../utils/api";                   ◁────┐ │   useQuery hook.
                                                              │ │
import BookablesList from "./BookablesList";            Import our data-fetching
import BookableDetails from "./BookableDetails";        utility function.
import PageSpinner from "../UI/PageSpinner";

                                                                   Call the
export default function BookablesView () {                         useQuery hook.
  const {data: bookables = [], status, error} = useQuery(  ◁────
    "bookables",                                       ◁────     Specify a key for
    () => getData("http://localhost:3001/bookables")   ◁──┐     the query.
  );                                                       │
                                                        Provide an asynchronous
  const {id} = useParams();                            data-fetching function.
  const bookable = bookables.find(
    b => b.id === parseInt(id, 10)
  ) || bookables[0];

  /* unchanged UI */
}
```

The only change to `BookablesView` in listing 10.11 is the switch from `useFetch` to `useQuery`.

## CHALLENGE 10.1

This is an easy one! Change the `BookingsPage` component so that it calls `useQuery` to load the bookables. Use `bookables` as the query key. This change has already been made on the 1004-use-query branch.

Because the Bookables page and the Bookings page use the same query key, whichever is loaded second will be able to grab the bookables data from the cache. With `BookablesView` and `BookingsPage` both calling `useQuery` with the same key, to see the cache in action, follow these steps:

1. Start `json-server` with a delay of two or three seconds.
2. Navigate to the Bookables page at /bookables. You should see the page-level loading spinner and then the list of bookables with the first bookable selected.
3. Click the Bookings link at the top left of the page. The Bookings page will be rendered straightaway, without a page-level loading spinner. React Query has used the bookables data from its cache.
4. Click the Bookables link at the top left of the page. The Bookables page will be rendered straightaway. Again, React Query provides the bookables data from its cache.

Because the Bookings page and the Bookables page use the same query key, `bookables`, when calling the `useQuery` hook, React Query knows to return the existing data for that key immediately. It refetches the data in the background and re-renders the component when the latest data arrives. The `useQuery` hook accepts more-complicated keys. For example, the `Bookings` and `BookingsGrid` components fetch bookings data dependent on a number of variables. Let's see how to fold multiple variables into the query key we pass to useQuery.

### USING AN ARRAY AS THE QUERY KEY

The Bookings page fetches booking data for a bookable between a start date and an end date. React Query needs to be able to track cached data for each combination of bookable, start date, and end date, so, when fetching bookings, we specify the query key as an array like this:

```
["bookings", bookableId, start, end]
```

If we specify a key that has previously been used (say, by clicking a bookable), then a second bookable, and then back to the first bookable, React Query can return data from the cache that matches the key.

The following listing shows the updated useBookings custom hook that Bookings and BookingsGrid use to fetch bookings.

> **Branch**: 1004-use-query, *File*: /src/components/Bookings/bookingsHooks.js
>
> **Listing 10.12**  useBookings **calling** useQuery

```
import {useQuery} from "react-query";

export function useBookings (bookableId, startDate, endDate) {
  const start = shortISO(startDate);
  const end = shortISO(endDate);

  const urlRoot = "http://localhost:3001/bookings";

  const queryString = `bookableId=${bookableId}` +          Call the useQuery hook.
    `&date_gte=${start}&date_lte=${end}`;

  const query = useQuery(                                    Specify an array as
    ["bookings", bookableId, start, end],                    the query key.
    () => getData(`${urlRoot}?${queryString}`)               Provide an asynchronous
  );                                                          data-fetching function.

  return {
    bookings: query.data ? transformBookings(query.data) : {},
    ...query
  };
}
```

The Bookings and BookingsGrid components call useBookings with the same arguments, resulting in equal keys. Now that we've switched to calling useQuery instead of useFetch, React Query sees that the keys are equal and merges the duplicate requests into one.

Navigate to the Bookings page and have a go at switching from one bookable to another and back again or from one week to another and back again. Because the query cache already contains the requested data, switching back to a previously selected bookable or week should instantly render the bookings for that selection. Such UI snappiness leads to user happiness!

**CHALLENGE 10.2**

The UserPicker and UsersList components both fetch the list of users from the database. Update their code to call useQuery instead of useFetch. Test the change by navigating to the Bookables page and then clicking the Users link. The Users page on the 1005-query-users branch should render immediately, without a loading spinner.

### 10.3.4 *Accessing data in the query cache*

The Bookables page now fetches the full list of bookables by calling the useQuery hook with a query key of bookables. For a period of time, React Query associates the key with the bookables data in its cache (check the docs for details on how and when the cached data is marked as stale). React Query makes the cache available should you want to access the fetched data directly or manipulate it in some way. In section 10.3.4, we update the cache when mutating the server state. In this section, we access the cache to improve the responsiveness of the Edit Bookable form.

In section 10.1, we used React Router to set up nested routes on the Bookables page. The routes let users view bookables, create new bookables, and edit existing bookables. To edit the bookable with an ID of 3, the user navigates to /bookables/3/edit. There are two ways of navigating:

- On the Bookables page, select a bookable and click the Edit button.
- Enter the URL directly in the browser's address bar.

Both options display the BookableEdit component, with the details of the specified bookable filled in and Delete, Cancel, and Save buttons, as shown in figure 10.8. The second option will need to load the bookable data from the server, showing a loading spinner while the bookable loads. But for the first option, the Bookables page will already have loaded the full list of bookables. Can the form just grab the existing data from the cache, avoiding the loading spinner?

React Query makes the cache available to components via the client object that we assigned to the provider in section 10.3.2. Call React Query's useQueryClient hook to get ahold of the client object:

```
const queryClient = useQueryClient();
```

We can use the associated query key and the getQueryData method to access already-fetched data. For example, to get the list of bookables in the cache:

```
const bookables = queryClient.getQueryData("bookables");
```

If we want a bookable with a specified ID, we call the find array method, like this:

```
const bookable = bookables?.find(b => b.id === id);
```

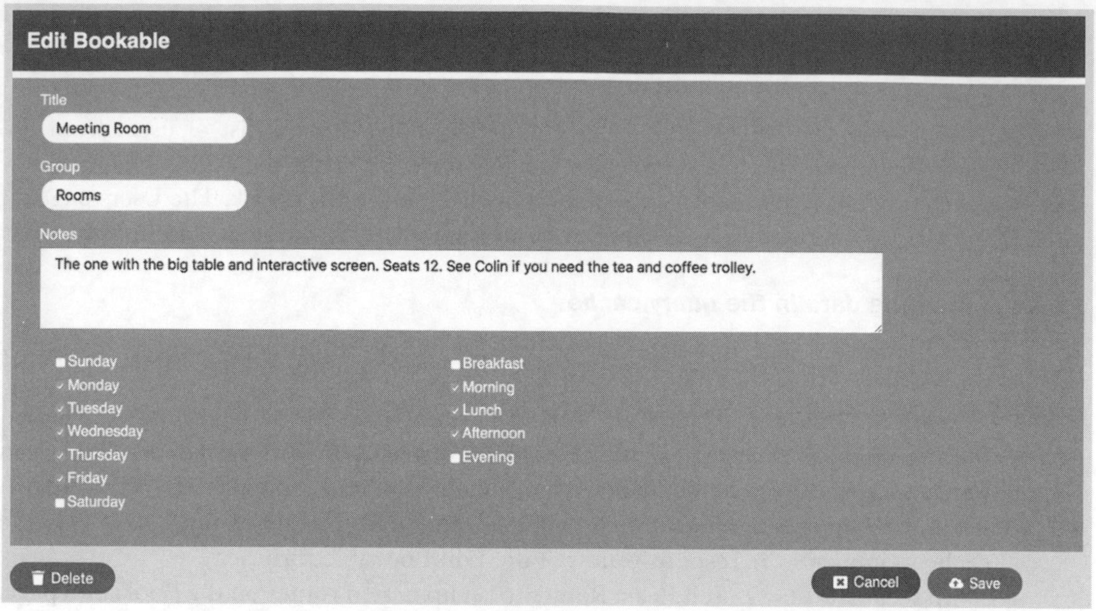

**Figure 10.8　The Edit Bookable form is populated with data from the selected bookable.**

So, we can retrieve a particular booking from the cache, but how do we tell useQuery to return the existing booking rather than fetching it from the server? The following listing shows the BookableEdit component calling useQuery with a third argument, a config object that includes an initialData property. We discuss it after the listing.

**Branch**: 1006-query-cache, **File**: /src/components/Bookables/BookableEdit.js

**Listing 10.13　The BookableEdit component accessing the cache**

```
import {useParams} from "react-router-dom";
import {useQueryClient, useQuery} from "react-query";          ◁—  Import the
                                                                    useQueryClient hook.
import useFormState from "./useFormState";
import getData from "../../utils/api";

import BookableForm from "./BookableForm";
import PageSpinner from "../UI/PageSpinner";

export default function BookableEdit () {                        Call the hook and assign
  const {id} = useParams();                                      the client to a variable.
  const queryClient = useQueryClient();          ◁—
                                                            Assign the initial data and subsequent
                                                            fetched data to the data variable.
  const {data, isLoading} = useQuery(          ◁—
    ["bookable", id],
    () => getData(`http://localhost:3001/bookables/${id}`),      Use the initialData
    {                                                            property to assign an
      initialData:                             ◁—                initial value to data.
```

```
        queryClient.getQueryData("bookables")
          ?.find(b => b.id === parseInt(id, 10))
    }
);

const formState = useFormState(data);

function handleDelete() {}
function handleSubmit() {}

if (isLoading) {
    return <PageSpinner/>
}

return (
    <BookableForm
      formState={formState}
      handleSubmit={handleSubmit}
      handleDelete={handleDelete}
    />
);
}
```

Use a key to get specific data from the cache.

Find the bookable for the specified ID.

Set the bookable data as the state for the form.

Use the isLoading Boolean returned by useQuery.

React Query's useQuery hook accepts a config object as a third argument:

```
const {data, isLoading} = useQuery(key, asyncFunction, config);
```

The config lets the calling code control all kinds of query-related functionality, such as cache expiry, retry policies when fetching-errors occur, callback functions, whether to work with Suspense and error boundaries (see chapter 11), and the setting of initial data. BookableEdit sets the initialData config property so that, when first called, and if the initial data exists, useQuery won't bother fetching the data from the server:

```
const {data, isLoading} = useQuery(
    ["bookable", id],
    () => getData(`http://localhost:3001/bookables/${id}`),
    {
      initialData:
        queryClient.getQueryData("bookables")
          ?.find(b => b.id === parseInt(id, 10))
    }
);
```

If the initial data is undefined (when a user loads the bookings app by navigating directly to the Edit Bookable form, for example) or on subsequent renders, useQuery will go ahead and fetch the data. useQuery sets properties on the object it returns, including Booleans for different status values. Just as an example, the BookableEdit component uses the isLoading Boolean to check for status === "loading".

The Edit Bookable and New Bookable forms use a custom useFormState hook and BookableForm component to manage and display the form fields. Fleshing out the forms here won't teach us anything new about hooks, so this is one of those moments where I ask you to take a look in the repo to get the necessary code and to see how they do their jobs. Notice also that the `BookableDetails` component now includes an Edit button to open the Edit Bookable form. Feel free to see the changes as a challenge and try implementing the forms before checking the repo.

So, we have an edit form that shows the existing bookable data. But how do we save any changes we make to the database? Instead of calling `useQuery`, we call `useMutation`. Let's get it working for new bookables.

### 10.3.5  *Updating server state with useMutation*

React Query helps us synchronize our React app UI with state stored on a server. We've seen how `useQuery` simplifies the process of fetching that state, caching it temporarily in the browser. We also want to update state on the server, and React Query provides the `useMutation` hook for that purpose.

On the Bookables page, we can bring up the New Bookable form and enter information in its fields, but we can't save our creations. We want to mutate that state! We need a function that'll send the new bookable to the server, something like this:

```
createBookable(newBookableFields);
```

The following listing shows the `BookableNew` component calling `createBookable` in its `handleSubmit` function. It gets the `createBookable` mutation function by calling `useMutation`, and we discuss the necessary syntax after the listing.

> **Branch**: 1007-use-mutation, *File*: /src/components/Bookables/BookableNew.js
>
> **Listing 10.14**  `BookableNew` saving data to the server with `useMutation`

```
import {useNavigate} from "react-router-dom";
import {useQueryClient, useMutation} from "react-query";        ← Import React
                                                                   Query hooks.
import useFormState from "./useFormState";
import {createItem} from "../../utils/api";        ← Import the createItem
                                                      API function.
import BookableForm from "./BookableForm";
import PageSpinner from "../UI/PageSpinner";

export default function BookableNew () {
  const navigate = useNavigate();
  const formState = useFormState();                Call useMutation, assigning
  const queryClient = useQueryClient();            the mutation function to the
                                                   createBookable variable.

  const {mutate: createBookable, status, error} = useMutation(    ←

      item => createItem("http://localhost:3001/bookables", item),

      {                                     Set an onSuccess callback.
        onSuccess: bookable => {            ←
          queryClient.setQueryData(         ←   Add the new bookable to the
            "bookables",                        "bookables" query cache.
```

Pass useMutation an asynchronous function. →

```
      old => [...(old || []), bookable]
    );

    navigate(`/bookables/${bookable.id}`);
  }
 }
);
```

Navigate to the newly created bookable.

```
function handleSubmit() {
  createBookable(formState.state);
}
```

Call the createBookable mutation function with the fields for the new bookable.

```
if (status === "error") {
  return <p>{error.message}</p>
}

if (status === "loading") {
  return <PageSpinner/>
}

return (
  <BookableForm
    formState={formState}
    handleSubmit={handleSubmit}
  />
);
}
```

The useMutation hook returns an object containing the mutate function and status values:

```
const {mutate, status, error} = useMutation(asyncFunction, config);
```

When you call mutate, React Query runs asyncFunction and updates the status properties (for example, status, error, data, and isLoading). When calling use-Mutation, the BookableNew component assigns the mutation function to a variable called createBookable:

```
const {mutate: createBookable, status, error} = useMutation(…);
```

BookableNew passes useMutation an asynchronous function to post the fields for the new bookable to the server. It uses the createItem function from /src/utils/api.js:

```
const {mutate: createBookable, status, error} = useMutation(

  item => createItem("http://localhost:3001/bookables", item),

  { /* config */ }
);
```

The config object includes an onSuccess property, a function that runs after the server state has been successfully changed. The function adds the new bookable to the bookables cache and navigates to the new bookable:

```
onSuccess: bookable => {                    ◁⎯⎯⎯  Receive the newly created
  queryClient.setQueryData(                         bookable from the server.
    "bookables",
    old => [...(old || []), bookable]       ◁⎯⎯⎯  Append the new bookable
  );                                                to the cache of bookables.

  navigate(`/bookables/${bookable.id}`);   ◁⎯⎯⎯  Navigate to the new
}                                                   bookable in the UI.
```

### CHALLENGE 10.3

Hook up the BookableEdit component so that it saves changes to bookables and allows the deletion of bookables. Create separate mutations for each action and call them from the handleSave and handleDelete functions. (You could add editItem and deleteItem methods to api.js and call those in the mutations.) The 1008-edit-bookable branch has solution code with lots of comments.

### CHALLENGE 10.4

This is a big one! Implement a BookingForm component so users can create, edit, and delete bookings on the Bookings page. The BookingDetails component should show either a Booking component with non-editable details of the selected booking, or the BookingForm component when a user wants to edit or create a booking. The solution branch, 1009-booking-form, creates custom hooks for the three mutations (useCreateBooking, useUpdateBooking, and useDeleteBooking) in the bookings-Hooks.js file.

> **NOTE**  I haven't implemented any form validation in the bookings app. In a real app, we'd add validation on both the client and the server.

> **NOTE**  The repo has two more branches for this chapter, 1010-react-spring and 1011-spring-challenge, that use the React Spring library to add animated transitions to the Bookings page, sliding the bookings grid down for switched bookables and across for switched dates. It's one fun extra use of third-party hooks.

## Summary

- With React Router, render the same component for routes that start with a specified path. For example, render BookablesPage for URLs that start with /bookables/:

  ```
  <Route path="/bookables/*" element={<BookablesPage/>}/>
  ```

- As an alternative to the `element` prop, wrap JSX within opening and closing `Route` tags:

```
<Route path="/bookables/*">
  <BookablesPage/>
</Route>
```

- Nest routes by including a `Routes` component in a component already matched by a `Route` higher up the component tree. For example, `BookablesPage` can include its own nested routes, with URLs /bookables and /bookables/new by returning UI like this:

```
<Routes>
  <Route path="/">
    <BookablesView/>
  </Route>
  <Route path="/new">
    <BookableNew/>
  </Route>
</Routes>
```

- Use parameters in routes by prepending parameter names with a colon:

```
<Route path="/:id" element={<BookablesView/>}/>
```

- Access the parameter in a component by calling React Router's `useParams` hook. `useParams` returns an object with parameters and their values. Destructure the parameters from the object:

```
const {id} = useParams();
```

- Navigate with React Router's `useNavigate` hook:

```
const navigate = useNavigate();
navigate("/url/of/page");
```

- Access search parameters in a URL's query string with React Router's `useSearchParams` hook:

```
const [searchParams, setSearchParams] = useSearchParams();
```

  For the URL /bookings?bookableId=1&date=2020-08-20, access the parameters like this:

```
searchParams.get("date");
searchParams.get("bookableId");
```

- Set the query string by passing an object to `setSearchParams`:

```
setSearchParams({
  date: "2020-06-26",
  bookableId: 3
});
```

- Use React Query to efficiently fetch and cache server state on the browser. Wrap your app JSX in a provider and pass the provider a client object:

```
const queryClient = new QueryClient();

export default function App () {
  return (
    <QueryClientProvider client={queryClient}>
      {/* app JSX */}
    </QueryClientProvider>
  );
}
```

- To fetch data, pass a key and a fetch function to the `useQuery` hook:

```
const {data, status, error} = useQuery(key, () => fetch(url));
```

- Pass a configuration object to `useQuery` as a third argument:

```
const {data, isLoading} = useQuery(key, asyncFunction, config);
```

- Set initial data by using the config object:

```
const {data, isLoading} = useQuery(key, asyncFn, {initialData: […]});
```

- Use the `getQueryData` method and a key to access previously fetched data from the `queryClient` object:

```
const queryClient = useQueryClient();
const {data, isLoading} = useQuery(
  currentKey,
  asyncFunction,
  {
    initialData: queryClient.getQueryData(otherKey)
  }
);
```

- Create a mutation function for updating server state by calling React Query's `useMutation` function:

```
const {mutate, status, error} = useMutation(asyncFunction, config);
```

- Use the mutation function to update state on the server:

```
mutate(updatedData);
```

# Part 2

React's evolution encompasses more than just hooks. The React team is working hard to make the experience of developing and using React applications as intuitive and enjoyable as possible by implementing flexible but powerful APIs that provide safe and sensible defaults. The team's motivations are driven in a large part by developing the Facebook application, but they also listen carefully to the community and take their time to get emerging models right.

The team has been working on Concurrent Mode for some time, and part 2 will give you insight into what's to come. Concurrent Mode lets React work on multiple versions of your UI simultaneously—pausing, restarting, and discarding rendering tasks to make your apps seem as responsive and predictable as possible.

Chapter 11 shows how you can use the `Suspense` component and error boundaries to decouple fallback UI from components for lazy loading and error reporting and recovery. Chapters 12 and 13 then head into more experimental territory, exploring how data fetching and image loading might integrate with Suspense and how you can use two further hooks, `useTransition` and `useDeferredValue`, to present the best UI to users as state changes in your apps.

# Code splitting
# with Suspense

**This chapter covers**

- Importing code dynamically with the `import` function
- Loading components when they're needed with `React.lazy`
- Specifying fallback UI declaratively with `Suspense` components
- Understanding how `lazy` and `Suspense` work together
- Specifying error fallback UI declaratively with error boundaries

It's common for app users to interact with some components more than others. In the bookings app, for example, users often visit the Bookings page without switching to the Bookables or Users pages, and on the Bookables page they may never bring up the New or Edit forms. To manage the amount of code loaded by the browser at any one time, we can use a technique called *code splitting*; rather than loading all of an app's code at once, we load it in *chunks*, as it's needed.

So far in this book, all of our examples have used *static imports*. At the top of each JavaScript file, we include `import` statements to specify *dependencies*, the code in external files that the current file uses. At build time, bundlers like webpack inspect our code, follow the paths to the imported files, and generate a *bundle*, a file that contains all the code the app actually uses. Our web pages then request the bundle.

This *tree-shaking* process, which avoids duplicate code and discards unused code, can help keep the bundle well organized and as small as possible. For larger applications and/or slower connections, "as small as possible" can still be big enough to take a while to load. Maybe loading all of the code up front isn't the best idea. If parts of the app are less likely to be used or contain particularly bulky components, it can be helpful to reduce the size of the initial bundle and then load further bundles only when the user visits a certain route or initiates a particular interaction.

In React, we work with components. We want to dynamically import some components into our applications only when they're needed. But React calls the components when it's time to render them. If the component isn't loaded when it's time to render it, what should React do? We don't want the whole app to pause and wait for the component. For bigger components or those that don't usually take part in initial user interactions, we can do these four things:

- Load the component code only when we try to render the component.
- Show a placeholder while the component loads.
- Continue rendering the rest of the app.
- Replace the placeholder with the component after it's loaded.

In this chapter, we look at how to put those four points into action by using React's `lazy` method and `Suspense` component. Our discussion of placeholder UI will also lead us to *error boundaries*, a way of giving React something to render if errors occur. First up, it'll be useful to understand how JavaScript lets us import code dynamically.

## 11.1 Importing code dynamically with the import function

In this section, we look at dynamically importing JavaScript from one module into another. We won't be using React, but the concepts are important for when we come to dynamically load components in our React apps. There are four subsections:

- Setting up a web page to load JavaScript when a button is clicked
- Making JavaScript available from a file using default and named exports
- Using static imports to load JavaScript
- Calling the `import` function to dynamically load JavaScript

### 11.1.1 Setting up a web page to load JavaScript when a button is clicked

Say we have an app that displays a button. When we click the button, two messages are displayed, as shown in figure 11.1.

To demonstrate module importing, let's split the app into three files: index.html, index.js, and helloModule.js. The following listing shows the HTML, including the

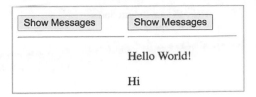

**Figure 11.1   Clicking the button shows two messages.**

button, two paragraphs to hold the two messages, and a script element to load the code file, index.js, that'll wire up the button to display the messages.

*Live:* https://vg0ke.csb.app, *Code:* https://codesandbox.io/s/jsstaticimport-vg0ke

**Listing 11.1   An HTML file for displaying two messages (index.html)**

```
<!DOCTYPE html>
<html>
  <head>
    <title>Dynamic Imports</title>
    <meta charset="UTF-8" />
  </head>

  <body>
    <button id="btnMessages">Show Messages</button>      ◁  Include a button to
    <hr />                                                   display the two messages.
    <p id="messagePara"></p>      Include paragraph elements
    <p id="hiPara"></p>           as targets for the messages.

    <script src="src/index.js"></script>   ◁  Load the script that'll
  </body>                                     wire up the button.
</html>
```

We don't yet have the index.js file, but we do know that it'll use some handy utility functions for injecting text into existing HTML elements. The utility functions live in their own module. Let's see that module and how it makes the functions available.

### 11.1.2   Using default and named exports

Our handy utility functions live in a JavaScript module, helloModule.js. The module is shown in the following listing and uses the export and default keywords to specify values that other files will be able to import. One of the messaging functions is the default export, and the other is a named export.

*Live:* https://vg0ke.csb.app, *Code:* https://codesandbox.io/s/jsstaticimport-vg0ke

**Listing 11.2   Creating a module with default and named exports (helloModule.js)**

```
export default function sayMessage (id, msg) {      ◁  Make the sayMessage
  document.getElementById(id).innerHTML = msg;         function the default
}                                                       export.
```

```
export function sayHi (id) {
  sayMessage(id, "Hi");
}
```
◁ **Make the sayHi function a named export.**

Files can have a single default export and multiple named exports. They don't have to export everything, only those values (in our case, functions) that they want other files to be able to import. We have our super-handy, message-injecting functions ready to go, so let's get importing!

### 11.1.3   *Using static imports to load JavaScript*

Our app performs the vital task of showing messages when the user clicks a button. The last file we need, index.js, sets up an event handler to wire up the button with the action of displaying the messages. But it doesn't start from scratch; we have some handy utility functions available, after all. So index.js imports the messaging functions from the helloModule.js module and calls them from the event handler. The standard approach to importing values exported from other modules is to import them statically at the top of a file, as shown in the following listing.

> **Live**: https://vg0ke.csb.app, **Code**: https://codesandbox.io/s/jsstaticimport-vg0ke
>
> **Listing 11.3   Static import (index.js)**

```
import showMessage, {sayHi} from "./helloModule";
```
◁ **Import the two messaging functions.**

```
function handleClick () {
  showMessage("messagePara", "Hello World!");
  sayHi("hiPara");
}
```
**Call the imported functions.**

```
document
  .getElementById("btnMessages")
  .addEventListener("click", handleClick);
```
◁ **Call the handler when the button is clicked.**

We assign the default export from `helloModule` to the local `showMessage` variable (we can choose the variable name), and assign the named export, `sayHi`, to a local variable using the matching variable name between curly braces—it's named `sayHi` in helloModule.js, so we have to use `sayHi` in index.js.

That all works as expected; it's a simple example. But say the module we want to import is a much bigger file (at least pretend it is for now), and say, too, that most users don't click the button very often. Can we avoid loading the hefty module unless it's needed? That would really help us load the main app more quickly.

### 11.1.4 *Calling the import function to dynamically load JavaScript*

How about loading the code that the button uses only if the button is clicked? The following listing shows index.js loading code dynamically with the `import` function.

**Listing 11.4  Dynamically loading code with the import function (index.js)**

```
function handleClick() {                    Call the import function to
  import("./helloModule")        ◁──┐       dynamically load a module.     Assign the module
    .then((module) => {                                                    to a local variable.
      module.default("messagePara", "Hello World!");     ◁────
      module.sayHi("hiPara");                                          Use the module properties to
    });                                                                call the exported functions.
}

document
  .getElementById("btnMessages")
  .addEventListener("click", handleClick);
```

There's no need to load a big file if it won't be used, so the module is loaded only when the button is clicked. The `handleClick` function uses the `import` function to load the module:

```
import("./helloModule")
```

The `import` function returns a promise that resolves to the exported module. We call the promise's `then` method to work with the module after it's loaded:

```
import("./helloModule").then((module) => { /* use module */ });
```

Alternatively, we can use `async`/`await` syntax:

```
async function handleClick() {
  const module = await import("./helloModule");
  // use module
}
```

The exported values (both functions, in our case) are available as properties of the `module` object. The default export is assigned to the `default` property, and named exports are assigned to properties of the same name. The helloModule.js file has a default export and a `sayHi` named export, so these are available as `module.default` and `module.sayHi`:

```
module.default("messagePara", "Hello World!");
module.sayHi("hiPara");
```

Rather than calling the functions as methods of the module object, we can destructure the module object as shown in the following listing.

---

**Listing 11.5   Destructuring module properties from a dynamic import**

```
function handleClick() {
  import("./helloModule")
    .then(({default: showMessage, sayHi}) => {
      showMessage("messagePara", "Hello World!");
      sayHi("hiPara");
    });
}

document
  .getElementById("btnMessages")
  .addEventListener("click", handleClick);
```

> Destructure the module, assigning exported functions to local variables.
>
> Use the local variables to call the exported functions.

Within the destructuring, we assign the default export to a variable with a more appropriate name, showMessage. Again, the async/await version is quite clean:

```
async function handleClick() {
  const {default: showMessage, sayHi} = await import("./helloModule");
  showMessage("messagePara", "Hello World!");
  sayHi("hiPara");
}
```

So, that's a quick introduction to dynamic imports. But we want to dynamically import React components; how can we delay the importing of components without breaking React's rendering process? Now that we need the knowledge, let's load up the lowdown on lazy.

## 11.2  *Importing components dynamically with lazy and Suspense*

In the preceding section, we used the import function to dynamically load JavaScript code. We loaded the code only when it was needed, when the user clicked a button. But we were also in control of rendering; we imperatively attached event handlers and tweaked the DOM with calls to addEventListener and getElementById and by setting the innerHTML property.

When working with React, we should concentrate on updating the state and let React manage the DOM. How can we combine lazily loading components with React's need to control the rendering process? We need some way of declaratively letting React know what to do if a component it wants to render is not yet ready. This section looks at the two pieces we can use to solve the problem, first separately and then together, before applying the solution to the bookings app example. Our four subsections are as follows:

- Converting a component to a lazy component with the lazy function
- Specifying fallback content with the Suspense component
- Understanding how lazy and Suspense work together
- Code splitting an app on its routes

First, we have a date with an overlarge calendar component in a news app. In its case, laziness is a virtue.

### 11.2.1 Converting a component to a lazy component with the lazy function

Say we have an app in the company that shows the latest company news and announcements. Coworkers check the app all the time to keep up-to-date. The app also includes a full-featured calendar component that can either be viewed on the main page along with the other content or opened in its own view.

However, coworkers check the calendar only from time to time. Rather than including the calendar component code when the app first loads, we want to load the calendar code only when a user clicks a Show Calendar button. Figure 11.2 roughly illustrates the setup, with a region for the main app and two ways of opening the calendar.

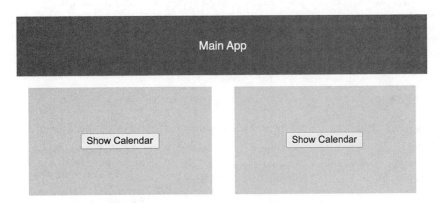

**Figure 11.2  Our company news app loads the `Calendar` component code only when a user clicks one of the Show Calendar buttons.**

We'll use the same component, `CalendarWrapper`, for the two calendar regions under the main app (but imagine one would open the calendar in place and the other would replace the current view). The following listing shows the JSX for the app's UI with a main region and the two calendar regions.

**Listing 11.6  The app includes a main region and two calendar regions**

```
<div className="App">
  <main>Main App</main>
  <aside>
    <CalendarWrapper />
    <CalendarWrapper />
  </aside>
</div>
```

The code for a `CalendarWrapper` component is in the following listing. The component starts by displaying the Show Calendar button. When a user clicks the button, `CalendarWrapper` switches to displaying a `LazyCalendar` component.

**Listing 11.7   A component with a button for displaying the calendar**

```
function CalendarWrapper() {
  const [isOn, setIsOn] = useState(false);
  return isOn ? (
    <LazyCalendar />                              ◁──── Include a lazily
  ) : (                                                 loaded component.
    <div>
      <button onClick={() => setIsOn(true)}>Show Calendar</button>
    </div>
  );
}
```

Listing 11.7 uses the `LazyCalendar` component, a special component that isn't imported until it's rendered for the first time. But where does that come from? Assuming we already have a `Calendar` component in a module called Calendar.js, we can combine a dynamic import with React's `lazy` function to convert `Calendar` into `LazyCalendar`:

```
const LazyCalendar = lazy(() => import("./Calendar.js"));
```

We pass `lazy` a function that returns a promise. More generally, the process looks like this:

```
const getPromise = () => import(modulePath);         ◁──── Create a function that
                                                            returns a promise.

const LazyComponent = lazy(getPromise);              ◁──── Pass the promise-generating
                                                            function to React.lazy.
```

We pass `lazy` a function, `getPromise`, that React calls when it's time to render the component for the first time. The `getPromise` function returns a promise that resolves to a module. The module's default export must be a component.

But we don't have a `Calendar` module (we're imagining it to be a large file) so, for the sake of our example, and to reinforce the idea that modules are objects with default and named properties, let's mock up a module and make it lazy by using the following code.

**Listing 11.8   Creating a pretend module and making its component lazy**

```
const module = {
  default: () => <div>Big Calendar</div>            ◁──── Assign a function component
};                                                        to the default property.

function getPromise() {
  return new Promise(
    (resolve) => setTimeout(() => resolve(module), 3000)    ◁── Return a promise that
                                                                resolves to our module.
```

```
  );
}
const LazyCalendar = lazy(getPromise);          ◁─┐ Create a lazy component by
                                                    │ passing getPromise to lazy.
```

Great! We have all the pieces in place to try out our first lazy component:

- A "huge" calendar component (() => <div>Big Calendar</div>)
- A module with the calendar component assigned to its default property
- A promise that resolves to the module (after three seconds)
- A function, getPromise, that creates and returns the promise
- A lazy component, LazyCalendar, created by passing getPromise to lazy
- A wrapper component, CalendarWrapper, that shows LazyCalendar only after a user clicks a button
- An App component that includes two CalenderWrapper components

The following listing puts all the pieces into place. It's part of a React application on CodeSandbox. The code to create and use the lazy component is in bold.

*Live:* **https://9qj5f.csb.app**, *Code:* **https://codesandbox.io/s/lazycalendarnosuspense-9qj5f**

**Listing 11.9   Running our app with a lazy component**

```
import React, { lazy, useState } from "react";
import "./styles.css";

const module = {                                ◁─┐ Set a component as the default
  default: () => <div>Big Calendar</div>            │ export from a module.
};

function getPromise() {
  return new Promise(                                    Resolve a promise
    (resolve) => setTimeout((() => resolve(module), 3000)   ◁── with the module.
  );
}
                                                ◁─┐ Convert the component-resolving
const LazyCalendar = lazy(getPromise);              │ promise into a lazy component.

function CalendarWrapper() {
  const [isOn, setIsOn] = useState(false);
  return isOn ? (
    <LazyCalendar />                ◁─┐ Use the lazy component
  ) : (                               │ like any other component.
    <div>
      <button onClick={() => setIsOn(true)}>Show Calendar</button>
    </div>
  );
}

export default function App() {
  return (
    <div className="App">
      <main>Main App</main>
```

```
        <aside>
          <CalendarWrapper />
          <CalendarWrapper />
        </aside>
      </div>
    );
}
```

Remember, for real modules we use a dynamic import; we pass `lazy` a function that calls the `import` function. So, if the `Calendar` component is the default export from a Calendar.js module, we'd create the lazy component like this:

```
const LazyCalendar = lazy(() => import("./Calendar.js"));
```

But wait! If you follow the link to CodeSandbox and click one of the Show Calendar buttons, you'll see we have a problem, an evil error! (Actually, like most React errors, it's quite a friendly error; it tells us exactly what we have to do.) The error is shown in figure 11.3. It tells us to "Add a <Suspense fallback=. . .> component higher in the tree to provide a loading indicator or placeholder to display." Let's follow its advice.

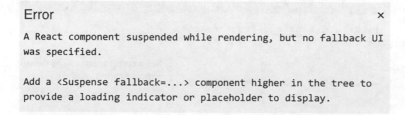

Figure 11.3 **Our app starts out fine, but clicking a Show Calendar button causes an error: "A React component suspended while rendering, but no fallback UI was specified."**

### 11.2.2 *Specifying fallback content with the Suspense component*

It takes time to load a component, and our imaginary `Calendar` component code is a big, beefy file. What should our app do when it's time to show the calendar but it hasn't yet loaded? We need some kind of loading indicator to let the user know the calendar is on the way. Maybe something as simple as in figure 11.4, just text saying "Loading . . . ".

Fortunately, as the error in figure 11.3 points out, React provides an easy way to specify fallback UI: the `Suspense` component. Use the `Suspense` component to wrap UI that contains one or more lazy components in its tree:

```
<Suspense fallback={<div>Loading...</div>}>
  <CalendarWrapper />
</Suspense>
```

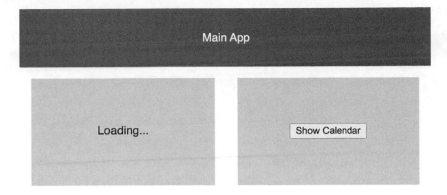

**Figure 11.4   When the user first clicks the Show Calendar button, the app displays a loading indicator until the component has loaded.**

Use the `fallback` prop to specify what you want the `Suspense` component to render until all its lazy descendants have returned some UI. In the following listing, we wrap both `CalendarWrapper` components in their own `Suspense` component so that the app knows what to do if one of the wrapper's `LazyCalendar` components is loading.

*Live:* **https://h0hgg.csb.app,** *Code:* **https://codesandbox.io/s/lazycalendar-h0hgg**

**Listing 11.10   Wrapping both calendar regions in `Suspense` components**

```
<div className="App">
  <main>Main App</main>
  <aside>
    <Suspense fallback={<div>Loading...</div>}>        ◁──  Wrap UI that contains
      <CalendarWrapper />                                   lazy components in
    </Suspense>                                             Suspense components.
    <Suspense fallback={<div>Loading...</div>}>        ◁──  Use the fallback prop to
      <CalendarWrapper />                                   specify placeholder UI.
    </Suspense>
  </aside>
</div>
```

If you follow the link to the new version on CodeSandbox and click the Show Calendar button, you'll see the "Loading . . . " fallback from figure 11.4 for three seconds and then the `Calendar` component will render, saying, "Big Calendar," as shown in figure 11.5.

Once the `Calendar` component has loaded, it doesn't need to load again, so clicking the second Show Calendar button will immediately render the second `Calendar` component. In listing 11.10, each `CalendarWrapper` component is wrapped in its own `Suspense` component. But a single `Suspense` component might be all you need. The following code snippet shows a single `Suspense` component for both `Calendar-Wrapper` components.

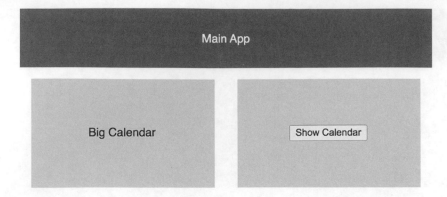

**Figure 11.5**   Once the `Calendar` component has loaded, it replaces the fallback content.

```
<Suspense fallback={<div>Loading...</div>}>
  <CalendarWrapper />
  <CalendarWrapper />
</Suspense>
```

If you wrap both components in this way, clicking a Show Calendar button for the first time will display the shared "Loading . . . " fallback shown in figure 11.6.

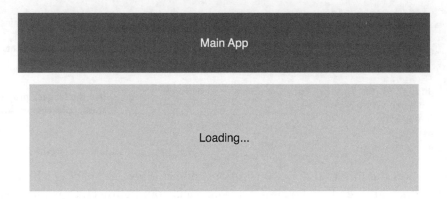

**Figure 11.6**   Multiple components can be wrapped in a single `Suspense` component. The fallback content is shown if any descendant is loading.

When a lazy component is first rendered, React will look all the way up the component tree and use the first `Suspense` component that it finds. That `Suspense` component will render its fallback UI in place of its children. If no `Suspense` component is found, React will throw the error we saw back in figure 11.3.

The ability to specify fallback UI separate from the components that are loading gives us greater flexibility when tweaking our UI for the best possible user experience. But how do the separate components work together? How exactly does React look up the component tree for a Suspense component? What mechanism do lazy components use to either render a loaded component or pass rendering to parents? Well, I'm here to help. I'll tell you how they do it, and that's a promise.

### 11.2.3 *Understanding how lazy and Suspense work together*

We can think of lazy components as having an internal status of uninitialized, pending, resolved, or rejected. When React first tries to render a lazy component, the component is uninitialized but has a promise-returning function React calls to load the module. For example, here the promise-returning function is getPromise:

```
const getPromise = () => import("./Calendar");
const LazyCalendar = lazy(getPromise);
```

The promise should resolve to a module whose default property is the component. Once it's resolved, React can set the status of the lazy component to resolved and return the component, ready to be rendered, something like this:

```
if (status === "resolved") {
  return component;
} else {
  throw promise;
}
```

The else clause contains the key to communicating with Suspense components further up the tree: if the promise has not resolved, React will throw it, just as you'd throw an error. Suspense components are set up to catch promises, rendering fallback UI if the promise is pending.

To recap, table 11.1 shows the steps React takes when it encounters a lazy component in the tree. It performs the first action it can.

**Table 11.1  The steps React takes when it encounters a lazy component**

| If the LazyComponent object contains | Actions |
| --- | --- |
| A component | Call the component. |
| An unresolved promise | Throw the promise. |
| A function that returns a promise | Call the function to get the promise. |
| | Store the promise in the LazyComponent object. |
| | Call the promise's then method so that when the promise resolves, the component is stored in the LazyComponent object. |
| | Throw the promise. |

Seasoned promise-wranglers may be wondering what happens if the promise is rejected, maybe because of a network error. Suspense components don't handle the UI for errors; that's the remit of the error boundary, which we discuss in section 11.3. Before that, let's split the booking app into lazy-loaded routes.

### 11.2.4  Code splitting an app on its routes

You now know how to split our app into separate bundles by lazy-loading some of the components. There's no need to load a lot of code if it's not going to be used. Instead, as the user opts to use certain functionality, the code for that functionality can be loaded, with some fallback UI displayed while it loads.

Our booking app example is already split into separate routes for bookings, bookables, and users. The routes seem like a sensible place to start splitting our code. The following listing updates the App component, lazy-loading each page component and wrapping the Routes component in a Suspense component.

> **Branch**: 1101-lazy-suspense, *File*: /src/components/App.js
>
> **Listing 11.11   Lazy-loading page components in App**

```
import {lazy, Suspense} from "react";          ◁──── Import the lazy function and
                                                     the Suspense component.
// previous imports with the three pages removed

import PageSpinner from "./UI/PageSpinner";

const BookablesPage = lazy(() => import("./Bookables/BookablesPage"));   ◁ Lazy-load the
const BookingsPage = lazy(() => import("./Bookings/BookingsPage"));         three page
const UsersPage = lazy(() => import("./Users/UsersPage"));                  components.

const queryClient = new QueryClient();

export default function App () {
  return (
    <QueryClientProvider client={queryClient}>
      <UserProvider>
        <Router>
          <div className="App">
            <header>
              <nav>
                {/* unchanged */}
              </nav>

              <UserPicker/>
            </header>
                                                       Wrap the page routes in a
                                                       Suspense component with
            <Suspense fallback={<PageSpinner/>}>   ◁── PageSpinner fallback.
              <Routes>
                <Route path="/bookings" element={<BookingsPage/>}/>
                <Route path="/bookables/*" element={<BookablesPage/>}/>
                <Route path="/users" element={<UsersPage/>}/>
              </Routes>
```

Use the lazy-loaded
page components
just like any other.

```
        </Suspense>
      </div>
    </Router>
   </UserProvider>
  </QueryClientProvider>
 );
}
```

Now, if a user first visits the Users page, say, only the code for the App component, the UsersPage component, and their dependencies is loaded. Code for BookingsPage and BookablesPage is not included. While the components load, our usual Page-Spinner component is rendered under the top menu bar.

The BookablesPage component includes some nested routes, and the user might navigate directly to any one of them without choosing to visit the others. Loading all of the code at once is unnecessary, so let's get lazy once again in the following listing.

---

**Branch**: 1101-lazy-suspense, *File*: /src/components/Bookables/BookablesPage.js

**Listing 11.12   Lazy-loading nested components for** BookablesPage

```
import {lazy} from "react";
import {Routes, Route} from "react-router-dom";

const BookablesView = lazy(() => import("./BookablesView"));    ◁── Lazy-load the
const BookableEdit = lazy(() => import("./BookableEdit"));         components.
const BookableNew = lazy(() => import("./BookableNew"));

export default function BookablesPage () {
  return (
    <Routes>
      <Route path="/:id">
        <BookablesView/>                    ◁──┐
      </Route>
      <Route path="/">
        <BookablesView/>                    ◁──┤   Use the components
      </Route>                                      in exactly the same
      <Route path="/:id/edit">                      way as before.
        <BookableEdit/>                     ◁──┤
      </Route>
      <Route path="/new">
        <BookableNew/>                      ◁──┘
      </Route>
    </Routes>
  );
}
```

This time, we don't wrap the routes in a Suspense component. Our existing fallback in App will happily deal with any *suspending* components (components that throw pending promises) below it in the tree. The PageSpinner is an appropriate fallback because all three components—BookablesView, BookablesEdit, and BookablesNew—are page-level components. They all replace whatever was on the page before them (excluding the ever-present menu bar at the top). Feel free to experiment with adding Suspense components around the nested routes; a "Loading Edit Form . . . " message might be useful.

Suspense components handle pending promises. What happens when a component throws a rejected promise or, more conventionally, throws an error while rendering? If Suspense components don't want to know, what does? It's time to set some boundaries for those pesky errors.

## 11.3   Catching errors with error boundaries

React doesn't provide a component for catching errors thrown in child components. But it does provide a couple of life-cycle methods that class components can implement if they want to catch and report errors. If one of your class components implements one or both of those methods, it is considered an *error boundary*.

If you wrap all or part of the component tree in the error boundary, it will render fallback UI if one of the wrapped components throws an error. Figure 11.7 shows the kind of fallback UI we might use in the bookings app if an error is thrown by one of the page components or one of their descendants.

**Figure 11.7    Rather than unmounting the app, an error boundary can show some fallback UI if an error occurs.**

Say we have such an error boundary component, ErrorBoundary, and we want it to catch errors for any of our routes in the bookings app. We want to be able to specify where the error boundary goes, and which components are replaced by the fallback UI when an error is thrown. We want to use ErrorBoundary like this:

```
<UserProvider>
  <Router>
    <div className="App">
      <header>{/* unchanged menu */}</header>        ⟵  Leave some UI outside
                                                          the error boundary.
Use an error
boundary to
catch errors    ⟶  <ErrorBoundary>                    Catch promises from
from wrapped         <Suspense fallback={<PageSpinner/>}>  ⟵  wrapped components.
components.            <Routes>{/* unchanged */}</Routes>   ⟵
                     </Suspense>                       Render wrapped
                   </ErrorBoundary>                    components when
                                                       all is well.

    </div>
  </Router>
</UserProvider>
```

Only the page components are replaced by the fallback; the app continues to show the menu in the `header` element, as you can see at the top of figure 11.7. The figure also shows the fallback UI, the message "Something went wrong," that the app displays in response to an error in a child component.

But where does that UI come from? And what are the life-cycle methods we have to implement in our error boundary class component? A good place to start (as always) is in the React docs.

### 11.3.1 Checking out the error boundary example in the React docs

To catch any errors thrown when our child components render, we need a class component that implements one or both of the life-cycle methods `getDerivedState-FromError` and `componentDidCatch`. The following listing shows an error boundary component that implements those methods, from the React docs on reactjs.org. It has the hardcoded fallback UI shown in figure 11.7.

> *React docs:* https://reactjs.org/docs/error-boundaries.html
>
> **Listing 11.13  The `ErrorBoundary` component on reactjs.org**

```
class ErrorBoundary extends React.Component {         ⟵  Extend React's Component class
  constructor(props) {                                     to create an error boundary.
    super(props);
    this.state = { hasError: false };                 ⟵  Include a hasError
  }                                                        property in state.

Return                                                
new state    ⟶  static getDerivedStateFromError(error) {
when an          // Update state so the next render will show the fallback UI.
error is         return { hasError: true };
caught.        }
                                                      Logs errors if
                                                      they are caught.
  componentDidCatch(error, errorInfo) {               ⟵
    // You can also log the error to an error reporting service
    logErrorToMyService(error, errorInfo);
  }
```

```
  render() {
    if (this.state.hasError) {
      // You can render any custom fallback UI
      return <h1>Something went wrong.</h1>;        ◁──┐   Renders fallback UI
    }                                                       if there's an error.

    return this.props.children;     ◁──┐   Render the wrapped components
  }                                         if there's no error.
}
```

The component manages state with a `hasError` property that flags whether or not the component has caught an error. The `componentDidCatch` method also logs any error information to an external logging service. Finally, the `render` method returns the wrapped components or, if the `getDerivedStateFromError` method has set the error flag to `true`, hardcoded fallback UI:

```
<h1>Something went wrong.</h1>
```

But listing 11.13 is just an example error boundary. Let's make our own.

### 11.3.2   Creating our own error boundary

The error boundary from the React docs is just one possibility. We may want something tailored more to our apps. The fallback UI in figure 11.8, for example, includes an instruction for the user to "Try reloading the page."

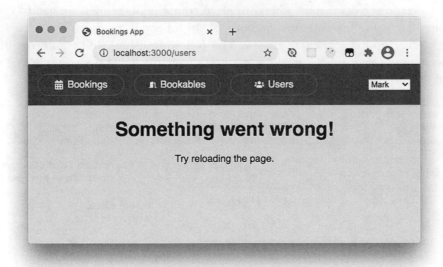

**Figure 11.8   Our `ErrorBoundary` component allows us to specify custom UI as the fallback when an error occurs.**

Rather than just switching one hardcoded message for another, let's have a go at implementing an error boundary that lets us specify different fallbacks each time we use it. The following listing shows just such a component. We're not going to log any errors, so we leave out the `componentDidCatch` method, and users of the component can specify UI in a `fallback` prop.

---

*Branch*: 1102-error-boundary, *File*: /src/components/UI/ErrorBoundary.js

**Listing 11.14** A simple, customizable `ErrorBoundary` component

```
import {Component} from "react";

export default class ErrorBoundary extends Component {
  constructor (props) {
    super(props);
    this.state = {hasError: false};
  }

  static getDerivedStateFromError () {
    return {hasError: true};
  }

  render() {
    const {
      children,                                          ← Get the wrapped
                                                            components from props.
      fallback = <h1>Something went wrong.</h1>          ← Get the fallback
    } = this.props;                                         from props, or use a
                                                            default fallback.
    return this.state.hasError ? fallback : children;    ← Render the fallback
  }                                                         or the wrapped
}                                                           components.
```

We'll put the new error boundary to use straightaway in the bookings app, as a catch-all for errors thrown on any of our three pages. In the following listing, the App component now wraps the `Suspense` and `Routes` components with `ErrorBoundary`.

---

*Branch*: 1102-error-boundary, *File*: /src/components/App.js

**Listing 11.15** App with an error boundary

```
// other imports, including Fragment
                                          ← Import our error
import ErrorBoundary from "./UI/ErrorBoundary";  boundary.

const BookablesPage = lazy(() => import("./Bookables/BookablesPage"));
const BookingsPage = lazy(() => import("./Bookings/BookingsPage"));
const UsersPage = lazy(() => import("./Users/UsersPage"));

const queryClient = new QueryClient();

export default function App () {
  return (
    <QueryClientProvider client={queryClient}>
      <UserProvider>
        <Router>
```

```
                   <div className="App">
Wrap the main         <header>{/* unchanged */}</header>
routes in the
error boundary.    <ErrorBoundary
                    fallback={
Provide some          <Fragment>
fallback UI.            <h1>Something went wrong!</h1>          Maybe include advice
                        <p>Try reloading the page.</p>         on what to do.
                      </Fragment>
                    }
                   >
                    <Suspense fallback={<PageSpinner/>}>
                      <Routes>
                        <Route path="/bookings" element={<BookingsPage/>}/>
                        <Route path="/bookables/*" element={<BookablesPage/>}/>
                        <Route path="/users" element={<UsersPage/>}/>
                      </Routes>
                    </Suspense>
                   </ErrorBoundary>              Wrap the main routes
                                                 in the error boundary.
                 </div>
               </Router>
             </UserProvider>
           </QueryClientProvider>
         );
       }
```

We wrap the app's main routes in an error boundary. To test it out, let's throw an error from a descendant component. In the `BookableForm` component, just before it returns its UI, add this line:

```
throw new Error("Noooo!");
```

Now, reload the app, navigate to the Bookables page, and click the New button under the list of bookables or the Edit button at the top right of the bookable details header. Dismiss the error overlay shown in figure 11.9; it's added by Create React App and won't appear in production. You should see the fallback UI in figure 11.8.

If a single page of an app includes multiple components and the failure of one component doesn't break the others—the user can keep using the page—then consider wrapping that component in its own error boundary. There's no need to bar users from working functionality elsewhere when error boundaries can safely quarantine wobbly widgets. It would be nice to be able to stabilize the wobbly ones, though, and we can further customize our error boundary components to make it easier to recover from errors.

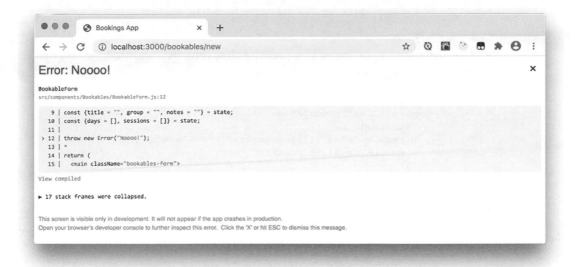

**Figure 11.9   In development mode, Create React App's server overlays the page with an error message. Press Esc or click the X to dismiss the overlay, revealing the error boundary's fallback UI.**

### 11.3.3 *Recovering from errors*

Asking users to refresh the page is one approach that might work for errors not caught lower down the component tree. But, especially for error boundaries around specific widgets within the main app, like chat windows or stock tickers, or social media streams, you might want to give the users a button to click to try resetting or reloading a specific component within the app. In chapter 12, we'll use a prebuilt error boundary package from npm called `react-error-boundary`. It provides handy extra functionality to make its error boundary more flexible and reusable. Check it out on GitHub at https://github.com/bvaughn/react-error-boundary.

Chapter 12 continues this chapter's theme of giving React something to render while it waits for the final UI to be ready. Rather than waiting for components to load, we'll be waiting for data or images. Join me there for our first explorations of experimental React features.

### *Summary*

- Include dependencies as static imports at the top of a JavaScript file. Bundlers like webpack can then perform tree shaking to create a bundle, a single file containing all the code that the app uses.
- To load JavaScript dependencies only in response to a user action or other event, dynamically load modules with the `import` function:

```
function handleClick() {
  import("./helloModule")
```

```
      .then(module => {/* use module */});
  }
```

- The dynamic import returns a promise that returns a module. Access default and named exports on the module object:

```
function handleClick() {
  import("./helloModule")
    .then(module => {
      module.default("messagePara", "Hello World!");
      module.sayHi("hiPara");
    });
}
```

- Use `React.lazy` to load components only when they are first rendered. Pass `lazy` a function that returns the promise from a dynamic import. The promise must resolve to a module whose default property is a component:

```
const LazyComponent = React.lazy(() => import("./MyComponent"));
```

- Use `Suspense` components to tell React what to render while waiting for lazy components to load. (`Suspense` components catch pending promises thrown by not-yet-loaded components.)

```
<Suspense fallback={<p>Just one moment...</p>}>
  { /* UI that could contain a lazy component */ }
</Suspense>
```

- Use error boundary components to tell React what to render if an error occurs while rendering a child component. Error boundaries are class components that implement one or both of the life-cycle methods `getDerivedStateFrom-Error` and `componentDidCatch`:

```
<ErrorBoundary>
  { /* App or subtree */ }
</ErrorBoundary>
```

- Customize error boundaries to provide tailored fallback UI and error-recovery strategies.

# 12

# Integrating data fetching with Suspense

## This chapter covers

- Wrapping promises to access their status
- Throwing promises and errors when fetching data
- Using `Suspense` components to specify fallback UI when loading data and images
- Fetching data and resources as early as possible
- Recovering from errors when using error boundaries

The React team has a mission to maintain and develop a product that makes it as easy as possible for developers to create great user experiences. In addition to writing comprehensive documentation, providing intuitive and instructive developer tools, authoring descriptive and easily actionable error messages, and ensuring incremental upgrade paths, the team wants React to make it easy to provide fast-loading, responsive, and scalable applications. Concurrent Mode and Suspense offer ways to improve the user experience, orchestrating the loading of code and resources, enabling simpler, intentional loading states, and prioritizing updates that let users get on with their work or play.

But the React team doesn't want hooking into Concurrent Mode to be a burden on developers; they want as many of the benefits as possible to be automatic and any new APIs to be intuitive and in step with existing mindsets. So, Concurrent Mode is still flagged as experimental as the APIs are tested and tweaked. Hopefully, we won't be kept in ~~suspense~~ for much longer! [*No! We agreed, no suspense jokes—ed*]

We'll get into more of the philosophy and promise of Concurrent Mode in chapter 13. This chapter's a bit of a bridge between the stable, production use of lazy components and Suspense from chapter 11 and the tentative APIs of deferred rendering, transitions, and SuspenseList components in chapter 13. Here we use the ideas about thrown promises to consider what data fetching with Suspense might look like. The code examples are not for production but offer an insight into what library authors might need to consider in order to work well with Concurrent Mode and Suspense.

## 12.1  *Data fetching with Suspense*

In chapter 11, we saw that Suspense components show fallback UI when they catch a thrown promise. There, we were lazy-loading components, and React coordinated the throwing of promises via the lazy function and dynamic imports:

```
const LazyCalendar = lazy(() => import("./Calendar"));
```

When trying to render the lazy component, React first checks the component's status; if the dynamically imported component has loaded, React goes ahead and renders it, but if it's pending, React throws the dynamic import promise. If the promise is rejected, we need an error boundary to catch the error and show appropriate fallback UI:

```
<ErrorBoundary>
  <Suspense fallback="Loading...">
    <LazyCalendar/>
  </Suspense>
</ErrorBoundary>
```

On reaching the LazyCalendar component, React can use the loaded component, throw an existing pending promise, or start the dynamic import and throw the new pending promise.

We want something similar for components that load data from a server. Say we have a Message component that loads and displays a message. In figure 12.1, the Message component has loaded the message "Hello Data!" and is displaying it.

Hello Data!

**Figure 12.1**   **The Message component loads a message and displays it.**

While data is loading, we want to use a Suspense component to display a fallback like the one in figure 12.2 which says, "Loading message . . . ".

**Figure 12.2** While the data is loading, a `Suspense` component displays a fallback message.

And if there's an error, we want an `ErrorBoundary` component to display a fallback like the one in figure 12.3, which says, "Oops!"

Oops!

**Figure 12.3** If there's an error, an `ErrorBoundary` component displays an error message.

The JSX to match our expectations will be something like this:

```
<ErrorBoundary fallback="Oops!">
  <Suspense fallback="Loading message...">
    <Message/>
  </Suspense>
</ErrorBoundary>
```

But while we have the `lazy` function for lazy components, there is no stable, built-in mechanism for components that are loading data. (There is a `react-cache` package, but it's experimental and unstable.)

Maybe we can come up with a way of loading data that throws promises or errors as appropriate. In doing so, we'll gain a little insight into some of the steps that data-fetching libraries will need to implement, but it's just an insight and definitely not a recommendation for production code. (Once Concurrent Mode and data-fetching strategies for React have settled, and battle-testing has defeated real-world issues and edge cases, look to the libraries like Relay, Apollo, and React Query for efficient, flexible, fully integrated data fetching.) Take a look at the following listing for our `Message` component. It includes a speculative `getMessageOrThrow` function.

**Listing 12.1** The `Message` component calls a function to retrieve data

```
function Message () {
  const data = getMessageOrThrow();
  return <p className="message">{data.message}</p>;
}
```

⟵ Call a function that returns data or throws a promise or error.

⟵ Include the data in the UI.

We want the `getMessageOrThrow` function to return the data if it's available. If there's a promise that hasn't yet resolved to our data, the function should throw it. If the promise has been rejected, the function should throw an error.

The problem is, if there's a promise for our data (like the one the browser's fetch API returns, for example), we don't have a way of checking its status. Is it pending? Has it resolved? Has it been rejected? We need to wrap the promise in code that'll report its status.

### 12.1.1 *Upgrading promises to include their status*

To work with `Suspense` and `ErrorBoundary` components, we need to use the status of a promise to dictate our actions. Table 12.1 matches the status with the required action.

**Table 12.1  The action for each promise status**

| Status of promise | Action |
| --- | --- |
| Pending | Throw the promise. |
| Resolved | Return the resolved value—our data. |
| Rejected | Throw the rejection error. |

The promise won't report its own status, so we want some kind of `checkStatus` function that returns the current status of the promise and its resolved value or rejection error if available. Something like this:

```
const {promise, status, data, error} = checkStatus();
```

Or, because we'll never get `data` and `error` at the same time, something like this:

```
const {promise, status, result} = checkStatus();
```

We'd then be able to use conditionals like `if (status === "pending")` to decide whether to throw promises or errors or to return values.

The following listing shows a `getStatusChecker` function that takes a promise and returns a function that gives us access to the promise's status.

**Listing 12.2  Getting a function to access the status of a promise**

```
export function getStatusChecker (promiseIn) {        ◁──┐ Pass in the promise whose
  let status = "pending";                    ◁──────────┘ status we want to track.
  let result;                  ◁── Set up a variable for   Set up a variable to hold
                                   the resolved value      the status of the promise.
  const promise = promiseIn        or rejection error.
    .then((response) => {    ◁──┐
      status = "success";        │ On success, assign the
      result = response;         │ resolved value to result.
    })
```

```
  .catch((error) => {          ◁── On error, assign the
    status = "error";             rejection error to result.
    result = error;
  });
                                              Return a function to
  return () => ({promise, status, result});  ◁── access the current
}                                             status and result.
```

Using the `getStatusChecker` function, we can get the `checkStatus` function we need to track the status of a promise and react accordingly. For example, if we have a `fetch-Message` function that returns a promise and loads message data, we could get a status-tracking function like this:

```
const checkStatus = getStatusChecker(fetchMessage());
```

Okay, that's great; we have a promise-status-tracking function. To integrate with Suspense, we need our data-fetching function to use that promise status to either return data, throw a promise, or throw an error.

### 12.1.2 Using the promise status to integrate with Suspense

Here's our `Message` component again:

```
function Message () {
  const data = getMessageOrThrow();
  return <p className="message">{data.message}</p>;
}
```

We want to be able to call a data-fetching function—in this case, `getMessageOr-Throw`—that automatically integrates with Suspense by throwing promises or errors as appropriate or returns our data after it's loaded. The following listing shows the `make-Thrower` function that takes a promise and returns just such a function, one that uses the promise's status to act appropriately.

#### Listing 12.3   Returning a data-fetching function that throws as appropriate

```
                                                  Pass in the data-
                                                  fetching promise.
export function makeThrower (promiseIn) {     ◁──
  const checkStatus = getStatusChecker(promiseIn);  ◁──  Get a status-
                                                         tracking function
  return function () {                                   for the promise.
    const {promise, status, result} = checkStatus();

    if (status === "pending") throw promise;        Use the status to
    if (status === "error") throw result;           throw or return.
    return result;
  };
}
```

*Return a function that can throw.*

*Get the latest status whenever the function is called.*

For the `Message` component, we'll use `makeThrower` to transform the promise that the `fetchMessage` function returns into a data-fetching function that can throw promises or errors:

```
const getMessageOrThrow = makeThrower(fetchMessage());
```

But when do we start fetching? Where do we put that line of code?

### 12.1.3 *Fetching data as early as possible*

We don't have to wait until a component has rendered to start loading the data it needs. We can kick off fetching outside the component, using the fetch promise to build a throw-ready data-access function that the component can use. Listing 12.4 shows a full `App` example for our `Message` component. The browser executes the code when it loads, starting the data fetch. Once React renders `App` and then the nested `Message`, `Message` calls `getMessageOrThrow`, which accesses the existing promise.

> *Live:* **https://t1lsy.csb.app,** *Code:* **https://codesandbox.io/s/suspensefordata-t1lsy**
>
> **Listing 12.4   Using the `Message` component**

```
import React, {Suspense} from "react";
import {ErrorBoundary} from "react-error-boundary";
import fetchMessage from "./api";
import {makeThrower} from "./utils";
import "./styles.css";

function ErrorFallback ({error}) {
  return <p className="error">{error}</p>;
}

const getMessageOrThrow = makeThrower(fetchMessage());    ⟵   Start fetching as
                                                              soon as possible.

function Message () {
  const data = getMessageOrThrow();             ⟵   Access the data or throw
  return <p className="message">{data.message}</p>;        an error or promise.
}                                                  ⟵   Use the data if
                                                          available.

export default function App () {
  return (
    <div className="App">
      <ErrorBoundary FallbackComponent={ErrorFallback}>    ⟵   Catch thrown
        <Suspense                                              errors.
          fallback={<p className="loading">Loading message...</p>}
        >
          <Message />
        </Suspense>
      </ErrorBoundary>
    </div>
  );
}
```

Catch thrown promises.

Our error boundary is the ErrorBoundary component from the react-error-boundary package, mentioned in chapter 11. We specify its fallback by setting the Fallback-Component prop. The fetchMessage function accepts two arguments to help you test the Suspense and ErrorBoundary fallbacks: a delay in milliseconds and a canError Boolean to randomly cause errors. If you want the request to take three seconds and sometimes fail, then change the call to the following:

```
const getMessageOrThrow = makeThrower(fetchMessage(3000, true));
```

In listing 12.4, the Message component can call getMessageOrThrow because it's in the same scope. That won't always be the case, so you may want to pass the data-access function to Message as a prop. You may also want to load new data in response to a user action. Let's see how to work with props and events to make the data-fetching more flexible.

### 12.1.4  Fetching new data

Say we want to upgrade our Message component to include a Next button, as shown in figure 12.4.

**Figure 12.4   The Message component now displays a Next button.**

Clicking the Next button will load and display a new message. While the new message is loading, Message will *suspend* (the getMessageOrThrow function or its equivalent will throw its promise), and the Suspense component will show the "Loading message . . ." fallback UI from figure 12.2 again. Once the promise resolves, Message will display the newly loaded message, "Bonjour," as shown in figure 12.5.

**Figure 12.5   Clicking the Next button loads a new message.**

For each new message that we load, we need a new promise and a new data-fetching function that can throw. In listing 12.6, we'll update the `Message` component to accept the data-fetching function as a prop. First, listing 12.5 shows the `App` component managing the current data-fetching function in state and passing it to `Message`.

**Live:** https://xue0l.csb.app, **Code:** https://codesandbox.io/s/suspensefordata2-xue0l

**Listing 12.5** The `App` component holds the current `getMessage` function in state

```
const getFirstMessage = makeThrower(fetchMessage());      ◁┈ Fetch the first message
                                                              straight away.
export default function App () {
  const [getMessage, setGetMessage] = useState(() => getFirstMessage);   ◁┈
                                                          Keep the current data-
                                                          fetching function in state.
  function next () {
    const nextPromise = fetchNextMessage();
    const getNextMessage = makeThrower(nextPromise);      ◁┈ Get a data-fetching
    setGetMessage(() => getNextMessage);                  ◁┈    function that can throw
  }                                                             the promise or error.

                                                          Update the state to
                                                          hold the latest data-
  return (                                                fetching function.
    <div className="App">
      <ErrorBoundary FallbackComponent={ErrorFallback}>
        <Suspense
          fallback={<p className="loading">Loading message...</p>}
        >
          <Message
            getMessage={getMessage}      ◁┈ Pass the current data-fetching
            next={next}                       function to the Message component.
          />
        </Suspense>                      Give the Message
      </ErrorBoundary>                   component a way to
    </div>                               request the next message.
  );
}
```

Start fetching the next message. ┈▷ (annotation for `const nextPromise = fetchNextMessage();`)

We pass `useState` an initialization function that returns the data-fetching function for the first message, `getFirstMessage`. Notice, we don't call `getFirstMessage`; we return it, setting it as the initial state.

App also provides a `next` function for loading the next message and placing the new data-fetching function in state. The first thing the `next` function does is start fetching the next message:

```
const nextPromise = fetchNextMessage();
```

Our API on CodeSandbox includes the `fetchNextMessage` function that requests the next message and returns a promise. To integrate with Suspense by throwing a pending promise, `next` needs to get a promise-throwing function for the data-fetching promise:

```
const getNextMessage = makeThrower(nextPromise);
```

The final step is to update the state; it's holding the current promise-throwing function. Both useState and the updater function it returns, setGetMessage in this case, accept a function as an argument. If you pass them a function, they call useState to get its initial state and setGetMessage to get the new state. Because the state value we're trying to store is a function itself, we can't pass it directly to these state-setting functions. We don't do this:

```
useState(getFirstMessage); // NOT THIS
```

And we don't do this:

```
setGetMessage(getNextMessage);  // NOT THIS
```

Instead, we pass useState and setGetMessage functions that return the functions we want to set as state:

```
useState(() => getFirstMessage);  // Return the initial state, a function
```

And we use this:

```
setGetMessage(() => getNextMessage);  // Return the new state, a function
```

We don't want to call getNextMessage here; we just want to set it as the new state value. Setting the state value causes App to re-render, passing Message the latest data-fetching function as the getMessage prop.

The updated Message component is in the following listing. It shows the component accepting getMessage and next as props and includes the Next button in the UI.

---

*Live:* **https://xue0l.csb.app,** *Code:* **https://codesandbox.io/s/suspensefordata2-xue0l**

**Listing 12.6   Pass Message props for data fetching**

```
function Message ({getMessage, next}) {          Accept the data-fetching function
  const data = getMessage();                     and button handler as props.
  return (
    <>
      <p className="message">{data.message}</p>
      <button onClick={next}>Next</button>        Include a Next
    </>                                            button in the UI.
  );
}
```

Message calls getMessage, which returns the new message data or throws. When a user clicks the Next button, Message calls next, starting to fetch the next message straightaway. And re-rendering straightaway. We're using the *render-as-you-fetch* approach, specifying Suspense and ErrorBoundary fallbacks for React to render when components throw promises or errors.

Speaking of errors, our `App` component is using the `ErrorBoundary` component from the `react-error-boundary` package. It has a few more tricks up its sleeve, including easy error recovery. Let's cast our next spell.

### 12.1.5 Recovering from errors

Figure 12.6 shows what we're after; when an error occurs, we want to give users a Try Again button to click, to reset the error state and try rendering the app again.

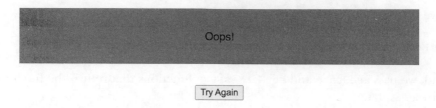

**Figure 12.6   The `ErrorBoundary` component UI now includes a Try Again button to reset the error boundary and load the next message.**

In listing 12.5, we assigned the `ErrorFallback` component as the `FallbackComponent` prop for the `ErrorBoundary`:

```
<ErrorBoundary FallbackComponent={ErrorFallback}>
  {/* app UI */}
</ErrorBoundary>
```

The following listing shows a new version of our `ErrorFallback` component. When `ErrorBoundary` catches an error and renders the fallback, it automatically passes a `resetErrorBoundary` function to `ErrorFallback`.

**Live: https://7i89e.csb.app/, Code: https://codesandbox.io/s/errorrecovery-7i89e**

**Listing 12.7   Adding a button to `ErrorFallback`**

```
function ErrorFallback ({error, resetErrorBoundary}) {     ◁   Receive the resetError-
  return (                                                      Boundary function from
    <>                                                          ErrorBoundary as a prop.
      <p className="error">{error}</p>
      <button onClick={resetErrorBoundary}>Try Again</button>   ◁
    </>
  );                                              Include a button that calls
}                                                    resetErrorBoundary.
```

The `ErrorFallback` UI now includes a Try Again button that calls the `resetError-Boundary` function to remove the error state and render the error boundary's children rather than the error fallback UI. In addition to resetting the error state on the error boundary, `resetErrorBoundary` will also call any reset function that we assign to the error boundary's onReset prop. In the following listing, we tell ErrorBoundary to call our next function and load the next message whenever we reset the boundary.

*Live:* **https://7i89e.csb.app/,** *Code:* **https://codesandbox.io/s/errorrecovery-7i89e**

Listing 12.8 Adding an onReset prop to ErrorBoundary

```
export default function App () {
  const [getMessage, setGetMessage] = useState(() => getFirstMessage);

  function next () {/* unchanged */}

  return (
    <div className="App">
      <ErrorBoundary
        FallbackComponent={ErrorFallback}
        onReset={next}                           Include an onReset function
      >                                      ◄─  that ErrorBoundary will call
        <Suspense                                if reset.
          fallback={<p className="loading">Loading message...</p>}
        >
          <Message getMessage={getMessage} next={next} />
        </Suspense>
      </ErrorBoundary>
    </div>
  );
}
```

The error boundary now does something to try to shake the app's error state: it tries to load the next message. Here are the steps it goes through when the Message component throws an error trying to load a message:

1 The Message component throws an error.
2 ErrorBoundary catches the error and renders the ErrorFallback component, including the Try Again button.
3 The user clicks the Try Again button.
4 The button calls resetErrorBoundary, removing the error state from the boundary.
5 The error boundary re-renders its children and calls next to load the next message.

Check out the GitHub repository for react-error-boundary to see the rest of its super-helpful error-related tricks: https://github.com/bvaughn/react-error-boundary.

### 12.1.6 *Checking the React docs*

In our brief foray into one experimental way of integrating data fetching with Suspense, we created two key functions:

- getStatusChecker—Provides a window into the status of a promise
- makeThrower—Upgrades a promise into one that returns data or that throws an error or promise

We used `makeThrower` to create functions like `getMessageOrThrow` that the `Message` component used to get the latest message, throw an error, or throw a promise (suspend). We stored the data-fetching functions in state and passed them to children via props.

The React docs also have an experimental, just for information, be careful—no, really be careful—example of integrating our own promises with Suspense, shown in the following listing, that does the job of our `getStatusChecker` and `makeThrower` functions in one `wrapPromise` function. Read the rationale behind the code in the docs: http://mng.bz/JDBK.

---

**Code: https://codesandbox.io/s/frosty-hermann-bztrp?file=/src/fakeApi.js**

**Listing 12.9    The `wrapPromise` function from the React docs examples**

```
// Suspense integrations like Relay implement          ◁──── The code is for
// a contract like this to integrate with React.             interest rather than
// Real implementations can be significantly more complex.   production use.
// Don't copy-paste this into your project!
function wrapPromise(promise) {
  let status = "pending";
  let result;
  let suspender = promise.then(        ◁──── The code names the
    r => {                                   wrapped promise a
      status = "success";                    suspender.
      result = r;
    },
    e => {
      status = "error";
      result = e;
    }
  );                          The function returns
  return {                    an object with a
    read() {        ◁──────   read method.
      if (status === "pending") {
        throw suspender;
      } else if (status === "error") {
        throw result;
      } else if (status === "success") {
        return result;
      }
    }
  };
}
```

The `wrapPromise` function doesn't return a function directly; it returns an object with a `read` method. So, rather than assigning a *function* to a local variable, `getMessage`, like this

```
const getMessage = makeThrower(fetchMessage());        ◁──── Assign the data-fetching
                                                             function to getMessage.
function Message () {              Call getMessage to
  const data = getMessage();  ◁── get data or throw.
```

```
    // return UI that shows data
}
```

we assign an *object* to a local variable, `messageResource`, like this:

```
const messageResource = wrapPromise(fetchMessage());          ◁——  Assign the object with
                                                                    data-fetching method
function Message () {                                                to messageResource.
  const data = messageResource.read();        ◁——
                                                     Call the read method
    // return UI that shows data                     to get data or throw.
}
```

Which approach is better? Well, I bet the React team thought carefully about its examples and considered many more scenarios in which the concept of a *resource* with a read method was found to be easier to think about and work with than directly storing, passing, and calling naked data-fetching functions. Having said that, I think our step-by-step exploration of the concepts and procedures involved in integrating data fetching with Suspense has been useful.

Ultimately, this is all still theoretical and experimental and is highly likely to change. Unless you're a data-fetching library author yourself, you'll find the nitty-gritty details will be handled by the libraries you use. We've been using React Query for our data work; does it integrate with Suspense?

## 12.2 Using Suspense and error boundaries with React Query

React Query provides an experimental config option to switch on Suspense for queries. Rather than returning status and error information, queries will throw promises and errors. You can find out more about the experimental Suspense integration in the React Query documentation (http://mng.bz/w9A2).

For the bookings app, we've been using the `status` value that `useQuery` returns to conditionally render loading spinners and error messages. All of our data-loading components have code like this:

```
const {data, status, error} = useQuery(          ◁——  When loading data,
  "key",                                                assign status value to
  () => getData(url)                                    a local variable.
);

if (status === "error") {          ◁——
  return <p>{error.message}</p>          Check status
}                                        and return
                                         appropriate UI.
if (status === "loading") {        ◁——
  return <PageSpinner/>
}

return ({/* UI with data */});
```

But we've now seen how `Suspense` and `ErrorBoundary` components let us decouple the loading and error UI from individual components. The bookings app has page-level `Suspense` and `ErrorBoundary` components in place, so let's switch over our queries to use the existing components.

---

*Branch*: **1201-suspense-data**, *File*: **/src/components/Bookables/BookablesView.js**

**Listing 12.10   The `BookablesView` component with Suspense integration**

```
import {Link, useParams} from "react-router-dom";
import {FaPlus} from "react-icons/fa";

import {useQuery} from "react-query";
import getData from "../../utils/api";

import BookablesList from "./BookablesList";
import BookableDetails from "./BookableDetails";
// no need to import PageSpinner

export default function BookablesView () {
  const {data: bookables = []} = useQuery(
    "bookables",
    () => getData("http://localhost:3001/bookables"),
    {
      suspense: true          ⟵──┐  Pass a config object with
    }                            │  suspense set to true.
  );

  const {id} = useParams();
  const bookable = bookables.find(
    b => b.id === parseInt(id, 10)
  ) || bookables[0];

  // no status checks or loading/error UI    ⟵──┐  Remove the status-checking
                                                │  code for loading and error
  return ({/* unchanged UI */});               │  states.
}
```

The updated `BookablesView` component passes a configuration option to `useQuery` when loading the bookables data:

```
const {data: bookables = []} = useQuery(
  "bookables",
  () => getData("http://localhost:3001/bookables"),
  {
    suspense: true
  }
);
```

That config option tells `useQuery` to suspend (throw a promise) when loading its initial data and to throw an error if something goes wrong.

CHALLENGE 12.1
Update the `BookingsPage` and `UsersList` components to use Suspense when loading their data. Remove any unnecessary loading and error state UI that's embedded within the components. The current branch includes the changes: 1201-suspense-data.

## 12.3　*Loading images with Suspense*

Suspense works great with lazily-loaded components and, at least tentatively, can be integrated with the promises that arise naturally when loading data. How about other resources like scripts and images, for example? The key is the promise: if we can wrap our requests in promises, we can (at least experimentally) work with Suspense and error boundaries to provide fallback UI. Let's look at a scenario for integrating image loading with Suspense.

Your boss is keen for you to make the Users page more useful, wanting you to include an avatar image for each user and, later, details of each user's bookings and tasks. We'll get to the bookings and tasks in the next chapter. Here, we aim to include an avatar image like the Japanese castle shown in figure 12.7.

**Figure 12.7　The `UserDetails` component includes an avatar image for each user.**

The 1202-user-avatar branch of the GitHub repo includes separate components for the list of users and the details of the selected user, `UsersList` and `UserDetails`, with management of the selected user in the `UsersPage` component. The repo also has avatar images in the /public/img folder. `UsersPage` now passes `UserDetails` just the ID of the selected user, and the `UserDetails` component loads the user's details and then renders the avatar as a standard `img` element:

```
<div className="user-avatar">
  <img src={`http://localhost:3001/img/${user.img}`} alt={user.name}/>
</div>
```

Unfortunately, at slow network speeds and with large avatar image files, the images can take a while to load, leading to the poor user experience shown in figure 12.8, where the image (a butterfly on a flower) appears bit by bit. You can use your browser's developer tools to throttle the network speed.

**Figure 12.8   When switching users, the avatar image might take a while to load, potentially resulting in a poor user experience. Here, only half of the image has loaded so far.**

In this section, we explore a couple of ways of improving the user experience for slow-loading images within our user interface:

- Using React Query and Suspense to provide an image-loading fallback
- Prefetching images and data with React Query

Together, the two approaches help provide users with a predictable user interface where, hopefully, slow-loading assets won't call attention to themselves, degrading the experience of using the app.

### 12.3.1   Using React Query and Suspense to provide an image-loading fallback

We want to show some kind of fallback while images load, maybe a shared avatar placeholder with a small file size, like the head silhouette image shown in figure 12.9.

**Figure 12.9   While the avatar image is loading, we can show a placeholder image that has a small file size and that could be loaded earlier.**

To integrate with Suspense, we need an image-loading process that throws a promise until the image is ready to use. We create the promise manually, around the DOM `HTMLImageElement Image` constructor like this:

```
const imagePromise = new Promise((resolve) => {
  const img = new Image();
  img.onload = () => resolve(img);
  img.src = "path/to/image/image.png"
});
```

Create a new
image object.

Start loading the image
by specifying its source.

Resolve the promise when
the image finishes loading.

We then need an image-loading function that throws the promise while it's pending:

```
const getImageOrThrow = makeThrower(imagePromise);
```

And, finally, a React component that calls the function, rendering the image after it
has loaded:

```
function Img () {
  const imgObject = getImageOrThrow();

  return <img src={imgObject.src} alt="avatar" />
}
```

Get the image object
or throw a promise.

Once the image is available,
render a standard img element.

But we don't want to be continually reloading the image on every render, so we need
some kind of cache. Well, we already have one of those built into React Query. So, rather
than building our own cache and throwing our own promises, let's hook into React
Query's Suspense integration (not forgetting that it's experimental). The following listing shows an `Img` component that throws pending promises until its image has loaded.

> **Branch: 1203-suspense-images**, *File: /src/components/Users/Avatar.js*
>
> **Listing 12.11  An `Img` component that uses React Query**

```
function Img ({src, alt, ...props}) {
  const {data: imgObject} = useQuery(
    src,
    () => new Promise((resolve) => {
      const img = new Image();
      img.onload = () => resolve(img);
      img.src = src;
    }),
    {suspense: true}
  );

  return <img src={imgObject.src} alt={alt} {...props}/>
}
```

Use React Query for caching,
deduping, and throwing.

Use the image src
as the query key.

Pass useQuery a function that
creates an image-loading promise.

Throw pending promises
and errors.

Return a standard
img element after the
image has loaded.

Using multiple `Img` components with the same source won't try to load the image multiple times; React Query will return the cached `Image` object. (The image itself will be
cached by the browser.)

In the bookings app, we want an `Avatar` component that uses Suspense to show a
fallback while the image is loading. The following listing uses the `Img` component
along with a `Suspense` component to achieve our goal.

**Branch**: 1203-suspense-images, *File*: /src/components/Users/Avatar.js

Listing 12.12   An `Avatar` component that uses `Img` and `Suspense`

```
import {Suspense} from "react";                                          Specify fallbackSrc
import {useQuery} from "react-query";                                     and src props.

export default function Avatar ({src, alt, fallbackSrc, ...props}) {    ◄─────
  return (
    <div className="user-avatar">
      <Suspense
        fallback={<img src={fallbackSrc} alt="Fallback Avatar"/>}       ◄─────
      >
                                                                         Use the
        <Img src={src} alt={alt} {...props}/>    ◄───                    fallbackSrc prop
      </Suspense>                                                        to show an image
    </div>                              Use the Img component             as a Suspense
  );                                    to integrate with the             fallback.
}                                       Suspense component.
```

The UserDetails component can now use an Avatar to show a fallback image until
the desired image has loaded, as implemented in the following listing.

**Branch**: 1203-suspense-images, *File*: /src/components/Users/UserDetails.js

Listing 12.13   Using the `Avatar` component in `UserDetails`

```
import {useQuery} from "react-query";
import getData from '../../utils/api';
import Avatar from "./Avatar";
                                                          Pass in the ID of
                                                          the user to show.
export default function UserDetails ({userID}) {    ◄──
  const {data: user} = useQuery(
    ["user", userID],
    () => getData(`http://localhost:3001/users/${userID}`),    ◄──   Load the
    {suspense: true}                                                 data for the
  );                                                                 specified user.

  return (
    <div className="item user">
      <div className="item-header">
        <h2>{user.name}</h2>                   Show an avatar,
      </div>                                    specifying the image
                                               and fallback sources.
      <Avatar                    ◄───
        src={`http://localhost:3001/img/${user.img}`}
        fallbackSrc="http://localhost:3001/img/avatar.gif"
        alt={user.name}
      />

      <div className="user-details">
        <h3>{user.title}</h3>
        <p>{user.notes}</p>
      </div>
    </div>
  )
}
```

We could even preload the fallback image by adding a link element with rel= "prefetch" to the page's head element, or by imperatively preloading it in a parent component. Let's look at preloading data and images now.

### 12.3.2 Prefetching images and data with React Query

At the moment, the UserDetails component doesn't render the Avatar until the user data has finished loading. We wait for the user data before requesting the image we need, creating a *waterfall*, as shown in figure 12.10.

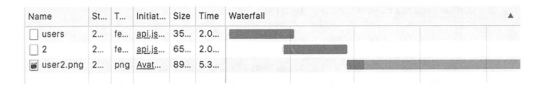

**Figure 12.10** The Waterfall panel shows that the image for user 2 (user2.png) isn't requested until the data for user 2 has finished loading.

The second row shows the data for user 2 loading. The third row shows the image for user 2, user2.png, loading. Here are the steps from click to image when we select a user in the users list:

1. A user is selected.
2. UserDetails loads the user information, suspending until the data loads.
3. Once the data has loaded, UserDetails renders its UI, including the Avatar component.
4. Avatar renders the Img component, which requests the image and suspends until the image has loaded.
5. Once the image has loaded, Img renders its UI, an img element.

The image doesn't start loading until the user data has arrived. But the image filename is predictable. Can we start loading the image at the same time as the user information, as shown in the last two rows of figure 12.11?

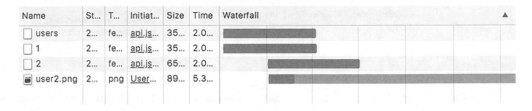

**Figure 12.11** We want the user 2 image and data to load concurrently, as in the last two rows of the figure.

The user selection is managed in the `UsersPage` component by the `switchUser` function. To get the concurrent loading shown in figure 12.11, let's get React Query to start fetching the user data and image at the same time. The following listing includes the two new `prefetchQuery` calls.

> **Branch**: 1204-prefetch-query, *File*: /src/components/Users/UsersPage.js
>
> **Listing 12.14    Preloading images and data on the Users page**

```
// other imports

import {useQueryClient} from "react-query";
import getData from "../../utils/api";

export default function UsersPage () {
  const [loggedInUser] = useUser();
  const [selectedUser, setSelectedUser] = useState(null);
  const user = selectedUser || loggedInUser;
  const queryClient = useQueryClient();

  function switchUser (nextUser) {
    setSelectedUser(nextUser);

    queryClient.prefetchQuery(          ⟵  Prefetch the user
      ["user", nextUser.id],                information.
      () => getData(`http://localhost:3001/users/${nextUser.id}`)
    );
                                        ⟵  Prefetch the user
    queryClient.prefetchQuery(             avatar image.
      `http://localhost:3001/img/${nextUser.img}`,
      () => new Promise((resolve) => {
        const img = new Image();
        img.onload = () => resolve(img);
        img.src = `http://localhost:3001/img/${nextUser.img}`;
      })
    );
  }

  return user ? (
    <main className="users-page">
      <UsersList user={user} setUser={switchUser}/>

      <Suspense fallback={<PageSpinner/>}>
        <UserDetails userID={user.id}/>    ⟵  Render the user details,
      </Suspense>                             including the avatar.
    </main>
  ) : null;
}
```

By fetching data and images as early as possible, we don't keep users waiting as long and reduce the chance of needing our fallback image. But switching to a new user still hits the visitor with a loading spinner (like the one in figure 12.12) if they haven't

**Figure 12.12  Switching to another user brings up a loading spinner on slower connections.**

viewed that user before. Switching from the details panel to a loading spinner and back to the next details panel is not the smoothest experience.

Rather than the jarring experience of replacing the details with a spinner, it would be better if we could hold off, and switch straight from one set of user details to another, avoiding the *receded* loading state, the feeling of *going back* to a spinner. React's Concurrent Mode promises to make such deferred transitions much easier, and you'll see how in chapter 13 when we introduce our last two hooks: useTransition and useDeferredValue.

## Summary

- Experiment with data-fetching integration for Suspense but don't use it in production code yet; it's not stable and will probably change.
- When the time comes, use well-tested, reliable data-fetching libraries to manage Suspense integration for you.
- To tentatively explore data fetching with Suspense, wrap promises with functions that can check their status:

```
const checkStatus = getStatusChecker(promise);
```

- To integrate with Suspense, data-fetching functions should throw pending promises and errors or return loaded data. Create a function to turn a data-fetching promise into one that throws as necessary:

```
const getMessageOrThrow = makeThrower(promise);
```

- Use the prepared data-fetching function within a component to get data for the UI or to throw as appropriate:

```
function Message () {
  const data = getMessageOrThrow();
  return <p>{data.message}</p>
}
```

- Start loading data as early as possible, maybe in event handlers.
- Provide ways for users to recover the app from error states. Libraries like `react-error-boundary` can help.
- Check out the React docs and its linked examples to gain further insight into these techniques and to see their use of resources with `read` methods (http://mng.bz/q9AJ).
- Use similar promise-wrangling techniques to load other resources like images or scripts.
- Harness libraries like React Query (in Suspense mode) to manage caching and multiple requests when fetching data or images.
- Load resources earlier by calling React Query's `queryClient.prefetchQuery` method.
- Avoid waterfalls, whereby later data-fetches wait for previous ones before starting, if possible.

# 13

# *Experimenting with useTransition, useDeferredValue, and SuspenseList*

**This chapter covers**

- Delaying UI updates with the `useTransition` hook
- Flagging inconsistent state and UI with the `isPending` Boolean
- Using old and new values simultaneously with the `useDeferredValue` hook
- Managing multiple fallbacks with the `SuspenseList` component
- Understanding the promise of Concurrent Mode

*Concurrent Mode* lets React work on multiple versions of our UI at once, showing older versions that are still fully interactive until newer versions are ready. This can mean that, for brief periods, the latest state doesn't match the current UI in the browser and React gives us some hooks and components to manage the feedback we give to our users. The aim is to improve the user experience of our apps, making them feel more responsive and orchestrating updates so our users immediately understand what is stale, what is updating, and what is fresh.

Concurrent Mode is still experimental, so the two new hooks we introduce in this chapter, `useTransition` and `useDeferredValue`, are experimental too. They give React permission to keep showing old UI or old values while components load new data or calculate new values. This helps us avoid *receded states,* whereby the UI falls back from a useful, interactive component to a previous loading state.

In the previous two chapters, we spent a lot of time wrapping components that could suspend in Suspense components, specifying appropriate fallbacks. As the number of Suspense components on a page increases, we risk infecting our users with fallback fever, making everything start spinning. One potential cure is the SuspenseList component, a soothing bandage that controls spinners, promoting them from a sickness to sign of health.

Let's explore these experimental solutions as we improve the Users page in the bookings app.

## 13.1    *Making smoother transitions between states*

When we first load the Users page, we see a spinner as the details for the current user load. That's fine; we might expect some spinners when first loading a page. But when we subsequently select a new user for the first time, the UI goes back to showing a spinner, as you can see in figure 13.1. (If necessary, start json-server with a delay to simulate slower connections.)

**Figure 13.1    Selecting a new user (Clarisse) in the list of users causes a spinner to replace the user details panel. This can be jarring; it feels like a backward step. We call it a *receded state*.**

Waiting for data to load may be unavoidable, but we can try to improve the perceived responsiveness of the page by avoiding the display of spinners, and continuing to show the old data while the new data loads.

In this section, we explore our last two built-in hooks, useTransition and use-DeferredValue, as ways of improving the user experience by delaying the update of the UI as data loads. To use these hooks, our app needs to be in Concurrent Mode, and for that we need the experimental version of React. Install it like this:

```
npm install react@experimental react-dom@experimental
```

If there is a problem with React Query insisting on a stable version of React, you could uninstall React Query before installing React's experimental release. Then reinstall React Query with the –force flag, like this:

```
npm install react-query --force
```

Then, update index.js to render the app as in the following listing.

> **Branch: 1301-use-transition, File: /src/index.js**
>
> **Listing 13.1   Enabling Concurrent Mode**

```
import ReactDOM from 'react-dom';
import App from './components/App.js';

const root = document.getElementById('root');
ReactDOM
  .unstable_createRoot(root)
  .render(<App />);
```

Use the element with ID "root" as the root of the app.

Render the App component into the root element.

### 13.1.1  Avoiding receded states with useTransition

Figure 13.2 shows an improved UI experience when selecting a new user on the Users page. While viewing the details for Mark, we've clicked Clarisse in the list of users, but the user details panel on the right continues to show the old UI, Mark's information, rather than dropping back to a spinner.

**Figure 13.2   A new user (Clarisse) is selected, but instead of immediately showing a receded loading spinner, the UI continues to show the old user (Mark).**

The following listing shows how to use the useTransition hook to give React permission to display old UI if a change of state (switching the user, for example) causes a child component to suspend.

---

**Branch**: 1301-use-transition, *File*: /src/components/Users/UsersPage.js

**Listing 13.2   Using a transition to improve UX on `UsersPage`**

```
import {
  useState,
  unstable_useTransition as useTransition,          ◁─┐  Import the
  Suspense                                             │  useTransition hook.
} from "react";

// unchanged imports

export default function UsersPage () {
  const [loggedInUser] = useUser();
  const [selectedUser, setSelectedUser] = useState(null);
  const user = selectedUser || loggedInUser;
  const queryClient = useQueryClient();
                                                        ┌  Get a transition function,
  const [startTransition] = useTransition()      ◁─┘  startTransition.

  function switchUser (nextUser) {                          ┌  Wrap the user
    startTransition(() => setSelectedUser(nextUser));   ◁─┤  state change in
                                                           └  the transition.
    queryClient.prefetchQuery(/* prefetch user details */);
    queryClient.prefetchQuery(/* prefetch user image */);
  }

  return user ? (
    <main className="users-page">
      <UsersList user={user} setUser={switchUser}/>

      <Suspense fallback={<PageSpinner/>}>        ◁─┐  Show a spinner while
        <UserDetails userID={user.id}/>             │  the first user loads.
      </Suspense>
    </main>
  ) : <PageSpinner/>;
}
```

To reinforce the fact that this is all experimental, the hook has an `unstable` prefix, so we import `unstable_useTransition` from the `react` package. We rename it `use-Transition`.

The `useTransition` hook returns an array whose first element is a function we use to wrap state changes that might cause components to suspend. We assign the function to the `startTransition` variable:

```
const [startTransition] = useTransition();
```

Our state change is in the `switchUser` function. Switching to a new user might cause the `UserDetails` component to suspend if React Query has not yet loaded that user's data. Wrapping the state change in `startTransition` tells React to keep showing the old UI rather than the `Suspense` fallback, until the data loads. If there isn't any old

UI—the component has not yet mounted—React will show the Suspense fallback while waiting for data:

```
startTransition(() => setSelectedUser(nextUser));
```

Not falling back to a spinner on state changes is an improvement as long as the data for the new state doesn't take long to load. If it does, the user is left in limbo, staring at the old UI. Has the app crashed? We need to give them some feedback to say the app is busy loading data.

### 13.1.2  *Giving users feedback with isPending*

The useTransition hook lets React show old UI while the state is changing. But inconsistent UIs might lead to confusion if they last too long. It would be good to give our users some feedback that a change is happening even if the UI continues to show some old values.

Something like figure 13.3 is what we're after; we've clicked a new user, Clarisse, in the users list, but our transition has kept the details for the old user, Mark, on the screen while Clarisse's information loads. We reduce the opacity of the user details panel to show that the details are stale.

**Figure 13.3   During a transition, the** isPending **value is used to set the class of the user details panel, allowing its opacity to be reduced via CSS. We don't have a receded spinner but do indicate a transition.**

Helpfully, useTransition also returns a Boolean value in its array to indicate a transition is ongoing. We can assign the Boolean to a local variable, isPending:

```
const [startTransition, isPending] = useTransition();
```

We can then use isPending to set a class name on the user details panel, for example, as shown in listing 13.3 for UsersPage and listing 13.4 for UserDetails.

**Branch**: 1302-is-pending, *File*: /src/components/Users/UsersPage.js

Listing 13.3    **Destructuring an** `isPending` **value to set a property during transitions**

```
export default function UsersPage () {
  // set up state

  const [startTransition, isPending] = useTransition();        ◁─┘  Assign pending
                                                                    flag to a local
                                                                    variable.
  function switchUser (nextUser) {
    startTransition(() => setSelectedUser(nextUser));          ◁─  Start the
                                                                   transition.
    // prefetch user details and image
  }

  return user ? (
    <main className="users-page">
      <UsersList user={user} setUser={switchUser}/>

      <Suspense fallback={<PageSpinner/>}>                          Pass the
        <UserDetails userID={user.id} isPending={isPending}/>  ◁─  pending flag to
      </Suspense>                                                   UserDetails.
    </main>
  ) : <PageSpinner/>;
}
```

**Branch**: 1302-is-pending, *File*: /src/components/Users/UserDetails.js

Listing 13.4    **Using** `isPending` **to set a class name in** `UserDetails`

```
export default function UserDetails ({userID, isPending}) {    ◁─  Get isPending
  const {data: user} = useQuery(/* fetch user details */);         flag from props.

  return (
    <div
      className={isPending ? "item user user-pending" : "item user"}   ◁─
    >
      {/* unchanged UI */}                                         Use isPending flag
    </div>                                                         to conditionally
  );                                                               set the class.
}
```

The `UserDetails` component for the new `userID` value will suspend while it fetches the user's data. While the transition takes place, however, React will continue to use the UI for the old user but will re-render it with `isPending` set to `true`. React manages two versions of the same component concurrently.

### 13.1.3 *Integrating transitions with common components*

When Concurrent Mode and its APIs become stable, we would expect to use transitions a lot to smooth switching states for potentially longer-running updates. But rather than inserting calls to `useTransition` all over the codebase, the React docs suggest we integrate the calls into our design system. Our buttons, for example, could wrap their event handlers in transitions.

Let's try using transition-ready buttons in our `UsersList` component; we can remove the transition and `isPending` code from `UsersPage` and `UserDetails`. Figure 13.4 shows what will happen when we click a new user, Clarisse. The button starts the transition to Clarisse and uses the `isPending` state to give feedback, showing spinners for the loading user. While the transition is ongoing, the old user, Mark, is still highlighted and his details are shown on the right.

**Figure 13.4   The buttons in the users list show spinners when their transition is underway.**

The following listing shows our new UI component, `ButtonPending`. It renders a button but also encapsulates the transition code. Clicking the button starts a transition, and spinners are shown by the button while the transition is in a pending state.

Branch: **1303-button-pending**, *File:* **/src/components/UI/ButtonPending.js**

Listing 13.5    A `ButtonPending` component that uses transitions

```
import {unstable_useTransition as useTransition} from 'react';
import Spinner from "./Spinner";

export default function ButtonPending ({children, onClick, ...props}) {      ◁─┐  Pass in a handler
  const [startTransition, isPending] = useTransition();                         │  that needs a
                                                                                │  transition.
  function handleClick () {
    startTransition(onClick);        ◁──  Wrap the handler
  }                                        in a transition.

  return (
    <button onClick={handleClick} {...props}>
      {isPending && <Spinner/>}            ◁─┐  Use the pending flag to indicate
      {children}                            │  a transition is in progress.
      {isPending && <Spinner/>}            ◁─┘
    </button>
  );
}
```

Replace the `button` in the `UsersList` component with `ButtonPending` (literally swap the names). Using the special button enables transitions! The CSS is set to fade in the spinners after a few hundred milliseconds; for quickly loaded data, you won't see the spinners.

### 13.1.4 *Holding on to old values with useDeferredValue*

There's one more tool we'll cover in our introduction to concurrent user interfaces: the `useDeferredValue` hook. We maintain old and new versions of a value and use both in our UI. Figure 13.5 shows what happens when we switch the user from Mark to Clarisse. The list of users immediately highlights the new user and shows a spinner, while the details panel continues to show details for the old user.

**Figure 13.5   The `UsersList` shows the latest selection (Clarisse) with inline spinners, but the user details panel still shows the old user (Mark), the deferred value.**

If switching to a new user, Clarisse, causes a delay in rendering the details panel, it will continue to use the old value, Mark, until the UI can be rendered for the new value. The new value has been *deferred*. The following listing updates `UsersPage` again, this time to pass a deferred value for the user to `UserDetails`.

Branch: 1304-deferred-value, *File*: /src/components/Users/UsersPage.js

Listing 13.6    Passing a deferred value to `UserDetails`

```
import {
  useState,
  unstable_useDeferredValue as useDeferredValue,
  Suspense
} from "react";

// other imports

export default function UsersPage () {
  const [loggedInUser] = useUser();
  const [selectedUser, setSelectedUser] = useState(null);
  const user = selectedUser || loggedInUser;
  const queryClient = useQueryClient();
```

```
                    const deferredUser = useDeferredValue(user) || user;        ◁──  Track the user value:
                                                                                     return the old if the
                    const isPending = deferredUser !== user;              ◁───       new delays rendering.

                    function switchUser(nextUser) {                   Create a pending flag that's true
                      setSelectedUser(nextUser);                      if the deferred value is stale.

                      queryClient.prefetchQuery(/* prefetch user details */);
                      queryClient.prefetchQuery(/* prefetch user image */);
                    }

                    return user ? (
                      <main className="users-page">
                        <UsersList                      Let the list know
                          user={user}                   the new user.
                          setUser={switchUser}     ◁──
                          isPending={isPending}    ◁───  Let the list know its user is
                        />                               inconsistent with UserDetails.

                        <Suspense fallback={<PageSpinner/>}>
                          <UserDetails              Show the old user details
                            userID={deferredUser.id}  ◁── while waiting for the new.
                            isPending={isPending}    ◁───
                          />                              Let UserDetails know
                        </Suspense>                       its user is stale.
                      </main>
                    ) : <PageSpinner/>;
                    }
```

Update the user value.

UsersPage gets the useDeferredValue hook to manage old and new user values. We call useDeferredValue with a value to track, like this:

```
const deferredValue = useDeferredValue(value);
```

The hook tracks a value. If the value changes from an old value to a new one, the hook can return either of the values. If React can successfully render a new UI with the new value, and no children suspend or delay rendering, the hook returns the new value, and React updates the UI. If the new value causes React to wait for a process to complete before finishing rendering, the hook returns the old value, and React displays the UI with the old value (while working in memory on the UI with the new value). deferredValue starts as undefined, so we add the || user at the end to make sure we use the initial user value as soon as it is set:

```
const deferredUser = useDeferredValue(user) || user;
```

In listing 13.6, we pass UsersList the newly selected user value while passing User-Details the potentially stale deferredUser value:

```
<UsersList
  user={user}
  setUser={switchUser}
```

```
      isPending={isPending}
    />

    <Suspense fallback={<PageSpinner/>}>
      <UserDetails
        userID={deferredUser.id}
        isPending={isPending}
      />
    </Suspense>
```

The UserDetails component continues to show the previous user while the new user loads. While the two user values are inconsistent, we set the isPending flag to true; UsersList will show spinners, and UserDetails will reduce its opacity, giving extra visual feedback to draw attention to the inconsistent UI state.

## 13.2    *Using SuspenseList to manage multiple fallbacks*

When we have multiple Suspense components in our UI, it can be useful to have a little more control over if and when to show their fallbacks; we don't want a full circus of spinners and acrobatic components jumping around the screen. We need a ringmaster to whip them into shape, introducing the pieces in a well-ordered manner. That ringmaster is the SuspenseList component.

Say the Users page now includes the bookings for the selected user and any to-dos they've been assigned. The UI might be something like figure 13.6 with the user info, bookings, and to-dos displayed as part of the user details panel.

In this section, we first update UserDetails to show the new information within separate Suspense components. Then we wrap the Suspense components inside a SuspenseList to better control the order in which we display their fallbacks.

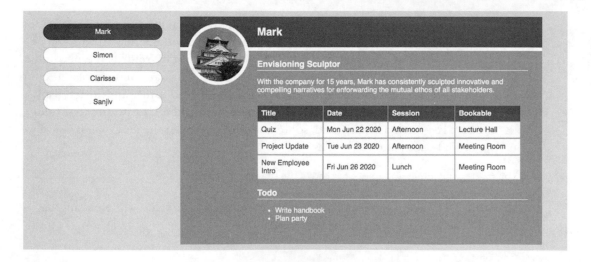

**Figure 13.6    The user details now include bookings and to-dos.**

### 13.2.1 Showing data from multiple sources

We want the `UserDetails` component to display user bookings and to-dos. While the data loads, we might see something like figure 13.7 with fallback messages, "Loading user bookings . . . " and "Loading user todos . . ." displayed by `Suspense` components.

**Figure 13.7**　**Showing fallbacks for loading bookings and to-dos**

Listing 13.7 adds `UserBookings` and `UserTodos` components to the `UserDetails` UI. Each loads its own data, so we wrap them in `Suspense` components with the appropriate fallback messages. Check the repo for the implementation of the new components; it's not important for the current discussion.

> *Branch*: 1305-multi-suspense, *File*: /src/components/Users/UserDetails.js
>
> **Listing 13.7**　**Including bookings and to-dos in `UserDetails`**

```
import {Suspense} from "react";
// other imports
import UserBookings from "./UserBookings";
import UserTodos from "./UserTodos";

export default function UserDetails ({userID, isPending}) {
  const {data: user} = useQuery(/* load user info */);

  return (
    <div className={isPending ? "item user user-pending" : "item user"}>
      <div className="item-header">
        <h2>{user.name}</h2>
      </div>

      <Avatar
        src={`http://localhost:3001/img/${user.img}`}
        fallbackSrc="http://localhost:3001/img/avatar.gif"
        alt={user.name}
      />

      <div className="user-details">
        <h3>{user.title}</h3>
```

```
                <p>{user.notes}</p>
            </div>
                                                                    ┐  Include a Suspense
            <Suspense fallback={<p>Loading user bookings...</p>}> ◄─┘  fallback for the
                                                                       bookings.
Show the ┌─▷   <UserBookings id={userID}/>
bookings.│    </Suspense>
         │                                                            Include a
         │                                                            Suspense fallback
            <Suspense fallback={<p>Loading user todos...</p>}> ◄───── for the to-dos.
               <UserTodos id={userID}/>       ◄───┐
            </Suspense>                           │ Show the to-dos.
        </div>
    );
}
```

A UI circus problem might arise because we can't predict how long each new compo-nent will take to load its data. Figure 13.8 shows what happens if the to-dos load first: the to-do list is rendered, but the fallback for the bookings is still showing above the list. When the bookings finally load, the to-dos, which we might be trying to read, will be shunted down the page by the incoming bookings.

**Figure 13.8    The to-dos are showing, but the bookings are still loading. Once the bookings load, they'll push the to-dos down.**

If we can either show both components at the same time or ensure that the bookings are displayed first, we'll improve the user experience. Let's see how SuspenseList helps us send the circus packing.

### 13.2.2  Controlling multiple fallbacks with SuspenseList

To avoid shifting components down when components above them render more slowly, we could specify that the components appear in order, top-down, even if the data for the later components loads first. For the Users page, we want to display the user's bookings first, as shown in figure 13.9, even if the to-dos data could load more quickly.

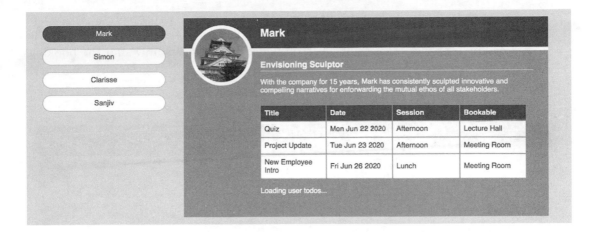

**Figure 13.9  With `SuspenseList`, we can set the reveal order to force the bookings to appear first.**

We'll use a `SuspenseList` component to manage our fallbacks. It's currently imported as `unstable_SuspenseList`:

```
import {Suspense, unstable_SuspenseList as SuspenseList} from "react";
```

The following listing shows the `UserBookings` and `UserTodos` components and their fallbacks wrapped in a `SuspenseList` with `revealOrder` set to `forwards`.

> *Branch*: 1306-suspense-list, *File*: /src/components/Users/UserDetails.js

> **Listing 13.8  Wrap the two `Suspense` components in a `SuspenseList`**

```
<SuspenseList                         ⟵┐  Wrap the Suspense components
    revealOrder="forwards"             │  in a SuspenseList.
>
    <Suspense fallback={<p>Loading user bookings...</p>}>
      <UserBookings id={userID}/>
    </Suspense>

    <Suspense fallback={<p>Loading user todos...</p>}>
      <UserTodos id={userID}/>
    </Suspense>
</SuspenseList>
```

*Specify the revealOrder.* (annotation pointing to `revealOrder="forwards"`)

We could also set `revealOrder` to `backwards` to show the to-dos first, or `together` to show bookings and to-dos at the same time.

We might not want multiple fallbacks to show, and `SuspenseList` also has a `tail` prop that if set to `collapsed` shows only one fallback at a time:

```
<SuspenseList revealOrder="forwards" tail="collapsed">
  {/* UI with Suspense components */}
</SuspenseList>
```

Figure 13.10 shows the user details panel when we set the `tail` prop on the `Suspense-List`. The user details panel shows just the "Loading user bookings . . ." fallback. The "Loading user todos . . . " fallback, as in figure 13.9, appears only after the bookings have rendered.

**Figure 13.10    Only one fallback is shown at a time: first the fallback for the bookings and then the fallback for the to-dos.**

`SuspenseList` is still experimental, and the ways in which it will help us orchestrate loading states will evolve in the coming months. Our Users page example could be improved with some judicious prefetching of data and a more careful combination of all of the techniques used in this chapter. But the examples should have given you a good feel for what's arriving in React soon.

## 13.3    *Concurrent Mode and the future*

With Concurrent Mode, React can work on rendering multiple versions of the UI in memory at the same time and update the DOM with only the most appropriate version for the current state, which might be in the process of change, waiting for updates that take time. This flexibility lets React interrupt rendering if higher-priority updates, like user interaction with form fields, are required. This helps keep the app responsive and improves the perceived performance of the app.

Being able to prepare updates in memory also gives React the ability to switch to an updated UI only when it has enough of it ready, whether that's a new page, a filtered list, or details for a user. The old UI can still be updated to display pending indicators to let the user know that change is afoot. Avoiding receded states and jarring spinners can make interacting with our apps feel smoother, helping users to stay focused on their tasks rather than frustrated with the app.

Concurrent Mode paves the way for more targeted, intentional loading of code, data, and resources, integrating server-side rendering more smoothly with the *hydration* of client-side components, the timely injection of resources to make components responsive just in time for user interaction.

Figure 13.11 shows many of the features that Concurrent Mode promises. It's taken from the React documentation at http://mng.bz/7VRe and includes a third mode, Blocking Mode, an intermediate step in adopting Concurrent Mode, that you can read about there, as well as the features we've covered in part 2 of this book.

## Feature Comparison

| | Legacy Mode | Blocking Mode | Concurrent Mode |
|---|---|---|---|
| String Refs | ✓ | ⊘ ** | ⊘ ** |
| Legacy Context | ✓ | ⊘ ** | ⊘ ** |
| findDOMNode | ✓ | ⊘ ** | ⊘ ** |
| Suspense | ✓ | ✓ | ✓ |
| SuspenseList | ⊘ | ✓ | ✓ |
| Suspense SSR + Hydration | ⊘ | ✓ | ✓ |
| Progressive Hydration | ⊘ | ✓ | ✓ |
| Selective Hydration | ⊘ | ⊘ | ✓ |
| Cooperative Multitasking | ⊘ | ⊘ | ✓ |
| Automatic batching of multiple setStates | ⊘ * | ✓ | ✓ |
| Priority-based Rendering | ⊘ | ⊘ | ✓ |
| Interruptible Prerendering | ⊘ | ⊘ | ✓ |
| useTransition | ⊘ | ⊘ | ✓ |
| useDeferredValue | ⊘ | ⊘ | ✓ |
| Suspense Reveal "Train" | ⊘ | ⊘ | ✓ |

**Figure 13.11  A feature comparison of Concurrent Mode, Blocking Mode, and Legacy Mode from the React docs page on adopting Concurrent Mode**

## *Summary*

- Remember, these APIs are experimental and are likely to change.
- Enable Concurrent Mode by updating how your app is initially rendered to the browser. Use `ReactDOM.unstable_createRoot` and render, like this:

```
const root = document.getElementById('root');
ReactDOM.unstable_createRoot(root).render(<App />);
```

- Delay rendering of new UI that's waiting for data by calling the `useTransition` hook:

```
const [startTransition, isPending] = useTransition();
```

- Wrap state changes that might cause components to suspend in the `start-Transition` function. React can continue to show the old UI until the new UI is ready.

```
startTransition(() => setSelectedUser(nextUser));
```

- Use the isPending Boolean, the second element in the array that useTransition returns, to update the old UI, letting the user know that the state is updating.
- Create design system components like custom buttons that automatically transition from one state to another by wrapping their event handlers with startTransition.
- When updating state, continue to use old values if the new value causes a delay, by calling the useDeferredValue hook to track the value:

```
const deferredValue = useDeferredValue(value);
```

- Components that can render immediately can use the new state, while those that might suspend can use the deferred value:

```
<QuickComponent value={value}/>

<Suspense fallback={<PageSpinner/>}>
  <UserDetails value={deferredValue}/>
</Suspense>
```

- Use the SuspenseList component to manage the order in which Suspense components display their fallbacks. Specify the revealOrder as forwards, backwards, or together, and, optionally, show only one fallback at a time by setting the tail prop.

```
<SuspenseList revealOrder="forwards" tail="collapsed">
  <Suspense fallback={<p>Loading 1...</p>}><Component1/></Suspense>
  <Suspense fallback={<p>Loading 2...</p>}><Component2/></Suspense>
</SuspenseList>
```

- Remember, these APIs are experimental and are likely to change.

# index

## RELATED MANNING TITLES

*Joy of JavaScript*
by Luis Atencio

ISBN 9781617295867
360 pages, $39.99
February 2021

*Secrets of the JavaScript Ninja*
by John Resig, Bear Bibeault, and Josip Maras

ISBN 9781617292859
464 pages, $44.99
August 2016

*React Quickly*
by Azat Mardan
Foreword by John Sonmez

ISBN 9781617293344
528 pages, $49.99
August 2017

*For ordering information go to www.manning.com*